© DISNEY

Using Multiple Gifts
to Build A Unified Vision

# Team Leadership

## in

## Christian Ministry

### Kenneth O. Gangel

**MOODY PRESS**
CHICAGO

*To my family—Betty, Jeff, and Julie—*
*still together after all these years*

---

# CONTENTS

## DIAGRAMS

# FOREWORD

O nce every few years, or perhaps once in a decade, I read a book that has a profound impact on my life and ministry. Without a doubt, *Team Leadership,* written by Dr. Kenneth Gangel, is that kind of book.

In a day in which books about leadership are being published at an unprecedented rate, there seems to be little evidence of their influence. We live in a culture which is crying out for effective leaders. "Where are the leaders?" is a question being asked in business, government, education—and even in the church.

I would suggest that this is not an ordinary book on leadership—nor does it convey a "fad" in current leadership theory. Quite to the contrary, this remarkable volume focuses on the biblical and practical theology of leadership.

This is a "how to" book in the very best sense. It is not to be browsed or read once and then set aside with the multiple books on leadership that most of us have in our libraries. To the contrary, *Team Leadership* is a resource to which the reader will want to return again and again. I know of no other book on leadership which contains so much helpful and insightful information on the vital subject of authentic Christian leadership.

I believe that our world desperately needs Christian leaders who lead like Jesus Christ. The Scriptures teach us some very graphic and practical principles of leadership. Kenneth Gangel has grasped those vital principles. He believes that the New Testament introduces us to a new, wonderful quality of *team leadership* that our Lord Jesus Christ both taught and practiced. Without a doubt, *team leadership* became the model for the New Testament church—and it is a model that is needed today.

Jesus Christ introduced a radically different kind of leadership model when He began to teach His disciples about leadership in His kingdom. "You know that the rulers of the Gentiles lord it over them, and their high officials exercise authority over them." As we know, "lording over" and "exercising authority" are still being practiced all around us—even in the church.

Jesus taught clearly that that approach was inappropriate for His kingdom. "Not so with you. Instead, whoever wants to become great among you must be your servant, and whoever wants to be first must be your slave." What an unusual and effectual leadership style Jesus communicated.

However, as we know, Jesus did not merely teach about this extraordinary and unnatural kind of leadership—He did it! He modeled it for us. "Just as the Son of Man did not come to be served, but to serve, and to give His life as a ransom for many" (Matthew 20:25-28 NIV).

In short, Jesus taught about servant leadership, and then He showed us how to do it. Dr. Gangel has focused on that important reality. This book not only informs us about servant leadership, it shows us how to do it—to lead as Jesus led!

A second principle of authentic Christian leadership is that in order to be effective leaders, we must first become committed followers. In both the Old and New Testaments, effectual leaders possessed that common denominator of being followers of God. Jesus understood that fact. He invites all of us to deny ourselves, take up our cross daily and *follow* Him (Luke 9:23). That, it seems to me, is the foundational step of authentic Christian leadership.

We must be following Jesus as Lord in order to be able to lead as He desires for us to lead. We need to follow the example of the New Testament leaders that Kenneth Gangel writes about with so much spiritual and practical insight. The apostle Paul stated that principle well when he encouraged the Corinthians "Follow me as I follow Christ" (1 Corinthians 11:1).

Without a doubt, our Lord is calling us to a distinctively Christ-centered kind of leadership. It is not "isolated" leadership or "egocentric" leadership. Quite to the contrary, what is needed is *team leadership*. We need committed Christian leaders who will lead by serving members of the team God has entrusted to them. And this *team leadership* must be facilitated with the love of Jesus Christ and the power of the Holy Spirit. Dr. Gangel communicates with passion and practical application how to do that.

This is a book for our time—and it is a book for leaders in every arena of Christian leadership. Pastors, along with local church, missions, parachurch, and denominational leaders, will benefit from this comprehensive study of Christian leadership.

Brothers and sisters, it is time to follow our Leader—and to encourage others to do the same. It is time to be used by our Lord Jesus Christ to lead His people in achieving the goals that He is giving to them—to the glory of God and to the advancement of His kingdom.

Paul A. Cedar
Chairman/CEO
Mission America

# INTRODUCTION

The field of leadership study is changing rapidly. Each passing year witnesses worthy additions to its growing body of literature. I have been involved directly in Christian education for nearly forty years as a college and seminary teacher/administrator, pastor, and consultant to many churches and Christian organizations. During that time I have taught countless students in leadership classes and written numerous articles and books on the subject.

As we approach the end of the century, one problem continues and perhaps even magnifies itself in the leadership vacuum all around us. That problem centers in a misunderstanding of leadership style that causes people and organizations to focus on individuals, prophets who will lead them (albeit sometimes blindly) out of the wilderness and into the promised land.

The Old Testament contains many stories of such individual leaders, but the New Testament changes the pattern dramatically. From the example of Jesus and the disciples through the last missionary journey, we see team leadership emerging as the consistent New Testament form. Yet hundreds of pastors and leaders of Christian organizations do not know how to build leadership teams or how to help others around them develop such teams in a church or organization. This book takes direct aim at that problem.

To be sure, leadership teams must be composed of competent individuals, but the attitudinal and philosophical differences between singular and multiple leadership are enormous. Furthermore, I have expanded this book well beyond the boundaries of the local church (though its predecessors focused only on local congregations). Certainly all evangelical leaders have congregational life as a common reference point. But I intend and pray that the message of this book penetrates colleges, seminaries, mission boards, and many other types of para-church Christian organizations.

Throughout the book I have attempted to make use of both secular and Christian leadership literature. Even secular literature has seen a strong movement away from the singularity of leadership, the strong person who possesses qualities to lead an organization. When one surveys current leadership literature, three elements come to the fore: leadership is an ability; leadership involves working with other people; and leadership involves progressing toward some kind of goal. These are all important and I have taken them into consideration throughout the book.

However, the biblical data hold considerably greater priority in framing a definition of leadership than does the body of human literature. I develop the concept at length in chapter 3, but it may be useful here to offer a simple, one-sentence definition of our subject: **Team leadership is the exercise of one's spiritual gifts under the call of God to serve a certain group of people in achieving the goals God has given them toward the end of glorifying Christ.**

One final thought before we begin. Churches and Christian organizations have survived and thrived for two millennia on the services of *volunteers*. In 1994, one in every five Americans was involved in volunteer work of some kind, 37 percent in churches and religious groups. I have made great efforts to emphasize this reality throughout the book. Churches and Christian organizations should not only gear up to find, train, and supervise volunteers, but they need to include them as a significant part of the overall leadership team.

# PART ONE

# FOUNDATIONS OF TEAM LEADERSHIP

# —1—
# The Context of
## Team Leadership

Teams—we see them all the time. We root for—or against —them. We function in them, both in the family and in the workplace. We watch them on TV—many of the currently popular TV shows depict teams, or groups of dissimilar people, bonding together. In that bonding, they face enemies without and conflicts within. Depending on the circumstances, differing members of the team may take starring or lead roles.

This elevation of teams, personal bonding, and leadership by gift hardly represents a new theme in literature or art. Nevertheless, the emphasis on individual giftedness or talent driving the leadership of a particular situation reflects a shift in general leadership philosophy. George Weber emphasizes that "the historic command-structure organization is dead" and reminds us:

> The successful leader of the future must have one more attribute that weighs perhaps as much as all the others on the scale of effectiveness; he or she must be a tireless, inventive, observant, risk-taking, and ever-hopeful builder and enabler of

management and leadership teams within and among the organization's constituent parts.[1]

Is this shift biblical? Many churches and Christian organizations have practiced authoritative, visionary leadership, top-down administrative policies since their inception, and have prospered in the doing. Does team leadership have a place in the church? Do we risk importing the idea from current secular literature without critical and biblical reflection? Or have those thinkers discerned the truth of leadership principles in a way that is thoroughly biblical?

My bias, as a supporter of team leadership, shows itself immediately. Years of study and practice have demonstrated to me that this sound biblical concept is a biblical mandate as well.

Our understanding of Christian leadership must properly proceed from theology to philosophy to practical implementation. Therefore, a book about team leadership should begin with a theological examination of the church itself as the context and matrix of leadership.

Much of the confusion we face today stems from the lack of a clear-cut ministry philosophy, carrying with it the weight of specific objectives that have their truth and value laid firmly in the Word of God. Christian leadership should be competent; even more essential, however, is that it be thoroughly biblical.

## CONTEMPORARY CONFUSION REGARDING THE NATURE OF THE CHURCH

### Secular Analysis

In the 1950s, 1960s, and into the 1970s, abundant literature provided a sociological analysis of the church's problems from such noted educators as Gibson Winter, Martin Marty, and R. J. Havighurst. The religious book market was flooded with volumes analyzing the church as though it were the local supermarket or a branch of a major industry. From such examination

16

the church can well learn some of the organizational defects into which it has fallen through the years. We have had ample opportunity to study its alleged irrelevance, tradition-bound immobility, and inability to meet the needs of modern society. Some of the criticism was deserved and much of it, helpful. Nevertheless, one basic erroneous note flowed through most of the literature dissecting the church during those decades. It viewed the church largely as *organization* and failed to realize that it is also *organism*.

## The Distorted Image of Fiction

Another problem the church has faced today is the image it has inherited in contemporary fiction and cinema. The picture of Jonathan Edwards thundering the truth of God to a people who trembled before His sovereignty has now given way to *Leap of Faith*—the movie about a phony con man, grasping for personal profit in religious merchandise. After identifying modern man as confused, complacent, chaotic, rebellious, and desperately in need of help, the writers of twentieth-century fiction have been able to construct nothing better than a "picaresque saint." The voices of Kafka and Camus, of Coppola, Lear, and Allen, have been heard more clearly on college campuses than the voice of God. Even the educated American has nearly lost sight of what the New Testament church was all about.

## The Gospel of a Cause

Still another voice clamoring to be heard in the darkness is what may be called "The Gospel of a Cause." Strangely enough, prophets of this position can be found in the ranks of variant theological extremes. Their paths differ and their traveling gear seems diverse, but they end up at the same crossroads— the banner of a *cause*. Some tell us the church must become more involved in human rights, using the influence of pastor and parish to push for affirmative action, school integration, equal job opportunities, and a dozen other aspects of pressing social problems.

Others would press the church into the battle for world peace. Only in such a noble and worldwide cause for the benefit of the human race, they threaten, can the church redeem itself from its years of apathy and injustice. Still others tell us that the church must be in the foreground, fighting abortion and homosexuality in the public arena.

But many of the above causes (and dozens more like them) have often failed to distinguish between the supernatural work of regeneration and its accompanying results in individual behavior and society. Human rights on earth are not to be equated with heavenly citizenship; world peace, though a noble cause, forms a shoddy substitute for the eternal peace of God in the human heart; and American democracy dare not be equated with biblical Christianity. The problem of the gospel of a cause, therefore, is that it offers itself as a substitute for the gospel of the Cross!

## Polarization of a Philosophy of Ministry

A number of beliefs and behaviors have divided evangelicals throughout the twentieth century—levels and extent of separation of church and state; arguments over prophecy; disputes related to systems of biblical interpretation; and positions on the doctrine of inerrancy. Increasingly obvious as a divisive force is the attitude toward how the church should minister and what forms that ministry should take. Part of the issue, for example, is size. One wing of conservative Christianity focuses on what we have come to call the "megachurch." On the other hand, the "metachurch" stresses the importance of small groups, discipleship training, and a heavy emphasis on "sharing." Obviously, local churches represent almost every point on a continuum line between those views, and people feel comfortable in many and varied ministerial styles. In a future chapter I will address the issue of ministry philosophy.

## THE MEANING OF THE WORD "CHURCH"

### The English Words

The English word *church* is one of the most abused and misused words in the twentieth-century vocabulary. Unfortunately, like Caesar, it suffers more at the hands of its friends than its enemies. Let's look at the four common uses that many Christians make of the word *church,* some within and some without its proper biblical context.

*Building.* Many people refer to the building in which the congregation assembles as the "church." A man may say to his wife, "I am going down to the church to pick up my hat, which I left there after the morning service," fully knowing that no other person will likely be in the building at the time he arrives.

*Denomination.* It is quite common to speak of a collection of churches which have assembled themselves together in some kind of organization or association as "the Baptist church," "the Methodist church," or "the Presbyterian church."

*Universal church.* The universal church refers to all members of the body of Christ in all places and all ages. Some theologians have referred to this as the "church invisible," but in actuality the church has never been invisible.

*Local church.* The local church is a given geographical representation of the universal church. This usage of the word is most in focus throughout the pages of this book.

Of the four common usages of the word *church* mentioned above, only two are biblical. The first two have grown up in the jargon of ecclesiastical years. It is not necessarily a great error to use the word *church* in these ways, unless by so doing one forgets the emphasis of the New Testament—that the church is always people. The last two uses, universal and local, are the only scriptural usages of the concept of church; we will examine these further below.

## The Greek Word

The Greek word used in the New Testament to designate either universal church or local church is *ecclesia*. To the Greeks the word indicated an assembly of free citizens; however, to the Jews it had more theocratic connotations. In the New Testament the word takes three basic uses:

1. *A political assembly of free citizens.* The word *ecclesia* appears in this context in Acts 19:32, 39, 41. The English word used in the Authorized translation is *assembly,* which is quite proper in describing the situation. God had worked various miracles through Paul at Ephesus, and Demetrius, representative of the silversmiths in Ephesus, expressed their fear that their patron deity was in jeopardy because of the increasing number of people turning to the gospel. In the confusion that followed, mob violence was averted by the speech of the town clerk. When the mob is in complete chaos (and when it is formally dismissed by the town clerk), it is referred to as an *ecclesia*.

2. *Jewish assembly of the Old Testament.* In his sermon just before his martyrdom, Stephen speaks of Moses and "the church in the wilderness" (Acts 7:38 KJV). The word *ecclesia* in this context obviously cannot be a reference to the New Testament church but speaks in a general way of the congregation or the gathering of Israelites in the wilderness under the leadership of Moses.

3. *The Christian church.* Almost all other New Testament passages deal with the Christian church in either its universal or local form. Because of the extreme importance of this concept, one cannot properly perceive of the doctrine of the church without a thorough understanding of these two uses of the word *ecclesia*. The universal church contains only true believers, whereas the local church may include those who profess Christianity but who have not yet had an experience of regeneration.

## The Universal Church

The Old Testament presented the church in typological form. Sample types might include Ruth, the Gentile bride and Israel, God's remnant in the world.

In the Gospels God's revelation of the church proceeds to prophetic form as Jesus Himself pronounces, "Upon this rock I will build My church" (Matt. 16:18 NASB). The book of Acts describes the history of the church in its early days; the spread of the gospel through the church, beginning at Jerusalem and continuing today around the world, is a literal fulfillment of Acts 1:8.

It is not until we read the Epistles, however, that we confront any kind of formalized church doctrine, since God's sovereign plan largely confined such information to the writings of the apostle Paul. The crown of church doctrine comes in the epistle to the church at Ephesus and its most glittering jewel, chapter 4, a passage which comes into focus frequently in any study of Christian leadership.

The universal church includes all Christians (1 Cor. 1:1–2), only Christians (Eph. 5:23–27), and is represented by those brought together through the Holy Spirit. The teaching on spiritual gifts in 1 Corinthians 12 and Romans 12 offers clear evidence of the nature of the church as organism. The universal church is, in the language of the apostle Paul, "the body of Christ."

## The Local Church

God's pattern has always designed the local church to manifest the universal church (Rom. 16:16), and Acts 2:41–47 represents the local church at Jerusalem carrying out the purposes and program of the universal church. No evidence in the Word of God suggests that Christ ever abandoned the program and format of the local church as the basic foundation for all forms of Christian mission in the world.

*Membership.* Membership in the local church seems to have been taken for granted by New Testament believers. Various passages seem to indicate that specific rolls were kept, but there is very little clear-cut teaching on the nature of those rolls (Acts 1:15; 2:41; 6:2–5; 1 Cor. 5:13; 1 Tim. 5:9).

*Organization.* Like the matter of membership, church organization is not specifically outlined in the New Testament. The Lord somewhat assumes it in Matthew 18 when He talks about establishing the facts of a dispute through collective hearing by the church. As apostolic authority passed off the scene, team leadership seems to have taken its place. In Acts 8, for example, Peter remonstrates with Simon the sorcerer on the basis of unilateral authority. Just a few years later Paul writes to the church at Corinth that they have the collective responsibility to judge wicked persons in their midst (1 Cor. 5:13).

Another characteristic of organization in the early church is that it arose largely in response to the needs and problems that the church encountered. The selection of the deacons in Acts 6 provides the most obvious example of this. In a sense, the indigenous principle of missions is a more refined development of this earliest principle of organization.

*Government.* An important part of organization in the local church is its government. Although evangelicals differ regarding the significance of such words as *episkopos* (bishop or overseer) and *presbuteros* (elder), several biblical principles of church government are enunciated in the New Testament. We will explore these issues more fully in chapters 3 and 4.

ASPECTS OF CHURCH GOVERNMENT

*Church Government Should Be Biblical in Constitution*

Young Timothy represents early church leadership, and to him the apostle Paul writes that leaders should constantly conform to "sound words, those of our Lord Jesus Christ, and with the doctrine conforming to godliness" (1 Tim. 6:3 NASB). Of course some would immediately point out that "words" here refers to the words of the living Son of God and not to the words written in the Bible. Nevertheless, our understanding of the words of Christ exclusively depends upon God's inspired record of those words. One of the great errors of liberal theology through the years has been a fabricated separation of the written Word from the incarnate Word.

## Church Government Should Be Participatory in Form

The existence of numerous evangelical denominations with varying attitudes regarding church government demonstrates that the Scriptures do not detail the issue. Some interpret the New Testament to teach congregational government, others favor a presbyterian form, and still others the more hierarchical Episcopalian structure. Quite obviously, each group will defend its preference from Scripture and history. The only point I wish to make here, therefore, is the renewed emphasis on the church as people. Evidence throughout the book of Acts strongly suggests that whatever emphasis we may place on the role of elders, the New Testament will never let us forget the participatory role of people in team leadership of the church. That omission came about by later corruption of medieval forms.

## Church Government Should Be Representative in Function

How easy it could have been in Acts 6 for the apostles themselves to select those seven men whom they desired to serve in the "daily ministration" (KJV). Nevertheless, they carefully restrained themselves and asked the entire group to make the selection. The statement of verse 5 is quite clear: "The whole multitude . . . chose" (KJV).

*Church Government Should Be Spiritual in Function*

The biblical, participatory, and spiritual aspects of church administration find their clearest practical application in the selection of the first missionaries. It seems clear in Acts 13 that the process of selecting and sending those missionaries depended solely upon the sovereignty of the Holy Spirit through prayer. The Holy Spirit selected the missionaries, and the Holy Spirit sent them to a particular place. The local church served as an intermediary agency, a physical representation of the hand of God in His world.

## THE PURPOSE OF THE CHURCH

Without a clear-cut set of objectives, any organization suffers. The church has been less than outstanding in its clarification of mission in the late twentieth century. Not all church leaders have been silent, however, and at least one leading educator has specified in print an attempt to answer the question, "What is the church for?"

> The answer is no mystery. Scripture makes it plain that the church is to be a worshipping body, committed to "show forth the praises of him who has called (it) out of darkness into his marvelous light"; that it is to proclaim the saving gospel of Jesus Christ to all the world; and that it is to obey all the teachings of Jesus Christ, its great head and Lord.[2]

For thirty years Dr. Frank E. Gaebelein gave careful thought to the issues of Christian education and philosophy. Unfortunately, however, no one individual can speak for all local churches. Each body of believers must reassess the purpose of its own existence and clarify its relationship to the universal church. The New Testament seems to set forth four basic objectives for the church, though church leaders may verbalize them differently.

## The Church Structures a Climate for Worship

A host of passages invites our attention to the subject of the church promoting worship. It may be beneficial, however, to confine our observation to the epistle of Ephesians. In chapter 1 Paul immediately declares that the purpose of God's predestination and adoption is that His people might be "to the praise of the glory of His grace" (NASB). Lest his readers miss the emphasis, the apostle repeats the worship theme in verses 12 and 14. The great benediction of chapter 3 also focuses on the concept of worship as Paul writes, "To him be glory in the church and in Christ Jesus throughout all generations, for ever and ever! Amen" (Eph. 3:21).

To say that the church purposes to worship does not guarantee that the church fully accomplishes this objective. Providing opportunities for believers to pray, sing, hear Scripture, read publicly, or engage in any other kind of physical or verbal activity is just the beginning. As a matter of fact, worship is not primarily an *activity* but rather an *attitude* of heart and mind which comprehends God and rejoices in the realization.

## The Church Provides the Setting for Fellowship

A little phrase in Ephesians 3:18 is often overlooked: "with all the saints." These words speak volumes regarding the nature of the church. Isolationism has never been God's way, and biblical separation today should be interpreted neither as *isolation* from others nor as *insulation* from the very world that needs the witness of the church. The apostle John writes of fellowship in his first epistle: "What we have seen and heard we proclaim to you also, so that you too may have fellowship with us; and indeed our fellowship is with the Father, and with His Son Jesus Christ" (1 John 1:3 NASB). In other words, horizontal fellowship among God's people depends upon vertical fellowship between individual Christians and their Lord. The world must see Christians living together in harmonious love demonstrative of the Christ whom they serve (John 13:35).

## The Church Develops a Strategy for Evangelism

Biblically, evangelism is the clear proclamation of the gospel of Jesus Christ, leaving the results entirely up to the sovereignty of the Holy Spirit. Some churches have viewed evangelism as the *only* task of the church and have subordinated all other purposes to it. Unfortunately, such churches fill their rolls with baby Christians who, instead of growing week by week on the milk, bread, and meat of the Word, receive only a constant barrage of the elementary principles of the gospel.

Such excesses, however, should not cloud the fact that evangelism is a legitimate task of the church. Surely some have a special gift of evangelism, but their ministry does not excuse the responsibility of every Christian to communicate the gospel. Paul speaks for the church in Ephesians 3:8 when he says of himself, "This grace was given me: to preach to the Gentiles the unsearchable riches of Christ." In Acts 8:4, when the apostles remained at Jerusalem for some reason during a mass persecution, Luke records that the church "went about preaching the word" (NASB).

Some would prefer to describe this concept of the church's purpose as "service," a more inclusive word. God's people render varied kinds of service through the church, and not all of them have to do directly with evangelism. Perhaps we can say that the church both *has* a mission in the world and *is* a mission in the world.

## The Church Maintains a Ministry of Education

Some would say that the church has a responsibility for instruction or edification. The Great Commission is a teaching commission (Matt. 28:19–20; Acts 2:42). James Deforest Murch, in a classic book title, once warned us to "Teach or Perish." It seems inappropriate to move on to matters of team leadership before examining that golden deposit of truth, Ephesians 4:11–16, which speaks so clearly regarding the church's educational task. Note carefully the *New International Version* translation of the passage:

> It was he who gave some to be apostles, some to be prophets, some to be evangelists, and some to be pastors and teachers, to prepare God's people for works of service, so that the body of Christ may be built up until we all reach unity in the faith and in the knowledge of the Son of God and become mature, attaining to the whole measure of the fullness of Christ.
>
> Then we will no longer be infants, tossed back and forth by the waves, and blown here and there by every wind of teaching and by the cunning and craftiness of men in their deceitful scheming. Instead, speaking the truth in love, we will in all things grow up into him who is the Head, that is, Christ. From him the whole body, joined and held together by every supporting ligament, grows and builds itself up in love, as each part does its work.

In this passage several facts form a biblical basis for the church's ministry:

1. The church's ministry is carried on by those first gifted by the Holy Spirit to lead and then given to the church for that purpose (v. 11).
2. A major purpose of the church's ministry is to help God's people mature so that they can minister. Maturation is edification, a "building up" process (v. 12).
3. Properly carried out, the church's ministry will result in a harmonious relationship among believers. The process of growing into this maturity and harmony is one of becoming more like Jesus Christ (v. 13).
4. The church's ministry is highly theological, producing discerning students of truth who are able—because of

their understanding of truth—to detect and avoid error (v. 14).
5. A properly functioning church will effectively combine truth and love without sacrificing either on the altar of the other. A mature Christian (v. 15) will be like his Lord, "full of grace and truth" (John 1:14).

To state it simply and yet biblically, *the overwhelming and all-encompassing objective of the church is total Christian maturity for all its members*. Total Christian maturity includes an individual and collective life of biblical worship, biblical fellowship, and biblical evangelism, all of which are stimulated by and produced through properly functioning team leadership.

## FOR FURTHER READING

Colson, Charles. *Kingdoms in Conflict*. Grand Rapids: William Morrow/Zondervan, 1987.

Koivsto, Rex A. *One Lord, One Faith*. Wheaton, Ill.: Victor, 1993.

MacArthur, John, Jr. *The Church, the Body of Christ*. Grand Rapids: Zondervan, 1973.

Saucy, Robert L. *The Church in God's Program*. Chicago: Moody, 1972.

Snyder, Howard A. *The Community of the King*. Downers Grove, Ill.: InterVarsity, 1977.

Stedman, Ray C. *Body Life*. Rev. ed. Glendale, Calif.: Regal, 1977.

## NOTES

1. George B. Weber, "Growing Tomorrow's Leaders" in *The Leader of the Future*, ed. Frances Hesselbein, Marshall Goldsmith, and Richard Beckhard (San Francisco: Jossey-Bass, 1996), 309.

2. Frank E. Gaebelein, *A Varied Harvest* (Grand Rapids: Eerdmans, 1967), 160.

# —2—
# UNITY AND COMMUNITY
## IN THE BODY

W hat is the greatest problem the church faces today? Traditionally, it has been a threat to orthodox theology by militant liberalism. Certainly that threat is always present, but in these declining years of the twentieth century evangelical churches seem to be much more troubled by the immature behavior of Christians *within* their ranks than they are by the heresy from *without*. Issues of ecclesiology have formed the battleground of recent decades, and a book attempting to describe biblical ways God's people work together in team leadership should emphasize issues of unity and community within the body of Christ.

We have already seen that the "universal church" refers to the spiritual unity of the redeemed in all ages and places. It includes believing Jews or Gentiles, women and men, people of all colors, those in heaven and on earth, and stretches historically from the origin of the church at Pentecost to the final day when we shall be in heaven with the Lord. The focal point of that unity, as Paul clearly declares in Ephesians 1, is a common redemption through the Atonement of Calvary and a corporate demonstration of the grace and glory of Jesus Christ.

## UNDERSTANDING THE CHURCH

In recent years defining and describing a philosophy of ministry has created much confusion and no little controversy. Yet as we study the New Testament, we seem to find at least a minimal boundary of inclusion/exclusion to help us understand the local church. Writing from the context of congregational polity, I would like to suggest that the local church is a *body of confessed believers joining together for worship, fellowship, instruction, and evangelism; led in its efforts by biblical officers (elders and deacons); and including, as part of its life and ministry, observance of the ordinances, discipline, and mutual edification.*

Theologian Robert Culver enumerates six characteristics of a local church: spiritual vitality, doctrinal instruction, fellowship, observance of the Lord's Supper, prayer, and Christian testimony.[1] The popular apologist Francis Schaeffer indicated eight ingredients that must be a part of "the polity of the church as a church":

1. Local congregations made up of Christians
2. Special meetings on the first day of the week
3. Church officers (elders) who have responsibility for the local churches
4. Deacons responsible for the community of the church in the area of material things
5. A serious view of discipline
6. Specific qualifications for elders and deacons
7. A place for form on a wider basis than the local church
8. The observance of two sacraments—baptism and the Lord's Supper[2]

I could fill hundreds of additional pages with various other views as well as biblical exposition of the nature of the universal and local church, but that is not the primary purpose of this volume. My concern is that readers recognize the validity and essentiality of the local church *as a visible, contemporaneous demonstration of the universal church and the primary importance that unity and community be demonstrated in its interpersonal relations.*

One theological concept closely aligned here is the priesthood of believers. Actually only five passages in two books of the New Testament refer directly to the priesthood of believers; they are few enough to be reproduced here.

> You also, like living stones, are being built into a spiritual house to be a holy priesthood, offering spiritual sacrifices acceptable to God through Jesus Christ. (1 Peter 2:5)

> But you are a chosen people, a royal priesthood, a holy nation, a people belonging to God, that you may declare the praises of him who called you out of darkness into his wonderful light. (1 Peter 2:9)

> To him who loves us and has freed us from our sins by his blood, and has made us to be a kingdom and priests to serve his God and Father—to him be glory and power for ever and ever! Amen. (Revelation 1:5b–6)

> You are worthy to take the scroll and to open its seals, because you were slain, and with your blood you purchased men for God from every tribe and language and people and nation. You have made them to be a kingdom and priests to serve our God, and they will reign on the earth. (Revelation 5:9–10)

> Blessed and holy are those who have part in the first resurrection. The second death has no power over them, but they will be priests of God and of Christ and will reign with him for a thousand years. (Revelation 20:6)

One writer draws from these Scriptures five principles that speak to the relationship of believers in community as they seek to worship and serve God together:

1. The priesthood of the believer must be held in healthy tension with other basic concepts; it is not an absolute.
2. The believer can delegate some of the authority of his life and ministry to other believers.
3. The priesthood of the believer is conditioned by the gifts and roles in the life of the fellowship.
4. The priesthood of the believer implies shared responsibility and ministry as well as shared authority.
5. The priesthood of the believer is the basis for decision making in the church.[3]

Team leadership, commitment to shared responsibility and authority, depends on a proper understanding of what it means to be the body of Christ. It emphasizes again the truth of being "laborers together," not only with God but also with each other, in carrying out the tasks of the church and establishing its witness in the world (Rom. 12:5).

## PAUL'S CONCEPT OF THE BODY

Perhaps no visual idea of the church receives more attention today than the image of the body described by Paul in 1 Corinthians 12. On every hand we hear about "body life," "body truth," and the exercise of spiritual gifts within the body. This healthy emphasis will help us look again at corporate notions that the early church had of itself and at the cardinal principles that governed its life and ministry in the first century.

Paul probably wrote the first Corinthian epistle from Ephesus about A.D. 57. A metropolis of the Roman province of Achaia, Corinth was a great commercial center in the Mediterranean world. Paul had visited the city twice and found it living up to its reputation as a center of sin and depravity. Corinth presented an enormous challenge to the gospel. One could reasonably expect the principles of Christian faith to operate at Jerusalem, where the members of the early church had been schooled for years in Old Testament truth. To motivate that kind of behavior in pagan Corinth, however, presented unique challenges.

Deplorable factions had split the Corinthian church into hostile fragments. Some believers claimed to follow Paul, others Apollos, others Peter, and some claimed such self-righteous piety that they wished to bypass all contemporary leaders and refer themselves directly back to Christ. Paul addresses a number of the problems resulting from the schism that had drained both unity and community at Corinth. In chapter 12 he makes an explanation of the nature and use of spiritual gifts. Interestingly, however, the bulk of the chapter does not deal with the specification of gifts, but rather with the kind of people who will be ministering them. The words of the old hymn "Onward, Christian Soldiers" well depict the intent of 1 Corinthians 12. They remind the church, "We are not divided; all one body we, One in hope and doctrine, One in charity."

## The Body Metaphor

Typically, Paul used common illustrations to explain difficult spiritual truths. First Corinthians 12 demonstrates in detail how the unity of a *physical* body offers a model for the kind of unity that ought to radiate from Christ's *spiritual* body. In verse 13 the apostle points out that the baptismal ministry of the Holy Spirit places people into the universal body of Christ, the church. Most evangelical scholars agree that the treatment of baptism here is less likely a reference to the ritual act of water baptism than to the spiritual act of implantation into the body of believers. We should always remember that symbolical acts exist only to emphasize spiritual reality.

The essence of this chapter is the old philosophical principle that "the whole is greater than the sum of its parts." Diversity of parts characterizes the operating body, but unity and community of the members allow the body to function properly. Paul draws the argument to ridiculous extremes in order to make his point: "If the whole body were an eye, where would the sense of hearing be? If the whole body were an ear, where would the sense of smell be?" (v. 17). What kind of a functioning organism would one's body be were it composed of nothing but one giant eye? Or perhaps one giant ear and no nose? Apparently autocratic leaders already were manifesting their power in the early church. People whose strong personalities overwhelm the body of Christ and dominate its life and ministry have plagued the church from the first century. Such overpowering control by any one member, or by a select inside group, shows an inaccurate concept of the church and a failure to understand team leadership.

After he focuses our attention on the functions of the physical body, Paul nails down the argument he really intends to make in this section of the epistle: *God has a place for everyone in the church, and everyone's place is important.* Remember the context of this passage—the use of spiritual gifts. Every Christian has a spiritual gift, and some may have more than one. And just as all members have spiritual gifts, all members have distinct functions. God gifts people for carrying on the work of the church and then places them in the body for a particular purpose of ministry. Not only that, but He does it in His own divine sovereignty, just as He arranged the organs of the physical body to create the best possible working relationship! Only when all members of the physical body do their tasks does that body function properly. The same is true of the church.

## The Broken Body

Ministry unity and community break down when some fail to exercise their proper gifts and roles in the body, or when certain members are considered to be weaker or stronger, more necessary or less necessary. Mutual care in the body can eliminate discord, but a ruptured organ can destroy the entire system. An oversized gland creates abnormality, causing the entire organism (or organization) to suffer desperately.

In verse 26, Paul points out that the unity of the body is most apparent during a time of pain or suffering. A broken leg sends splinters of pain throughout the entire system. Even the common cold can simultaneously produce a runny nose, red and tired eyes, an earache, an aching head, a sore throat, an upset stomach, and general discomfort throughout the entire body. In the same way, all members of the spiritual body share the suffering and unhappiness of each other. Since a unified body enjoys community, when one of its members feels well or receives some particular benefits, the entire body rejoices. As Paul wrote in another letter, "Rejoice with those who rejoice, and weep with those who weep" (Rom. 12:15 NASB).

The crucial application comes in 1 Corinthians 12:27: "Now you are Christ's body, and individually members of it" (NASB). Note the emphasis on the word *you*. Even this fractured Corinthian church, with all its doctrinal confusion and personal bickering, could demonstrate the body of Christ to the world! The "bookends" of this passage (vv. 12–27) fit classic Pauline logic: "For even as the body is one" (v. 12 NASB) and "Now you are Christ's body" (v. 27 NASB). Alan Redpath suggests that the kind of unity Paul describes in this chapter "is only possible as we recognize that within the church we have fellowship in our diversity, as we learn to love and to care for our brethren who are different, always recognizing the utter futility of identity."[4]

Francis Schaeffer wrote often about community. He emphasized that horizontal relationship can only follow vertical relationship because a Christian community can only be made up of individual Christians.

> Therefore, as we meet in our groups, we know who we are. We are not like those who march in our streets and do not know who they are—who call for community but have no basis for community beyond biological continuity. Now we are ready to begin real personal living, to practice the orthodoxy of commu-

nity corporately as a community. Real personal Christian living individually and corporately as a community that rests upon the individual's and the community's personal relationship with a personal God gives us the possibility of Christian community before the eye of an observing world.[5]

## THE IMPLEMENTATION OF UNITY AND COMMUNITY

It is tempting to spend the rest of the chapter continuing the discussion of the biblical nature of the "communited" church. But this book deals with team leadership. Up to this point, I have tried to draw some biblical implications regarding the relationships we must maintain if we expect leadership teams to work together effectively in the body of believers, whether that be in the local church or in other Christian organizations. Now I will deal briefly with four concepts that help form a pattern of ministry based, if not on specific verses of 1 Corinthians 12, at least upon the general New Testament concept of the church as a unified body.

### A People-Centered Ministry

In one sense we could say that the church should be the most person-centered organization in the world. But the church must be God-centered before it can be person-centered. Finding the proper balance between these two very important ingredients of biblical life has proven too great a responsibility for some congregations. They have slipped from the path either to the left (an overemphasis on human relationships to the neglect of God's sovereignty) or to the right (a greater concern for "souls" than for people).

*Christian love always finds its outworking within the context of relationships.* Yet precisely at this point many Christian leaders go sour. Our problems testify not so much to our inability to perform publicly as to our inability to get along with people in private, interpersonal relations. The church is and always has

36

been people, and service in it at any given time requires necessary relationship with those people. Adequate team leadership requires awareness of and sensitivity to human need all around us, as well as an appreciation of how we can meet that need through the supernatural dynamics of God's truth and Spirit.

Consider, for example, a pastor who finds his self-satisfaction and fulfillment amid the books in his study, where he spends all his time. Although his theology may be orthodox and his sermons scholarly, a dimension of reality could be missing from his ministry. His lifeline to meaningful ministry demands constant contact with people, so that he can learn to relate God's truth to real problems in real lives.

Our Lord's ministry always centered on people; He focused on meeting their spiritual and eternal needs. But this priority did not keep Him from showing interest in temporal and physical needs as well. If our various "body parts" properly function together, it will be because we have discovered and implemented a new-covenant view of interpersonal relations.

## The Gift of Leading

In conjunction with the spiritual gift of administration (*kubernesis*), a gift of leadership appears as well in Romans 12:8 where Paul uses the word *prohistemi*.[6] It literally means "to put before" or "to go before." Originally it had the connotation of presiding, conducting, directing, or governing. I have often asked myself whether *kubernesis* and *prohistemi* represent two different gifts or two dimensions of the same gift, namely, congregational leadership. As closely as these ideas are linked, we probably must recognize them as two different gifts, both essential to effective ministry.

In spite of today's popular emphasis on prestige and publicity, *the New Testament concept of leadership emphasizes service.* Those who utilize the gift of leadership (or administration) must exemplify service and unity as models for the body. Somehow we must balance delegated authority and loving concern in our constant quest for biblical leadership.

D. Swan Haworth identifies three interesting concepts of staff relationships:

1. A loosely organized staff which may have several "soloists" but no director, no regular rehearsals, and consequently very little harmony; people on such a staff relate to each other only by necessity;
2. An integrated staff held together by one commander; or
3. A colleague relationship in which "each staff member trusts the others, despite their difference. This colleague relationship requires each member of the team to be a responsible person."[7]

Relationships of the professional staff stand as a model for any Christian ministry. Confusion and bickering at the top will not only destroy the working effectiveness of the management team, but will filter down the ranks to distort interpersonal relationships between other workers all the way up and down the line.

### The Requirement of a Biblical Lifestyle

The Christian leader's behavior toward other people is determined by inner qualities. To put it another way, interpersonal relations on a horizontal plane arise from interpersonal relations with God on a vertical plane. We face so many people problems in the church because we have somehow confused ourselves into thinking that what we *do* for God is more important than what we *are* before God. A distinctly Christian lifestyle, with shared ministries in a communal setting, requires the grace of mutual acceptance, a willingness to enter into mutual burden bearing, and a generous dose of active love.

Understanding one's fellow leaders involves seeing and

knowing them as persons rather than merely as "employees." Paul Tournier points out two great fears that keep people from understanding each other: fear of being judged and fear of being advised.[8] Harsh criticism and flippant answers to troubling problems are two clubs that can bludgeon human relations to death. For example, some adults have no ministry with teenagers because they greet every attempt at communication with a handy "Oh yes, I used to feel like that. You'll get over it."

The immorality of manipulation is not confined to Madison Avenue. It is just as wrong for Christian leaders as for the advertising executive who designs television commercials geared to trick people into buying what they do not need and cannot afford.

In our pressure-cooker society, we find it difficult to grasp and practice the biblical concept of patience. We tend to be obsessive and compulsive about our behavior, and frequently "come on too strong" in relationships with other people. I like the way Robert Lofton Hudson put it: "Impatience is a heresy of the soul and an apostasy of the disposition."[9]

Schaeffer called unity in love "the mark of the Christian" and referred to that unity as "the final apologetic." He pointed out that the world cares nothing for doctrine but has been given the authority to judge the effectiveness and authenticity of the church on the evidence of a loving lifestyle among members in its community.

## Understanding Interpersonal Encounters

In one sense, we can think of the whole social order as a communications framework. If we want to realize unity and community, a third concept—communication (a term obviously related to the first two)—must function properly (see chapter 24 for more on communication). Communication can be verbal or nonverbal and should not be confused with the information theory of hardware and software systems. Some sociologists remind us that no one person can be held responsible for communication; it is always a mutual process. The word *mutuality* becomes very important in recognizing the interrelated nature of communication.

Another term frequently used in sociological literature is *simultaneity.* Communication is not like a Ping-Pong game in which messages are batted back and forth. Rather, the ongoing relationship between communicating people forms a simultaneous process. People who effectively relate to other people recognize that both what they say and what they hear pass through an emotional and cultural grid.

When a Sunday school superintendent speaks to a teacher, the meaning of her words is not so much inherent in what she says, as in the way the teacher interprets them. These two people are simultaneously active in the communication process and therefore mutually responsible for what happens in their dialogue. Each loads up little trucks (words) with cargo (ideas) and sends them on their way. At the same time, each one is unloading the trucks sent by the other person.

Sociology assumes that human beings develop their human abilities through social interaction. The community (church, school, or other institution) provides the context for an analysis of relationships. We might also add that it provides the context for believers to function as the body of Christ, in keeping with the kind of patterns delineated in 1 Corinthians 12 and similar passages in the New Testament. We are certainly not passive recipients of everything sociology and psychology tell us about human relationships. But we must be astute discerners of truth and willing to integrate information that fits our understanding of the special revelation of God's Word.

Perhaps this chapter should end where it began—with the church. Surely, any recognition of relationship styles must stand under a proper delineation of the Lordship of Christ. Walter Liefeld has written:

A local church . . . functions as a body of disciples devoted to their Lord and transmitting His teaching. The church remembers the past, insofar as it reminds itself and the world of its origin in the death and resurrection of Christ. It faces the future as an eschatological community in which the characteristics of the kingdom and the presence of the king are realized in its daily life.[10]

## FOR FURTHER READING

Coppedge, Allan. *The Biblical Principles of Discipleship.* Grand Rapids: Francis Asbury, 1989.

Getz, Gene. *Loving One Another.* Wheaton, Ill.: Victor, 1979.

Madsen, Paul O. *The Small Church—Valid, Vital, Victorious.* Valley Forge, Pa.: Judson, 1975.

Malphurs, Aubrey. *Pouring New Wine into Old Wineskins.* Grand Rapids: Baker, 1993.

Stedman, Ray C. *Body Life.* Rev. ed. Glendale, Calif.: Regal, 1977.

## NOTES

1. Ecclesiology class notes. Deerfield, Ill.: Trinity Evangelical Divinity School, 1970.

2. Francis Schaeffer, *The Church at the End of the Twentieth Century* (Downers Grove, Ill.: InterVarsity, 1970), 62–66.

3. Ernest White, "Applying the Priesthood of the Believer to the Life and Work of a Church," *Search 2,* no. 2 (Winter 1972): 13–18.

4. Alan Redpath, *The Royal Route to Heaven* (Westwood, N.J.: Revell, 1960), 152.

5. Schaeffer, *The Church at the End of the Twentieth Century,* 56.

6. For other appearances of *prohistemi* see 1 Thessalonians 5:12; 1 Timothy 3:4, 12; 5:17; Titus 3:8, 14.

7. D. Swan Haworth, *How Church Staff Members Relate* (Nashville: Southern Baptist Sunday School Board, 1969),1.

8. Paul Tournier, *To Understand Each Other* (Richmond, Va.: John Knox, 1966), 19–25.

9. Robert Lofton Hudson, *What Makes for Patience?* (Nashville: Southern Baptist Sunday School Board, 1970), 7.

10. Walter Liefeld, "The Church: What Did Jesus Intend?" Trinity Evangelical Divinity School, 1970. Unpublished class notes.

# —3—

# A BIBLICAL THEOLOGY
## OF LEADERSHIP

In 1980, Lawrence Richards and Clyde Hoeldtke authored a significant volume that attempted to force readers "into Scripture for an understanding of leadership in Christ's church."[1] Yet the work took an essentially deductive approach and offered virtually no information from the Old Testament. Since the appearance of that volume, evangelicals have offered the literature virtually no serious treatment of biblical concepts. We borrow ideas and popular themes from secular writers; we quickly jump on trendy terminology; but we do not courageously shoulder the burden of putting every discipline—certainly one as crucial as leadership studies—through the sieve of integrated theology. And I am hardly without blame.

In small portions of two works I attempted to develop some inductive analysis of significant passages, but hardly anything qualifying as a theological overview.[2] *Feeding and Leading* (Victor, 1989) attempted to show how information can be derived inductively, but I provided only the slightest examples in

43

the five categories identified: Old Testament models, New Testament models, example of Jesus, teaching of Jesus, and teaching of other New Testament writers.[3]

Even here I must urge readers to understand that the boundaries of this chapter allow only the most cursory overview of the topic. These paragraphs make no attempt at either a systematic theology nor a biblical exegesis of leadership. What follows takes the outline of a "biblical theology," defined by Ryrie as "that branch of theological science which deals systematically with the historically conditioned progress of the self-revelation of God as deposited in the Bible."[4] This chapter simply seeks some systematic overview of the progressive revelation of God regarding how He considers leadership to be practiced and taught among His people on earth.

The other key term of this chapter's title resists definition with even greater vigor. In an earlier work I identified Christian leadership as "the exercise of one's spiritual gifts under the call of God to serve a certain group of people in achieving the goals God has given them toward the end of glorifying Christ."[5] Robert Clinton offers this definition: "Leadership is a dynamic process in which a man or woman with God-given capacity influences a specific group of God's people toward His purposes for the group."[6] And James Means expands the idea but captures the same essence:

> Spiritual leadership is the development of relationship with the people of a Christian institution or body in such a way that individuals and the group are enabled to formulate and achieve biblically compatible goals that meet real needs. By their ethical influence, spiritual leaders serve to motivate and enable others to achieve what otherwise would never be achieved.[7]

Countless other examples could be given, but these three lead us on the right track as we prepare to analyze briefly five segments of Scripture toward developing a biblical theology of leadership.

## LEADERSHIP IN THE PENTATEUCH

The early centuries of Israel's life formed a corporate pattern displaying how God dealt with individuals before the forming of the nation. Finding people whose hearts were right toward Him (Noah, Abraham), He developed a vertical relationship with those leaders, which affected their horizontal relationship with others. Like most Old Testament theology, a theology of leadership is best learned by the study of the lives of people whom God used. Eugene Habecker argues that "leaders ought to view their leadership assignment as stewardship of a temporary trust from the Lord rather than as something to be permanently clung to."[8] Furthermore, a clear link exists between the requirements of leadership and those of followership, a most interesting pattern in view of recent research which once again finds those two inseparable.

### Key Words

My studies began with an examination of crucial terms such as *episkopos, presbyteros,* and *prohistemi.* For example, 48 of the 150 times *episkeptomai* is used in the Pentateuch, it appears in the book of Numbers where tribes and families are reviewed. The verb form tends to take the meaning of appointment for supervision. The Septuagint (the Greek version of the Old Testament) uses the word "group" derived from the root *presb* to refer both to age and to those within a tribe or people who held special responsibilities. Sometimes *presbeutes* and *presbys* denote "ambassador" or "negotiator" in the classic sense of spokesman for a defined group. More on this later.

### Character Studies

Of course the chief leader of the Old Testament, especially in the Pentateuch, is God Himself. He rules the heaven-designed theocracy (Ex. 13:17; 15:13; Num. 14:8). But He shares His role with mortals so that Moses can spell out accountability for "all of you [who] are standing today in the presence of the Lord your God—your leaders and chief men, your elders and officials, and all the other men of Israel" (Deut. 29:10). Though no Hebrew nor English words for "lead" appear in conjunction with Abraham, he certainly demonstrates distinctiveness of call, the unique choosing of God for a specific leadership.

> The Lord had said to Abram, "Leave your country, your people and your father's household and go to the land I will show you. I will make you into a great nation and I will bless you; I will make your name great, and you will be a blessing. I will bless those who bless you, and whoever curses you I will curse; and all peoples on earth will be blessed through you." (Genesis 12:1–3)

But Moses clearly stands as the dominant human leader in the Pentateuch. Indeed, God so often reminds him of his leadership task that he responds, "You have been telling me, 'Lead these people,' but you have not let me know whom you will send with me" (Ex. 33:12). Moses, under the tutelage of his father-in-law, Jethro, then learns to share his leadership with others. The dynamic eighteenth chapter of Exodus describes his appointment of numerous leaders.

> He chose capable men from all Israel and made them leaders of the people, officials over thousands, hundreds, fifties and tens. They served as judges for the people at all times. The difficult cases they brought to Moses, but the simple ones they decided themselves. (Exodus 18:25–26)

### Derived Principles

What can we learn from the way God dealt with His people from Creation to the death of Moses? During this period, leadership spread from the embryonic role of Adam supervising

Seth to the later military endeavors of a nation preparing to invade the territory of other peoples (Deut. 20:5–9). Several lessons seem to stand out.

1. *Biblical leadership comes by divine appointment.* Whether we observe Noah, Abraham, Moses, or Aaron, we see the Lord God designating in some clear-cut form those whom He wishes to exercise leadership over others. In every case, the call seems clear both to the intended leader and those who follow.

2. *Leadership moves from singular to multiple.* Noah and Abraham seem to stand alone as they each defy the onslaughts of a pagan world, but once God forms the nation of Israel, Moses parcels out leadership responsibilities to others, sharing his authority, and exercising what we might call today a participatory leadership style. We read about "the leaders of the community" (Ex. 16:22); "leaders of the people" (Ex. 18:25); "leaders of the Israelites" (Num. 13:3); and "the leadership of Moses and Aaron" (Num. 33:1).

3. *Leadership requires definitive accountability.* The law spelled out the greater responsibility for those called by divine appointment: "When a leader sins unintentionally and does what is forbidden in any of the commands of the Lord his God, he is guilty" (Lev. 4:22). Miriam criticized and became leprous; Moses hit the rock in anger and was forbidden entry into the Promised Land; both minor rebellions and major anarchy, like that of Korah, were immediately put down from on high.

## LEADERSHIP IN THE HISTORICAL BOOKS

Much has been made of the appearance of the word *success* in the early verses of Joshua, a term obviously connected with prosperity and material things such as the conquest of the land. Morton Rose warns that the modern concept of success contradicts biblical understandings of leadership and seeks to redefine it by rejecting "material growth, organizational size, or powerful position" and reorienting toward "living the life of

Christ or finding and doing the will of God." He goes on to say, "Everything seems to revolve around the leader and is evaluated by how well that leader fares. If we think of success in terms of leader-greatness, we are on faulty ground. Success is to be measured by the greatness of the people of God not just the leaders."[9]

But in the Historical Books we see God's people focusing on the physical material acquisition and protection of land while at the same time maintaining spiritual devotion to the Lord God. God's leadership lessons for His people continue to evolve and grow.

### Key Words

In the Historical Books, *episcopos* and its variants continue to emphasize the root of observing or paying attention to something or someone, so Saul "sees" (1 Sam. 14:17), Samson "visits" (Judg. 15:1), and God "has come to the aid" of His elect people (Ruth 1:6). In 2 Chronicles 24:11, and especially in Nehemiah, the term relates to officers and governors (11:9, 14, 22). Sometimes particular persons hold these positions of authority, but often the word describes the power as well as the office. Writing in *The New International Dictionary of New Testament Theology*, Lothar Coenen notes that no connection may be "drawn between the OT and the later offices of *episcopos,* or bishop. For the various offices in Israel and their relationship to one another [we must turn to] *presbyteros.*"[10]

Turning to that second key word, however, we see relatively few examples in the Historical Books. Second Chronicles 32:31 shows us the spokesman idea. In the community of the nation, elders control local settlements (1 Sam. 16:4; Judg. 11:5; Ruth 4:2), responsible for judicial, political, and military decisions within their jurisdictions. A paragraph from Coenen's article is helpful here.

The title of "elder" continues to be applied to a ruling class of the individual tribes (cf. 2 Sam. 19:11) and of Israel as a whole. The elders make the decision to send the ark against the Philistines (1 Sam. 4:3). It is they who demand the introduction of the monarchy (1 Sam. 8:4ff.). . . . Their critical, occasionally conspiratorial, attitude toward the monarchy is doubtless due not least to the threat to their influence posed by the formation of a royal civil service and growth of dynastic power.[11]

_Prohistemi_ appears only eight times in the Septuagint; it is without Hebrew equivalent, and is aimed primarily at the role of leading a household (2 Sam. 13:17).

## Character Studies

As the Israeli community expands into a monarchy, we see numerous examples of those who followed the patterns of earlier leaders. Perhaps three stand out in the Historical Books. Joshua portrays the tribal leader assuming military command; David represents the theology of kingship; and Nehemiah shows us the quintessential Old Testament "lay leader," thrust into service without the kind of training afforded either Joshua or David.

The Lord God clearly tells Joshua "you will lead these people" (Josh. 1:6), and he does so by heading up numerous subordinates referred to variously as "the leaders of Israel" (8:10), "the leaders of the assembly" (9:18), and "the leaders of the community" (22:30). The intricacy of organization in the latter days of Joshua's control appears in 23:2 where we read about "elders, leaders, judges and officials."

By the time David comes on the scene, people appear quite prepared for the leadership role of a king. Indeed, they had asked Samuel to "appoint a king to lead us" (1 Sam. 8:5), and the old prophet told the people, "Now you have a king as your leader" (1 Sam. 12:2). Even while fleeing from Saul, David gathered a team: "all those who were in distress or in debt or discontented gathered around him, and he became their leader" (1 Sam. 22:2).

49

By 445 B.C. Nehemiah served as special cupbearer to the king, a noble representative of a people who by this point had long since forgotten leadership and could not recall how God had called them to lead other nations of the world. Nehemiah responds to the call and follows through on a strong sense of mission and accomplishment. Of Nehemiah's role in Jerusalem, Donald Campbell writes: "With such a leader at the helm of the affairs in Jerusalem small wonder the impossible dream soon became a reality. Our prayer today should be that God will raise up more like Nehemiah to serve as Christian leaders . . . the spiritual needs of our world cry out for more Nehemiahs."[12]

## Derived Principles

As the progressive revelation of leadership develops, we are almost overwhelmed with lessons learned from the lives of these and other people God used during the historical period. Perhaps a few can at least provide examples of the many.

1. *Leadership requires a time of preparation.* We see that in the life of Joshua, who served for years as Moses' servant. We see it in David, who trained in obedience and duty at home, then lived the life of an active soldier before his anointing as king. In Nehemiah we see the heart preparation essential to spiritual leadership.

2. *Leadership requires a heart sensitive to spiritual things* (1 Sam. 16:7). David was a skilled fighting man, handy with a sword and bow—but God selected him because of his heart

3. *Leadership requires organizational skills.* To be sure, the terms *leadership* and *administration* are not synonymous. But in God's service, there seems to be dynamic overlap, and Nehemiah provides a wonderful example of one who could organize, plan, delegate, supervise, arbitrate, recruit, train, and evaluate. As Habecker describes him, "God gives the leader the vision; the leader ascertains the facts; he then involves the relevant parties who will be involved in carrying the leadership vision; he shares

with these people his sense of God's call and also the king's response and then the leader waits for the people to respond."[13]

_Intended to instruct._

## LEADERSHIP IN THE POETS AND PROPHETS

Didactic material in the poets and prophets adds little to our understanding of leadership in the Old Testament. But then, Old Testament studies do not depend upon didactic material. We see constant reaffirmation that God calls and anoints certain individuals to carry out roles for Him. Like the ancient judges, the prophets were called. Like their forerunner Samuel, they carried enormous responsibility for the representation of the Lord God, though in far different roles than did the kings.

### Key Words

The linking of *leader* with *shepherd* takes on new meaning in both poets and prophets. The authoritarian oversight of the *episcopos* concept tends to be ameliorated, and we now see the warlike David in different images. The Shepherd Psalm reminds us of the coming Good Shepherd and the shepherding roles of New Testament elders.

_improved; made better_

We find the words *kybernaō* and *kubernēsis* a few places in the Wisdom Literature, and in Proverbs they take on the meaning of wise counsel essential for rulers (Prov. 1:5; 11:14). But the root can be used in the negative sense of the wicked (Prov. 12:5). Elders reappear after the monarchical system. Coenen discusses this in some detail.

> How deeply rooted was the position of the elders as demonstrated by what happened after the end of the monarchy and exile of large portions of the population. It was the elders who once again appeared as guardians and representatives of the Jewish communities both in exile (Jer. 29:1) and in the homeland (Ezek. 8:1ff.; cf. also the elders of the land who in Jeremiah 26:17 speak on behalf of the prophet). But there also was a

change which took place during this period. The clans were superseded by influential families, and influential families thus gained a position of eminence among the people as a whole. The heads of these appear now as an aristocratic ruling class.... At the table of the governor Nehemiah there is a daily gathering of 150 notables, who are without any recognizable legal function, but certainly not without influence.[14]

## Character Studies

A contrast of the prophetic leadership of Isaiah and Jeremiah was undertaken in some detail by Helen Doohan, to great benefit. Prophetic leadership, as noted earlier, is inseparably linked with the word of Yahweh, a rock-solid conviction which seems to free these leaders from the current necessity of popular approval. In Jeremiah's case, selection by God meant rejection by people.

> Both Isaiah and Jeremiah are affected in their leadership style by the theological convictions emanating from an understanding of covenant. Furthermore, they are professional irritants in the existential situation and respond to changing needs with appropriate reinterpretation of the basic message. Prophetic leaders know their world and are deeply involved in it. However, their religious convictions are the prime factor influencing their approach to leadership and to the world of their day. They give us a politics of faith.[15]

Far different yet equally enlightening is the life of Daniel. His leadership demonstrates not merely "politics of faith" but rather the exercise of faith while in politics. The sterling character of his personal life, the unshakable convictions of his godly behavior, and his reputation for unimpeachable integrity lift Daniel to a special place in leadership modeling among Old Testament saints.

*Derived Principles*

Once again, one could list pages of lessons in life and ministry available from these men and their colleagues, but we shall limit ourselves to only three.

1. *Leadership requires deep conviction in God's will for both leaders and followers.* We talk a great deal today about mission statements and long-range planning. The lives of the prophets were constantly futuristic, clearly committed to what God wished to do with them and with the people He had called them to serve.

2. *Leadership requires clear theological perspective.* On the surface, the casual reader might conclude that God sent His prophets only to pronounce doom and warn against judgment. In reality, however, they constantly served as national guardsmen, protecting the purity of the covenant and its essential doctrinal content. They regularly confronted false prophets and consistently defended the Lord God's word, often at the risk of their own lives.

3. *Leadership requires an awareness of contemporary surroundings.* To be sure, at times Ezekiel appeared to live in some distant world, never visited by his contemporaries. However, eccentricity was merely one of his character traits. Most of the prophets, notably Isaiah, Jeremiah, and Daniel, stayed sharply tuned to the needs and hurts of their day. They directed their messages with a profound sense of divine vocation. Indeed, the very meaning of the word "prophet," *nabi,* comes from a root meaning "one who is called."

## LEADERSHIP IN THE GOSPELS AND ACTS

According to Kennon Callahan, the key to effective church leadership lies in moving from what he calls "professional minister" to "missionary pastor." "The professional minister movement," he writes, "was a cultural reflection of the broader cultural movement toward professionalism. To be sure, much was gained. And it worked as long as the culture was a churched culture."

The professional minister, as described by Callahan, was reactive, passive, organizational, and institutional. The missionary pastor, on the other hand, is proactive, intentional, relational, and missional. Leadership then becomes the ability to lead a group toward discovery and fulfillment. Callahan concludes,

> Leadership is more than management, bosses, ennoblement, or charismatic direction. To be a leader is to be more than any of these. "More" here is not to be understood as "better." It is simply that the leader resonates with the whole of life; others resonate only with part of life. That is why the leader is the leader.[16]

This is an interesting idea. But our purpose is not to chase the rabbit trails of contemporary theory or cultural constructs; rather we want to see whether Callahan and others actually grasp the biblical handle on our subject.

## Key Words

As the funnel narrows, the importance of key words in the new covenant becomes ever more obvious. Here we encounter the exact statements made by our Lord to His disciples regarding how they should carry His mission in the world—how they must become leaders like Him. Of primary concern in the Gospels (as well as later in the Epistles) is the word *hegeomai*, which appears twenty-seven times in twenty different chapters of the New Testament. It simply means ruler or chief (Matt. 2:6; Acts 7:10; 14:12; 26:2).

But two uses stand out in this portion of Scripture (to our great profit) regarding the nature of new covenant leadership. The first appears in Luke 22:26, clearly a high-water mark on our subject. The disciples have been arguing among themselves on the very night of the Crucifixion. They have fallen into dispute, a *philoneikia*, literally meaning "rivalry." Because of their fondness for strife and personal gain, the disciples verbally attack one another in their attempt to gain political prominence in what they expected would be an immediately forthcoming earthly kingdom.

In the midst of their political power play, the Lord likens their behavior to the Hellenistic monarchs who ruled Egypt and Syria. He begins His statement in verse 26 with a strong contrast construction: "But you . . . not so." The full verse reads, "But you are not to be like that. Instead, the greatest among you should be like the youngest, and the one who rules [the *hegeomai*] like the one who serves."

Still another reference of importance appears in Acts 15:22, where we learn that after the resolution of the Gentile question at the Jerusalem Council the church "chose Judas (called Barsabbas) and Silas, two men who were leaders among the brothers." *The plurality of team leadership and significance of servanthood surface very early in the New Testament text.*

A second word of extreme importance in the New Testament is <u>*oikonomos*,</u> appearing in ten verses scattered over ten chapters from Luke to 1 Peter. The word commonly translates as "<u>steward</u>" (though "manager" is acceptable), and the verb form indicates someone who has been entrusted with responsibility. Paul himself is an *oikonomos* (1 Cor. 4:1) and fulfills the primary qualification of this leadership dimension—<u>faithfulness</u>.

As the word group derived from <u>*episcopos*</u> reaches the New Testament, we find almost a singular theme—<u>caring.</u> In five uses of the standard noun, four deal with the leader of the community (Acts 20:28; Phil. 1:1; 1 Tim. 3:2; Titus 1:7), and 1 Peter 2:25 refers to Christ as the guardian of souls. The verb <u>*episkep-tomai*</u> commonly describes the <u>loving and seeking care of God.</u> The word refers to Moses in Acts 7:23 and to Paul and Barnabas in Acts 15:36.

The Old Testament thrust of punishment seems completely replaced, giving way to a caring rather than ruling theme. Luke introduces the expression *presbyteroi* in Acts 11 to describe those who exercised leadership in the Jerusalem church. The word also appears in Acts 14:23 and Acts 20:17. In the latter context, *episcopos* and *presbyteros* are viewed as synonymous.

One other term requires mention here in view of modern preference for the term "pastor." The word is *poimen* (shepherd), and we learn early in the New Testament that the primary reference is to the Lord Himself (Matt. 26:31; John 10). Jeffrey Rada argues,

> Paul's leadership terminology was fluid enough that he did not feel compelled here (Eph. 4:11) to list every Greek word for leadership, nor in any other of his lists of the gifts. While, as we shall see later, the words for the eldership are interchangeable, there is no use of "pastor" *(poimen)* to compel us to equate it with either "preacher" or "minister." . . . Thus Paul's fluid use of leadership terminology is meant to denote the *emphasis* of each particular elder; not to hermetically compartmentalize his office and create an office for every function in the body. It then becomes unnecessary for us to invent a new office of "pastor" to legitimize such a compartmentalization of leadership responsibilities.[17]

Whether one agrees with Rada or not, it seems clear that we have fogged in the participatory and multiple nature of team leadership in the New Testament. *Any kind of focus on a dominant pastoral role which creates a single-leader church (a rather common concept in some church-growth literature of the late twentieth century) dilutes the biblical emphasis on team leadership.*

## Character Studies

Clearly the key to understanding Christian leadership requires learning to lead like the Lord. In the dramatic eleventh chapter of Matthew (vv. 25–30), Jesus describes His leadership as gentle and humble. In the chapter that follows, He quotes from Isaiah 42 to describe the chosen servant as one who "will not quarrel or cry out; no one will hear his voice in the streets. A bruised reed he will not break, and a smoldering wick he will not snuff out" (Matt. 12:19–20a). As I suggested in *Feeding and Leading*,

> Evangelical leaders following the gentleness and humility of Christ recognize they are neither the single nor final authority; they decentralize decision-making and develop the leadership qualities of their colleagues. The pastor is the coach, not the general manager, and certainly not the team owner.[18]

Our Lord's work with the disciples provides a pattern of group leadership worthy of the most diligent study. I find it amazing how few current Christian leaders have carefully worked their way through A. B. Bruce's *The Training of the Twelve*. James Hind notes, "If there was one modern management trait that carried Jesus Christ from a nobody to a somebody, it was His service to and for the benefit of others—His servant leadership."[19]

James, moderator of the Jerusalem church, provides a second valuable character study in the New Testament. He was Jesus' half brother and the author of the epistle of James. Though not directly trained by the Lord Himself, James modeled team leadership by moderating a public assembly with a broad view to the greatest possible benefit of the body of Christ; he allowed all viewpoints to be appropriately aired, summarizing the consensus of the assembly, and preserving the unity of the saints.

Finally we need to look at Barnabas, who rose from an apparent layman's role in Jerusalem to become leader of the second New Testament church at Antioch. He affords a brilliant example of unthreatened, secure leadership, willing to thrust others (Saul of Tarsus) toward the greatest potential of their gifts, never defending his own turf or holding on to position for personal prestige. God moved him out of his first and only "senior pastorate" after one year, and then Barnabas started out joyously to lead the first missionary journey. Yet leadership was soon passed to his former assistant and, though John Mark seems somewhat offended by the change, Barnabas never misses a stride.

Some would fault him for his argument with Paul at the end of Acts 15. But even there the positive note emphasizes his long-term commitment to John Mark and the ultimate results produced in that young man who became profitable for ministry under the tutelage and modeling of Barnabas. Richards and Hoeldtke write:

> The New Testament's picture of the servant as one who *does,* rather than one who adopts the leadership style of the world and *tells,* has a unique integrity. The Christian both hears the Word from his spiritual leader and sees the Word expressed in his person. The open life of leaders among—not over—the brothers and sisters is a revelation of the very face of Jesus. And to see Jesus expressing Himself in a human being brings the hope that transformation might be a possibility for me too.[20]

## *Derived Principles*

Perhaps here we should paraphrase John, suggesting that if every leadership principle available in the Gospels or in Acts were written down, perhaps the whole world would not have room for the books that would be written (John 21:25). But several things stand out with piercing impact for the needs of today's church.

1. *Leadership is servanthood.* Commenting on Matthew 20:25–28, Francis Cosgrove says: "This teaching of leading by serving continues to have an unfamiliar ring in an age that calls for us to do everything we can to climb to the top. The Bible teaches that to lead is to serve. We may recognize the truth of this concept and respond positively. The problem, however, is doing it day-to-day."[21] He goes on to suggest that when we define the concept biblically, a servant is a person who doesn't exercise his

own will but rather submits it in order to please his master. He also demonstrates the importance of serving another without any assurance of reward.[22] Someone once asked Lorne Sanny how it is possible to know whether one functions as a servant. Sanny replied, "By the way you react when people treat you like one."

_2. Leadership is stewardship._ We need not return to a detailed study of *oikonomos* to emphasize again the concept of stewardship. In the parable of the faithful and wise manager, we had better notice that the *oikonomos* is placed in charge of other servants, not to give them their orders but to distribute their food allowance. He holds an absolute responsibility for awareness of the master's will and carries out his tasks in light of the master's return.

_3. Leadership is shared power._ Current secular leadership literature talks a good bit about empowering others. Practically, leadership in business and politics centers on grasping, retaining, and using power. Such concepts run totally counter to the New Testament. John Stott correctly reminds us that "Christian leaders serve not their own interests but rather the interests of others" (Phil. 2:4). This simple principle should deliver the leader from excessive individualism, extreme isolation, and self-centered empire building. Leadership teams, therefore, are more healthy than solo leadership.[23]

My own view is well documented in my writings—the proper climate for leadership development emphasizes a decentralized institutional philosophy. Our goal is to push decision making and authority as far down the ranks as possible so that the people who live with actual implementation have a major voice in the decision.

> We must develop (a) a climate of respect focusing on individual worth and dignity and encouraging people to contribute their ideas; (b) a climate of trust in which people learn to trust their own abilities and those of others, unthreatened by constant changes and policy in program; (c) a climate of acceptance where, within the appropriate boundaries, people have room to

59

think and move, to consider changes in their own belief systems, and more important, in methods of ministry; (d) a climate of discovery which recognizes that new leaders will make mistakes, that alternative solutions need to be explored without the pressures of immediate answers, and with tolerance for ambiguity in tough problems; and (e) a climate of depth— depth of spiritual dimensions in individual and corporate leaders and also depth "on the bench."[24]

## LEADERSHIP IN THE EPISTLES AND REVELATION

If the Twelve demonstrated the practical outworking of Christ's teachings in the book of Acts, it was left for Paul and other epistle writers to formulate New Testament doctrine, including what we might call "a biblical theology of leadership."

### Key Words

The gift of leadership identified in Romans 12:8 by the Greek word *prohistemi* must occupy our attention for a moment. The word appears in eight verses throughout five chapters of the New Testament with special focus on the verb form ("manage") in the Pastoral Epistles.

In Romans 12:8 and 1 Thessalonians 5:12 we find a special emphasis on caring for others. This New Testament combination of caring and leading gives us the servant model of team leadership.

Though the noun form appears only three times in the New Testament, *kubernetes* is crucial to our overall study of leadership. Two passages (Acts 27:11; Rev. 18:17) use the word in its traditional classical sense of helmsman or manager of a ship. In 1 Corinthians 12:28 Paul takes the related term *kubernesis* and impregnates it with theological significance as the gift of administration.

Yet a third word occupies our attention here, one which has drawn enormous controversy in the late twentieth-century church. I refer to *kephale,* which occurs twelve times in the Epistles, most commonly designating Jesus as Head of the church. In the other instances, it refers to relationships between husbands and wives. Richards observes that, "Neither in any of these nor in Revelation's 18 uses of head is there any indication that 'headship' refers to leaders in the body of Christ!"[25] I include the word here to emphasize its *negation* in the New Testament. A serious commitment to the servant-steward-sharing model of New Testament leadership rejects authoritarian and autocratic roles for those who propose to lead God's people.

Finally we need to take a brief look at *diakonia,* often linked with various New Testament offices. The word commonly means "ministry" or "service," and it appears thirty-seven times in the verb form and thirty-four times as a noun in the New Testament. The masculine *diakonos* has an additional thirty references. The diversity ranges wide, from Matthew to Revelation, and most frequently the term means to serve or care for others. It takes particular poignancy in 1 Timothy 3 in relation to the office of a deacon (vv. 8, 10, 12–13) and in Paul's frequent use of the word in reference to himself (e.g., Col. 1:23–25). Viewpoints differ widely on this subject. As we have noted earlier, Rada insists that the New Testament cannot be made to say "that the role of 'minister' exists distinct from elders and that they were the prototypes of this office."[26]

Whatever position one adopts on that question, it seems clear that the concept of *diakonia* emphasizes again the servant leadership concept which Jesus initiated in the Gospels.

## Character Studies

It is impossible in this segment to bypass the apostle Paul. His constant activity of modeling and mentoring, encouraging and exhorting, teaching and training, exemplifies New Testament leadership at its zenith. He describes his own leadership in 1 Thessalonians, offering a contrast with first-century pagan understandings. In 2:1–6 he identifies what he did *not* do among the believers there. Then in 2:7–12 he describes a process of nurture and family care, depicting himself as a nursing mother, a patient schoolteacher, a mother bird, and a loving father. These metaphors, though uncommon to the modern North American ear, undeniably imprint the text.

As we follow Paul's trail it doesn't take us long to come to Timothy, the quintessential disciple, the end result of modeling and mentoring. How much of what we know about church leadership is embodied in this young man because of Paul's two letters! (In looking at the life of Timothy we learn that biblical servants avoid false doctrine; they aim toward godly living; they activate and use their spiritual gifts; and they accept the challenge God has placed before them in whatever leadership role He has prescribed.) From family preparation to pastoral problems, Timothy provides a brilliant example of how *leadership is learned behavior.*

Finally, we must note also the group we commonly call "the Ephesian elders," whose dramatic appearance in Acts 20 demonstrates for us what God expects of lay leaders in local congregations. These elders (v. 17) and overseers (v. 28) served as shepherds (*presbyteros, episcopos,* and *poimen* all appear in the same context and describe the same people). We link Acts 20 with Ephesians 4:11–16 to see precisely how this kind of leadership creates strength in the unified body of any given congregation.

## Derived Principles

At the risk of being accused of forced alliteration in both New Testament lists of principles, I find again a basic pattern developing among the dozens of leadership lessons found in the Epistles and Revelation.

1. *Leadership is ministry.* The emphasis on *diakonia* and the thrust of the gift of leadership in Romans 12:8 show us that if New Testament leadership means anything, it means serving

other people. With meekness, church leaders involve themselves in concert with other believers to engage in team ministry. Then the smog of selfishness and egoism lifts to make mutual ministry a biblical reality.

2. *Leadership is modeling behavior.* We've seen it clearly in the Paul-Timothy relationship (1 Tim. 4:11–16; 2 Tim. 3:10–15). Richards says it well: "The spiritual leader who is a servant does not demand. He *serves.* In his service the spiritual leader sets an example for the body—an example that has compelling power to motivate heart change."[27]

3. *Leadership is membership in the body.* Here we do not refer to the placement of one's name on the roll, but rather to the identification of the leader with all other parishioners. In Romans 12:4–5 Paul writes, "Just as each of us has one body with many members, and these members do not all have the same function, so in Christ we who are many form one body, and each member belongs to all the others." Relating to other people stands at the heart of an understanding of Christian leadership, the measure of which can only be shown when the leader serves the body in meekness and membership.

Lyle Schaller offers "long established congregations" three options for leadership:

> One is to rely on several compatible, redundant and mutually reinforcing organizing principles to undergird the life and unity of that fellowship. A second is to watch passively while existing organizing principles erode, fade away or become divisive with this erosion followed by a numerical decline. The third is to find a minister with a charismatic personality who is able and willing to serve as THE leader.[28]

Let us hope those three non-biblical options do not represent closure on the issue. In an interesting study of ministerial leadership, Jack Balswick and Walter Wright remind us that "the skills needed to lead persons at each of the maturity levels are not always given to every minister. Thus the complementarity of the body of Christ provides a variety of gifted leaders who together can empower believers for lives of service to the body of ministry in the community."[29]

From the narrow definitions of leadership offered in the introduction to this chapter we can now expand our horizons to incorporate the fifteen dimensions we have seen arise out of Scripture. Pooled together in a narrative paragraph they might look something like this:

> Biblical team leadership takes place when divinely appointed men and women accept responsibility for obedience to God's call. They recognize the importance of preparation time, allowing the Holy Spirit to develop tenderness of heart and skill of hands. They carry out their leadership roles with deep conviction of God's will, clear theological perspective from His Word, and an acute awareness of the contemporary issues which they and their followers face. Above all, they exercise leadership as servants and stewards, sharing authority with their followers and affirming that leadership is primarily ministry to others, modeling for others and mutual membership with others in Christ's body.

## FOR FURTHER READING

Bruce, A. B. *The Training of the Twelve*. New York: Harper, 1986.

Cedar, Paul. *Strength in Servant Leadership*. Waco, Tex.: Word, 1987.

Enroth, Ronald M. *Churches That Abuse*. Grand Rapids: Zondervan, 1992.

Habecker, Eugene B. *The Other Side of Leadership*. Wheaton, Ill.: Victor, 1987.

Means, James E. *Leadership in Christian Ministry*. Grand Rapids: Baker, 1989.

Richards, Lawrence O., and Clyde Hoeldtke. *A Theology of Church Leadership*. Grand Rapids: Zondervan, 1980.

## NOTES

1. Lawrence O. Richards and Clyde Hoeldtke, *A Theology of Church Leadership* (Grand Rapids: Zondervan, 1980), 10.

2. Kenneth O. Gangel, *Building Leaders for Church Education* (Chicago: Moody, 1981), 73–80; and *Feeding and Leading* (Wheaton, Ill.: Victor, 1989), 31–47.

3. Gangel, *Feeding and Leading,* 52.

4. Charles C. Ryrie, *Biblical Theology of the New Testament* (Chicago: Moody, 1959), 12.

5. Gangel, *Feeding and Leading,* 31.

6. Robert J. Clinton, *The Making of a Leader* (Colorado Springs: NavPress, 1988), 7.

7. James E. Means, *Leadership in Christian Ministry* (Grand Rapids: Baker, 1989), 58.

8. Eugene B. Habecker, *The Other Side of Leadership* (Wheaton, Ill.: Victor, 1987), 54.

9. Morton F. Rose, "Steps Toward Servant Leadership," *Search* (Spring 1990): 17.

10. Lothar Coenen, "Bishop, Presbyter, Elder," in *The New International Dictionary of New Testament Theology,* ed. Colin Brown, vol. 1 (Grand Rapids: Zondervan, 1979), 190.

11. Ibid., 195.

12. Donald K. Campbell, *Nehemiah: Man in Charge* (Wheaton, Ill.: Victor, 1979), 23.

13. Habecker, *The Other Side of Leadership,* 58.

14. Brown, *New International Dictionary,* 196.

15. Helen Doohan, "Contrasts in Prophetic Leadership: Isaiah and Jeremiah," *Biblical Theology Bulletin* 13, no. 2 (1983): 43.

16. Kennon Callahan, "The Key to Effective Church Leadership," *Pulpit Digest* 71:502 (March/April 1990): 79.

17. Jeffrey R. Rada, "Restoring New Testament Church Leadership," *Seminary Review* 28, no. 3 (September 1982): 116.

18. Gangel, *Feeding and Leading,* 57.

19. James F. Hind, *The Heart and Soul of Effective Management* (Wheaton, Ill.: Victor, 1989).

20. Richards and Hoeldtke, *Theology of Church Leadership,* 120.

21. Francis Cosgrove, "The Disciple Is a Servant," *Discipleship Journal* 30 (1985): 35.

22. Ibid., 36.

23. John R. W. Stott, "What Makes Leadership Christian?" *Christianity Today* (August 9, 1985): 27.

24. Kenneth O. Gangel, "Developing New Leaders for the Global Task," *Evangelical Missions Quarterly* (April 1989): 169.

25. Richards and Hoeldtke, *Theology of Church Leadership,* 17.

26. Rada, "New Testament Church Leadership," 112.

27. Richards and Hoeldtke, *Theology of Church Leadership,* 115.

28. Lyle Schaller, "Is Pastoral Ministry a Personality Cult?" *Church Management— The Clergy Journal* (February 1987): 35.

29. Jack Balswick and Walter Wright, "A Complementary–Empowering Model of Ministerial Leadership," *The Best in Theology* 4 (1989): 317–26.

# —4—

# TOWARD A NEW TESTAMENT
# VIEW OF LEADERSHIP

As Aesop tells the story, the frogs down on the pond wanted a king. They bothered Jupiter so much with their request that he finally tossed a log into the pond, and for a while the frogs were happy with the new leader.

Soon, however, they discovered they could jump up and down on the leader, run all over him, and he offered no resistance—not even a response. Not only that, but he had no direction or purpose to his behavior but just floated back and forth on the pond, a practice which exasperated the frogs, who were really sincere about wanting "strong leadership."

So back to Jupiter they went. They complained about their log leader and appealed for stronger administrative oversight. Jupiter, weary of the complaining frogs, this time gave them a stork, who stood tall above the members of the group and certainly had the appearance of a leader. The frogs were quite happy with the new situation. Their leader stalked around the pond making great noises and attracting attention. Soon, however, the frogs' joy turned to sorrow and ultimately to panic, for in a very short time the stork began to eat his subordinates.

One of the major problems in implementing team leadership in the church, or in any other kind of Christian community, is failure to recognize not only a functional, but also a biblical leadership style. Frequently we find ourselves gravitating to extremes and behaving like logs or storks in our relationship to the people with whom God allows us to work. The log was a "free-rein" leader, letting the followers do whatever they wanted to. The stork chose absolute autocracy.

In a *Harvard Business Review* article entitled "How to Choose a Leadership Pattern," authors Tannenbaum and Schmidt discuss the same problem with respect to secular functions of management science.

> The problem of how the modern manager can be "democratic" in his relations with subordinates and at the same time maintain the necessary authority and control in the organization for which he is responsible has come in to focus increasingly in recent years.
>
> Earlier in the century this problem was not so acutely felt. The successful executive was generally pictured as possessing intelligence, imagination, initiative, the capacity to make rapid (and generally wise) decisions, and the ability to inspire subordinates. People tended to think of the world as being divided into "leaders" and "followers."[1]

How interesting. The best elements of leadership style that have evolved from multimillions of dollars of research on the part of industrial management science are not far removed from the leadership style which Scripture delineates from the start! They recognize the inherent value of the individual and the worth of human relations not only as a means to an end, but as an end in itself within the Christian community. (In a very real sense, the church should be the most person-centered organization in the world.) Indeed, a congregation that has its vertical relationships in order (theocentricity) will generally follow with proper horizontal relationships (anthrocentricity). The church does not have to overemphasize the social gospel to recognize that "souls" are ethereal and invisible, but one sees people every day.

What is a biblical view of leadership? Without reviewing the details of chapter 3, perhaps we can best arrive at that answer by first dealing with the negative side of the question.

## WHAT NEW TESTAMENT LEADERSHIP IS NOT

A marvelous passage in Luke 22 holds some enormously valuable principles for helping us analyze our Lord's view of leadership. The passage itself appears in verses 24 through 27, but the context is of great importance also. The Lord has just ministered to the disciples in their final supper together in the Upper Room. Commentators differ about whether the foot washing had taken place before this conversation or followed it. One thing is clear: the disciples had just finished the bread and the cup and had experienced among themselves a worship relationship of the highest order with the incarnate God in their midst, and with the Father in heaven. It is almost unbelievable that this scene could have followed that experience.

> Also a dispute arose among them as to which of them was considered to be greatest. Jesus said to them, "The kings of the Gentiles lord it over them; and those who exercise authority over them call themselves Benefactors. But you are not to be like that. Instead, the greatest among you should be like the youngest, and the one who rules like the one who serves. For who is greater, the one who is at the table or the one who serves? Is it not the one who is at the table? But I am among you as one who serves." (Luke 22:24–27)

### *New Testament Leadership Is Not Political Power Play*

Immediately after sharing the symbolic representation of our Lord's flesh and blood, the disciples fell into a dispute. The word for <u>dispute is *philoneikia*</u> and literally means "<u>rivalry.</u>" Even more interesting, this word does not describe an accidental falling into argument on occasion, but rather the possession of a habitually contentious spirit. To put it another way, because of their fondness for strife, the disciples verbally attacked one another in an attempt to gain political prominence in what they expected would be an immediately forthcoming, earthly kingdom. Martin Buber once said that people's inability to "carry on authentic dialog with one another is the most acute symptom of the pathology of our time." Hardly a modern problem.

Political power play in Christian organizations is even more reprehensible than in the world. Yet even before the first church organized at Jerusalem; before a pastor ever candidated for appointment to a congregation; before an official board ever met to design a building program, the church knew how to fight! Toward the end of the first century, John bemoaned that in one local church a man named Diotrephes liked "to have the preeminence among them" (3 John 9 KJV). Unfortunately, the Diotrephesian tribe has multiplied in nineteen hundred years of history.

## *New Testament Leadership Is Not Authoritarian Attitude*

In chapter 3 we looked at Luke 22:27–29. Let's expand that further. Luke 22:25 records our Lord's reaction to the arguments of His disciples. He offers first a comparison, then a contrast. As I mentioned before, the comparison shows that their behavior at that moment paralleled the behavior of the Hellenistic monarchs who ruled Egypt and Syria. Their leadership style is described as "<u>exercising lordship</u>"—the word *kurieuō*, which appears frequently in the pages of the New Testament. At times it is used to describe the authority of God (Rom. 14:9). Paul uses it often to refer to <u>negative control, such as death's attempt to hold dominion over</u> Christ (Rom. 6:9); the power of sin in the life of the believer (Rom. 6:14); and the hold of the law on people freed by the gospel (Rom. 7:1).

A similar word, *katakurieuō,* describes Gentile rulers; the control of demons over people (Acts 19:16); and a negative example in prescribing the behavior of elders with saints in the church (1 Pet. 5:3). But the verb form is never used positively of Christian leadership. To put it simply, *Christian leadership is not authoritarian control over the minds and behavior of other people.* Peter remembered the lesson of this night, for in writing his epistle he warned the elders not to lord it over God's heritage.

The first part of Luke 22:26 is a strong contrast construction: "But ye . . . not so." The kings of the Gentiles wished to be called benefactors for any little deed of kindness they might show their subjects, although everyone knew they practiced autocracy and demagoguery. Team leadership rejects that kind of authoritarian control. As a matter of fact, in defiance of the culture of the time, our Lord says that the one who is greatest in the church actually behaves like the younger, and the boss behaves like a worker.

## New Testament Leadership Is Not Cultic Control

One beautiful word describing the work of the church is *diakanos.* It means "service," precisely what Christ did for His disciples in that Upper Room. The question of verse 27 seems to be rhetorical: Who is more important, the waiter or the dinner guest? Obvious answer: the dinner guest, of course! But wait a minute; who is the guest and who is the waiter at this Last Supper? Answer: "I am among you as one who serves." Conclusion: *New Testament leadership is not flashy public relations and platform personality, but humble service to the group.* The work of God is carried on by spiritual power, not personal magnetism, as Paul clearly points out in 1 Corinthians 1:26–31. Some leaders may serve the Word and some may serve tables—but all leaders serve (Acts 6)!

## THE POSITIVE PATTERN OF CHRIST

The positive pattern of Christ's developing leadership in

His disciples is clearly enunciated in A. B. Bruce's helpful book *The Training of the Twelve.*[2] He suggests that the total report of the Gospels covers only thirty-three or thirty-four days of our Lord's three-and-one-half-year ministry, and John records only eighteen days. What did Christ do the rest of the time? The clear implication of the Scriptures indicates that He trained team leaders. What kind of leaders did He train? How did He deal with them? What were the important principles of His leadership-development program?

1. *The leadership of our Lord focused on individuals.* Christ's personal conversation with Peter, recorded in John 21, offers a good example of the way He gave Himself to people in an attempt to build His life and ministry into them.

2. *The leadership of our Lord focused on the Scriptures.* His treatment of God's absolute truth was not diluted by relativistic philosophy. He held the Old Testament in highest esteem. The rabbis had distorted God's revelation, and the Leader of leaders now came to say, "You have heard that it was said, . . . but I tell you" (Matt. 5:21–48).

3. *The leadership of our Lord focused on Himself.* In John 14:9, Jesus finds it necessary to say to one of the disciples, "Philip have you been so long with Me and you still have not known the Father? Take a good look at Me because if you understand Me you understand the Father" (author's paraphrase).

4. *The leadership of our Lord focused on purpose.* Christ had clear-cut goals for His earthly ministry, and a limited time in which to achieve them. If you knew you had to leave your present ministry within three and one-half years and turn it over completely to subordinates, how would you prepare? You could do no better than follow the example of Jesus, and the result would probably look a great deal like the leadership which characterized the New Testament church.

## WHAT NEW TESTAMENT LEADERSHIP IS

In dealing with this issue, I am always inclined to turn to the book of Acts because of its vivid description of early church life. Yet the book of Acts gives us historical narrative, not a developed ecclesiology. We will be better helped by looking at the epistles of Paul, commissioned by the Spirit of God to organize local churches and to describe God's plan and pattern for the functioning of those churches. Some verses in 1 Thessalonians will serve us well as a model:

> As apostles of Christ we could have been a burden to you, but we were gentle among you, like a mother caring for her little children. We loved you so much that we were delighted to share with you not only the gospel of God but our lives as well, because you had become so dear to us. Surely you remember, brothers, our toil and hardship; we worked night and day in order not to be a burden to anyone while we preached the gospel of God to you. You are witnesses, and so is God, of how holy, righteous and blameless we were among you who believed. For you know that we dealt with each of you as a father deals with his own children, encouraging, comforting and urging you to live lives worthy of God, who calls you into his kingdom and glory. (1 Thessalonians 2:6–12)

### New Testament Church Leadership Is Nurture

Nurture is a botanical term which describes the care and feeding of a young plant so that it grows properly to maturity. In verses 7 and 8, Paul uses some distinctive words to describe nurture in the eyeball-to-eyeball relationships which accompany leadership responsibility.

He speaks of being "gentle," the word *herioi,* used often of a teacher, patient in the process of nurturing seemingly incorrigible students. As if that emphasis were not clear enough, he refers to the gentleness of a mother, not a hired baby-sitter. The word appears in the Old Testament to describe the Lord God's care of Israel, and in 2 Timothy 2:24 Paul uses the word to describe "the servant of the Lord" (KJV).

But there is more to this emphasis on nurture. A gentle mother "cares for her little children." The word "care" is *thalpē*, which literally means "to soften by heat" or "to keep warm." Deuteronomy 22:6, in the Septuagint, uses the word to describe a bird caring for its young by spreading its feathers over them in the nest. Such a mother loves those growing children (1 Thess. 2:7). Such yearning for the good of the group may ultimately result in a sacrifice on the part of the leader.

Where is assertiveness in all of this? The image of a sharp voice barking orders and running a tight ship? Again, a pagan culture distorts our understanding of spiritual reality. We identify leadership with toughness and ruggedness; God identifies it with tenderness. We think of leadership as "handling" adults; God thinks of it as nurturing children.

## New Testament Leadership Is Example

The hard work of Paul's leadership spills out in verse 9. Both day and night, with great effort, he worked among the believers. His own life, and those of his colleagues, provided examples of holiness, justice, and blamelessness before God. Note that this behavior took place *before the believers* to facilitate evangelism.

In 2:5–6, Paul assures the Thessalonians that their leaders are human, not some kind of ecclesiastical giants who want to run the organization by sheer executive skill and personal power. The plural pronouns throughout this passage affirm again the biblical reality of team leadership.

## New Testament Leadership Is Fatherhood

What does a father do? According to Ephesians 6:4, he, too, is responsible for the nurture of his children. In 1 Thessalonians 2:11 (KJV), the words rendered "exhorted" and "comfort-ed" are the words *parakalountes* and *paramuthoumenoi*, respec-tively. These commonly appear together in Paul's writing. The former is often used of divine ministry, but the latter is always a human word. Never used directly to mean God's comfort, it describes the way He works through people to minister to other people in the community of faith.

A father also "urges" his children (v. 12). The word car-ries the idea of admonishing or witnessing truth so that they will walk in patterns acceptable to God.

## PAUL'S EXAMPLE

Earlier, we noted the positive pattern of Christ in leadership training. A word or two about the example of the apostle Paul may also be helpful. The New Testament church multiplied from the few people described in Acts 1. Many church leaders were person-ally trained by the apostle Paul. He was, in effect, the "pilot pro-ject." Timothy, Silas, Titus, Epaphroditus, the Ephesian elders, and many others were spin-offs from his own life and ministry.

In some Christian organizations today, the great curse of a one-person ministry looks much like the worldly leadership con-demned by our Lord in Luke 22. If we would serve our own gen-eration with power and effectiveness, we must stop pretending that Christian leadership resembles the kings of the Gentiles.

### FOR FURTHER READING
Bratcher, Edward B. *The Walk-on-Water Syndrome.* Waco, Tex.: Word, 1984.

Engstrom, Ted W. *The Making of a Christian Leader.* Grand Rapids: Zondervan, 1976.

Gangel, Kenneth O. *Feeding and Leading.* Wheaton, Ill.: Victor, 1989.

Richards, Lawrence O., and Clyde Hoeldtke. *A Theology of Church Leadership.* Grand Rapids: Zondervan, 1980.

Stabbert, Bruce. *The Team Concept.* Tacoma, Wash.: Hegg Bros., 1982.

## NOTES

1. Robert Tannenbaum and Warren H. Schmidt, "How to Choose a Leadership Pattern," *Harvard Business Review* 36 (March-April 1958): 95.

2. A. B. Bruce, *The Training of the Twelve* (New York: Harper, 1986).

# —5—

# TEAM LEADERSHIP IN
# ORGANISM AND ORGANIZATION

W e have already noted that the church is both organism and organization. Organismically, it is the body
of Christ and partakes of the spiritual qualities of that mystical
assembly. Organizationally, it demonstrates many of the same
characteristics that mark other organizations: institutional goals,
trained personnel, budgets and accounts, hierarchy of leadership,
and basic organizational structures.

The major difference comes in the understanding of leadership. One must maintain one's attitude of serving in this unique
organism-organization. Contrast this with the secular response of
the kings of the Gentiles discussed in Luke 22 (see chapters 3 and
4). Despite the many points of similarity between Christian and
secular leadership, the differences are much more important. In
this chapter we will look at four of those differences: the source
of authority; the historical precedent of biblical examples; the
unique spiritual dynamic in leadership; and an analysis of
bureaucracy in biblical leadership.

## THE SOURCE OF AUTHORITY

### *Platonic Leadership*

Even preceding the Christian era, the great philosophers of ancient Greece grappled with the question of authority. Both Plato in *The Republic* and Aristotle in *Politics* concerned themselves with the questions of leadership, even though their interests related largely to questions of political leadership in Greece's democracy at that time.

When we analyze Plato's brand of philosophy, for example, we find that the Platonic concept views the leader as one possessed of special knowledge. This is not the knowledge of the cobbler, the pilot, or the shepherd, however; these have to do with a particular art or craft. We may call upon the river pilot to sail us safely across the water because the pilot's skill and knowledge are precisely proportionate to this particular task. But it would be foolish to ask him to mend a pair of shoes, to train horses, to till the earth, or to take care of sheep; and it would be even more foolish to ask his advice on how to conduct the policy of the state or to determine laws. In short, the Platonic source of authority is *the particular task or relationship one has to the total operation of the state.* We do well to remember this emphasis because leadership is always situational.

### *Catholic Leadership*

Throughout the history of the Roman Catholic Church, leadership has taken its authority from the church as its source. The doctrine of apostolic succession reflects this concept, and it carries through the entire hierarchical system of church leadership. People become leaders because the church has appointed them to an office. The church appoints them to an office because it has resident within it the authority to make such appointments.

## *Scriptural Leadership*

Another view of authority and leadership, however, varies from both of these. It holds that the principle of *sola scriptura*, recaptured for the church at the time of the Reformation, must today be the governing source of authority for Christian leadership. To determine what Christian leadership is, how people can be prepared for it, and how one exercises it within the community of the redeemed, the investigator must go directly to the inspired Word and develop therefrom a biblical perspective (see chapter 3). The underlying theological assumptions are the doctrines of plenary inspiration and special revelation. In *Basic Christian Doctrines* Addison Leitch clearly states the nature of this authority:

> This is the Bible record of God's mighty acts and his authoritative Word about the revelatory acts and about himself. This is the climax and fulfillment of God's word to us in the living Word, even Jesus Christ. Natural revelation gives us direction and confidence in our search for God; God's special revelation gives us final authority and assurance regarding his own nature and his will for man. As Calvin suggests, in the Bible we have the "divine spectacles" which bring the truths of natural theology into focus.[1]

We see from these words that Christian leadership must take its cue from the Bible, the only acceptable source of authority by which its definition and function can be determined. However, true Christian leadership is more than just adherence to a printed page. It embodies the Spirit and truth of God. As Richard Caemmerer says:

> His plan is that the small boys and their grandfathers and the whole church of God be people in whom He, God, is Himself at work and alive. Learning words and definitions help in the process, but that is only a help. The Bible is a means toward that end, but always only a means. The great objective of

Christian nurture is that people belong to God, that He and His Spirit and His Son are enthroned as rulers in their hearts, and that these people therefore carry out the purposes for which God has placed them in the world and recaptured them from sin and the devil to fulfill His purposes.[2]

Not all, however, accept a high view of Scripture as the source of authority for Christian leadership. Some attempt to reverse the position stated above by making quality of life a factor for determining truth rather than allowing the truth of God's revelation to shine upon the life of leadership. Allan Hart Jahsmann warns that

> the chief assumption of Sherrill, Miller, Munro, and their followers is that "the quality of life within a congregation is the most powerful mediator of God's grace," and that "we live ourselves into religious thinking far more than we think ourselves into religious living." This teaching is clearly debatable, for, as we hope to demonstrate, the one type of learning experience finds its meaning in the other.[3]

Jahsmann's complaint against the existential views of those writers he names is that they have made human experience the final judge in matters of truth and have therefore followed Dewey into the kingdom where human experience reigns. Of course, the views of Leitch and Caemmerer emphasize human experience also, but always as a *result* of the activity of God rather than a *producer* of that activity.

## BIBLICAL EXAMPLES: MOSES, JOSHUA, PAUL

### Moses

As the slave child who became prince and lawgiver, Moses possessed almost all the natural and educable attributes desirable in effective leadership. He grew up in Pharaoh's court and stood in the line of heirship to the Egyptian throne. The hand of God reached down, snatched him from the royalties of the palace, and thrust him by divine sovereignty into a position that he did not want. William Sanford LaSor pinpoints several leadership qualities of Moses, indicating such traits as singleness of purpose, organizational ability, faith, obedience, and faithfulness in service. LaSor notes that leadership potential was demonstrated early in Moses in that "he was able to gather around him the elders of the people of Israel, who by this time had been in Egypt many years. . . . Yet Moses was able to fire the imagination of these people and elders of Israel; he was able to convince them that God was bent upon their deliverance, and he made them follow him. That is leadership."[4]

## Joshua

The characteristics of godly leadership resident in Joshua are manifest in Joshua 1:1–8.

> Now it came about after the death of Moses the servant of the Lord, that the Lord spoke to Joshua the son of Nun, Moses' servant, saying, "Moses My servant is dead; now therefore arise, cross this Jordan, you and all this people, to the land which I am giving to them, to the sons of Israel. Every place on which the sole of your foot treads, I have given it to you, just as I spoke to Moses. From the wilderness and this Lebanon, even as far as the great river, the river Euphrates, all the land of the Hittites, and as far as the Great Sea toward the setting of the sun will be your territory. No man will be able to stand before you all the days of your life. Just as I have been with Moses, I will be with you; I will not fail you or forsake you. Be strong and courageous, for you shall give this people possession of the land which I swore to their fathers to give them. Only be strong and very courageous; be careful to do according to all the law which Moses My servant commanded you; do not turn from it to the right or to the left, so that you may have success wherever you go. This book of the law shall not depart from your mouth, but you shall meditate on it day and night, so that you may be careful to do according to all that is written in it; for

then you will make your way prosperous, and then you will have success." (NASB)

A number of elements in the above verses deserve delineation. First of all, Joshua was *called* to the task that he faced; he did not seek to advance himself in the ranks of Israel. He had been around for a long time and had held various subordinate positions of authority, but there is no indication whatsoever that he was pushing to become Moses' successor. As in all authentic cases of Christian leadership, God selected a person to fulfill ministry necessary to advance His cause at that time.

Joshua also *paid the price of preparation.* This man who heard the call of God had been "Moses' minister" (KJV). Although we do not know what it meant to be Moses' minister in those days, undoubtedly such a role included subordination and follower-ship. All those years of toil and service had prepared Joshua for the task of leadership that now lay before him. God prepared Moses alone in a remote area of the desert. He chose to prepare Joshua through constant apprenticeship so that his leadership with the people of Israel would be an extension of Jehovah's work through Moses.

Absolute dependence upon the Lord is clear in these verses. From the beginning God allowed Joshua to harbor no thoughts of self-sufficiency. Frequently throughout these verses we see the sovereign manipulation of the situation in such phrases as "I am about to give to them," "I will give you," "I will be with you," "I will never leave you." Team leadership requires that we always recognize our place of subordination within the spiritual line-staff relationships of the kingdom.

Joshua's leadership also demonstrates a definite emphasis on *courage* (vv. 6, 7, 9). Why does God give this triple command to His newly appointed captain? Because godly leadership then, as now, requires a continual courageous relationship based on God's faithfulness.

One final note of emphasis is Joshua's relationship to the Word, the special revelation as it had progressed to his time.

Verse 8 clearly indicates that Joshua should operate within the framework of the Mosaic Law. His leadership, in other words, was governed by the *authority of revelation*. Joshua's orders came not from his own ability and creativity but from a higher source, the world plan of the living God.

## *Paul*

In an excellent article in *Christianity Today* entitled "The Marks of Leadership," James Taylor, a Scottish Baptist pastor, wrote:

> We are looking for Christians who are developing the same traits of character that made the Apostle Paul such a dynamic leader in the early days of the Christian church. He was God's man for the church to lead her forward in outreach and understanding. What can he tell us, centuries later, of the essential characteristics of leadership?[5]

Taylor delineates several specific characteristics that should be found in Christian leaders today. He speaks first of "tenacity of mind," referring to specific objectives and aims that governed the apostle's life. The faithful Christian leader moves toward these goals with resolution of mind and will. Such tenacity includes conception of purpose and concentration of achievement. Paul's course did not deviate from one side to the other. When he testified that Christ controlled all his life, he recognized the practical implications in all that he did. Neither personal limitations, physical weakness, nor the adversities of life deterred Paul from continually pursuing his goal of being like his Master.

Taylor also finds "conviction of belief" an important mark of apostolic leadership. Paul knew that his message was an offense to many and that its proclamation threatened his very life. Yet he would not compromise, nor would he shirk the responsibility.

The apostle was characterized by "breadth and largeness

of vision." Today Paul would be called creative and visionary when he talked about communicating the gospel to the world. He put no stock in the view of those who would contain truth within the narrow confines of Judaism and cling to Old Testament legalism in the new life of grace. His vision spanned the Mediterranean to take in Asia Minor, Rome, and even Spain. No matter that he was a small man with no financial backing; he represented the sovereign God of the universe.

Taylor indicates two behavior patterns in the apostle Paul which point to distinctive team leadership: "He was a man of deep affection and he had a genius for friendship." Paul's ability to relate to people, to draw them to himself and to his Lord, demonstrated inner motivation that is essential to the Christian leader.

These three examples from both Old and New Testament days appear here only in brief form. However, the lessons indicated above are indicative of the many more which can be learned by studying Christian leadership through the biographies of people God used.

## THE DYNAMIC OF SPIRITUAL LEADERSHIP

The experiences of Joshua and Paul demonstrate spiritual characteristics or qualities of Christian leadership which take precedence over all sociological aspects of the leader's role. In reality, Christian leadership ought to be characterized by all the legitimate earmarks of effective secular leadership, plus factors that make it distinctively Christian.

The obvious spiritual elements include such matters as faith, reliance upon prayer, the reality of the Holy Spirit in the lives of leaders, and the absolute authority of God's inerrant Word as the basis for leadership. However, some less obvious factors mark a given exercise of leadership as "spiritual," compared to leadership which is either "natural" or "carnal," i.e., totally secular, or exercised in the flesh.

## Acceptance of Responsibility

Accepting responsibility is a basic discipline of all leadership which takes on added dimensions in terms of God's call upon a life. Every team leader should strive to earn a reputation for being a person whom others can count on. Someone has suggested that the best ability is dependability.

As a man settles finally to one woman who becomes his partner, so Christian leaders settle into the ministry to which God has called them. Sometimes this decision may push other legitimate and desirable things out of one's life. Such are the demands of leadership. During the days following the Resurrection, Peter may have thought fishing a more attractive occupation than evangelism. Ultimately, however, he had to face the claims of discipleship upon his life as the Master said to him, "Follow me."

## Meekness and Humility

The more mature we become in Christian life and service, the more we realize that when we have done the best job we possibly can and exerted all efforts to the task, we remain—when compared with the absolute perfection of God—dispensable servants (Luke 17:7–10). Team leaders cannot indulge in self-pity or dislike for others. They must minimize personality conflicts and allow the Spirit of God to work out an attitude of meekness before the Lord.

Christian leaders pattern their lives after the Word of God wherein lie countless examples of this kind of attitude in leadership. Moses disciplined himself for many years to listen patiently to the murmuring and complaining of the children of Israel. The Hebrew children in Babylon renounced all possible political advantage by refusing to be defiled by the king's meat. Daniel laid power and prestige on the line in prayer, despite his high governmental position. Paul's missionary endeavors frequently took him into hard places, caused him to renounce himself, and placed him in danger; the result was his complete commitment to Jesus Christ and His will.

## Teachableness

Someone has aptly remarked that the teacher who ceases to learn ceases to teach. The following selected verses from Psalm 25 pinpoint David's attitude toward his own leadership in the light of teachableness:

> Make me know Thy ways, O Lord; teach me Thy paths. Lead me in Thy truth and teach me, for Thou art the God of my salvation; for Thee I wait all the day.
> Good and upright is the Lord; therefore He instructs sinners in the way. He leads the humble in justice, and He teaches the humble His way.
> Who is the man who fears the Lord? He will instruct him in the way he should choose. His soul will abide in prosperity, and his descendants will inherit the land. (Psalm 25:4–5, 8–9, 12–13 NASB)

## Care for Followers

The team leader exercises an _agape_ relationship that is not a passive feeling but an aggressive commitment to the welfare of others. Such concern does not wither when people fail to do what the leader expects of them. It can weather disappointments and disillusionment in the difficult process of leadership. It reflects Moses' concern for the people of Israel, but shows an even greater resemblance to the life and ministry of the Son of God.

### BUREAUCRACY AND BIBLICAL LEADERSHIP

What does bureaucracy have to do with a Christian organization? First of all, we must recognize that bureaucracy is not the horrible specter of demonic control some portray it to be. In a discussion, a pastor friend of mine indicated that the church was "becoming too bureaucratic." I asked him if he had ever read anything which attempted to deal with bureaucracy in a theological context, and he said that he had never read anything about bureaucracy at all. It is one of those convenient words we have learned to use when we want to speak out against something too big for us to understand, much less handle.

Bureaucracy is necessary in free society and in a participatory organization. It is not *bureaucracy* that gives us the trouble, but rather the misuse and abuse of bureaucracy to the point that it becomes a hindrance rather than a help. Like many other tools of accomplishment, it makes the proverbial good servant but bad master.

Contrary to popular notions, bureaucracy can be very efficient and an almost necessary tool to productivity. Peter Blau suggests that the term describes a "type of organization designed to accomplish large-scale administrative tasks by systematically coordinating the work of many individuals."[6]

It is not bureaucracy but rather a misunderstanding of its inherent evils, as well as its helpfulness, that leads us astray. Thus our study might best take the form of pitting bureaucracy against several concepts generally considered contrary to it, in order to see the tension created when bureaucratic concentration of power destroys group processes.

## *Bureaucracy and a "Professional" View of Work*

The word *professional* appears in quotation marks in this heading because it represents a technical term when used in the jargon of management science. Studies indicate a distinction between the behavior of "a bureaucratic person" and that of "a professional person."

To be more bureaucratic does not necessarily mean to be less professional. The same person could be oriented toward both bureaucratic and professional goals, but the double orientation would necessitate a constant struggle to bring together two things that tend to polarize themselves. A "professional" administrator tends to emphasize individuals, research, freedom of relationships, skill development through training (rather than practice), decentralization of decision making, and team leadership, rather than the constant serving of organizational goals.

Corwin would argue that administrators in a college or seminary tend to be more bureaucratic (serving the organization), whereas faculty tend to be more professional (serving their academic disciplines). It should be easy for us to understand that a person serving her academic discipline can also serve the organization and, if a Christian, serve Christ above either.

On the other hand, notice how often a professional faculty member becomes a bureaucratic administrator when appointed to a post as dean or perhaps even department chairman. Or consider the professional pastor whose prior concerns have always been for the autonomy of the local congregation. Yet as a district superintendent, he seems to serve the goals and interests of the denomination, sometimes, it may seem, even to the detriment of individual congregations within his sphere of authority.

## Bureaucracy and Effectiveness

Most research done on the subject of bureaucracy tends to conclude that the purely bureaucratic administrative structure is, from a technical point of view, capable of attaining the highest degree of efficiency. The catch comes when we notice that efficiency is measured in terms of product output and achieving the goals of the organization.

At this point the concepts of Peter Drucker help us. He candidly offers a marked distinction between *efficiency* and *effectiveness* by suggesting that the former deals with doing things right, whereas the latter focuses on doing the right things. Drucker pinpoints what he calls five practices, or habits, of the effective executive:

1. Effective executives know where their time goes.
2. Effective executives focus on outward contribution.
3. Effective executives build on strengths.
4. Effective executives concentrate on the few major areas where superior performance will produce outstanding results.
5. Effective executives make effective decisions.[7]

It should not be difficult to note that bureaucracy tends to emphasize *efficiency,* because it focuses on doing things right (task specialization, standardization, etc.); but *effectiveness* concerns itself much more with achievement than with process.

## Bureaucracy and a Participatory View of Organization

A comparison of bureaucracy with democracy in organizational structure leads to profound implications, since bureaucracy is primarily concerned with systematizing the process of how one's own work fits together with the work of others. Blau's first chapter in *Bureaucracy in Modern Society* identifies three types of associations, all of which may describe the church and any other kind of Christian organization.

1. *The association that exists to produce certain end products and which, therefore, must concern itself with efficiency (doing things right).* Think about your organization for a moment. You may not actually create tangible products, but your service to those not in the organization (the witness to the pagan culture and the outreach of world mission) is equivalent to the marketing of an industrial company. We might also argue that the matter of "doing the right things" is important to the Christian if biblical absolutes define the way in which at least some of the work should be done.

2. *The association that is established for the purpose of finding intrinsic satisfaction in common activities.* Here efficiency is less relevant, since the members find the end result of their

togetherness in their relationship to each other. This we would call *koinonia,* and we think of it as both end and means. Note that bureaucracy is important here, as well.

3. *The association that exists for the purpose of deciding upon common goals and courses of actions.* Surely this also describes the church. To the extent that it has a job to do and a right way to do it, the church must of necessity be a bureaucratic organization. To the extent that the kind of team leadership defined for the church in the New Testament (see chapter 4) is essentially participatory when based on the concept of the universal priesthood of believers, the church must resist bureaucratization.

## *Bureaucracy and a Christian View of Society*

In his once-famous book, *The Lonely Crowd,* David Riesman delineated three periods in the development of any culture: the high-growth-potential period, characterized by tradition-direction; the transitional-growth period, characterized by inner-direction; and the incipient decline of population, characterized by other-direction. The essential point of the book is that American society in the last half of the twentieth century lives in the "other-directed" period. Therefore, the culture faces the responsibility to preserve individualism in the face of mass standardization.

Riesman suggests, "In large and bureaucratized organizations people's attention is focused more on products (whether these are goods, decisions, reports, or discoveries makes little difference) and less on the human element."[8] In this particular section of his book, Riesman talks about the economic and industrial orientation of an inner-directed society. His point is the overemphasis on efficiency. However, in discussing the matter of what he calls "the parental role in the stage of other-direction," Riesman argues, with Blau, that over-bureaucratizing stifles the individuality that people in the other-directed phase of society claim they want so desperately.

Team leaders in Christian organizations should focus on the real issue—involving people in a genuine and meaningful way rather than glossing over the situation with some thin veneer of plastic "human relationism."

When we pour Riesman's theories through the sieve of special revelation, we find ourselves committed to a direction of children in the home, parishioners in the church, and students in the school. This direction receives its impetus from a Power outside and beyond leadership in each of those organizations, and not merely from some kind of psychological gyroscope set into operation by the mature members of society.

## Bureaucracy and a Biblical View of Humanity

Let us stay with Riesman just a moment longer. One's philosophy of anything always grows out of theology, even if one does not admit to having a theology. This is notably true in education, and quite obviously, therefore, in the ministry of many Christian organizations, including the church. If one considers the social system to be in constant flux (which it certainly is), one is tempted to accept the presupposition of most secular psychologists and sociologists that the nature of people is therefore constantly formed by surrounding environmental factors.

But the "inner-direction" of which Riesman speaks is not generated from the turbulent waters of the social system itself. It arises, rather, from moving and influencing the hearts of Christians, both individually and collectively, so that their work, in the process of association, transcends the norms and standards of society rather than constantly being formed and controlled by them. Living according to absolutes in a relativistic cultural system is not easy, but it is definitely necessary for the Christian.

Team leadership may be considered the exercise of certain qualities and abilities given by the Spirit of God and based in Christian character, which the group member, acting upon the call of God and the authority of His Word, will offer in loving service to the group for the sake of Christ.

### FOR FURTHER READING

Armerding, Hudson T. *The Heart of Godly Leadership.* Wheaton, Ill.: Crossway, 1992.

Drucker, Peter F. *The New Realities.* New York: Harper & Row, 1989.

Gangel, Kenneth O. *Lessons in Leadership from the Bible.* Winona Lake, Ind.: BMH, 1980.

Hesselbein, Francis, Marshall Goldsmith, and Richard Beckhard, eds. *The Leader of the Future.* San Francisco: Jossey-Bass, 1996.

Koestenbaum, Peter. *Leadership—The Inner Side of Greatness.* San Francisco: Jossey-Bass, 1991.

Sanders, J. Oswald. *Spiritual Leadership.* Rev. ed. Chicago: Moody, 1980.

### NOTES

1. Addison Leitch, "The Knowledge of God: General and Special Revelation" in Carl F. H. Henry, *Basic Christian Doctrines* (New York: Holt, Rinehart & Winston, 1962), 5–6.

2. Richard R. Caemmerer, *Feeding and Leading* (St. Louis, Mo.: Concordia, 1962), 34.

3. Allan Hart Jahsmann, *What's Lutheran in Education* (St. Louis, Mo.: Concordia, 1960), 80.

4. William Sanford LaSor, *Great Personalities of the Old Testament* (Westwood, N.J.: Revell, 1959), 62.

5. James Taylor, "The Marks of Leadership," *Christianity Today* 8 (January 3, 1964): 5.

6. Peter Blau, *Bureaucracy in Modern Society* (Chicago: Univ. of Chicago, 1956), 14.

7. Peter Drucker, *The Effective Executive* (New York: Harper & Row, 1967), 23–24.

8. David Riesman, *The Lonely Crowd* (New Haven, Conn.: Yale Univ., 1950), 112.

# PART TWO

# Roles of the Team Leader

# —6—

# THE TEAM LEADER
## AS ADMINISTRATOR

A dministration is getting things done through people. The study of administration from a scientific viewpoint has received more attention in recent decades than perhaps in any other single period of history. Experts have worked to develop a theory of administration operable in all aspects of administrative work, including business, education, industry, and church work.

Although many resources appear in the secular domain, for a Christian leader the most essential source of administrative theory is the Scriptures. In many of these chapters we shall look more closely at what the Bible has to say about the functions of administration.

## DEFINITION OF ADMINISTRATION

What is administration? Ordway Tead's enduring definitions are still useful. He says that administration is "the direction of people in association to achieve some goal temporarily shared" and "the inclusive process of integrating human effort so that a desired result is obtained."[1] Both definitions are obviously based on team leadership, since administration cannot be divorced from leadership technique. On the other hand, when compared with an understanding of leadership, administration seems to put more emphasis on the task, and leadership more emphasis on the person. A transactional approach to this dualism teaches us that proper administration involves leadership of people toward a given goal. Perhaps it will be of some help here to designate two other words that are related to the concept of administration.

_Organization_ has to do with setting up the total task in its various aspects, particularly denoting an emphasis on planning and structuring the activities of the organization. _Supervision_ places emphasis upon the leader's guidance of people within the framework of the tasks they hold in the organization. Therefore, it might not be improper to say that a leader organizes the task, then supervises group members in the function of that task. More on that in later chapters.

_Administration_ signals the total process of the leader in relationship to the organization she serves. Along with Tead's definition stated above, here are some other approaches to describing the administration-management process:

> The stewardship of the talents of people God has entrusted to the leader's care.
> The purpose for bringing together of the means and the end.
> Not the direction of things, but the development of people.
> The work a person does to enable people to work most effectively together.

Creative leadership is the opposite of custodial management. The creative administrator seeks new solutions and does not base decision making on tradition, or on present or standard controls. He steadfastly resists slogans and clichés that destroy initiative and bog down ideation. She applies herself to the total task, in full recognition that most people in the organization already view administration as a necessary evil to be tolerated but never liked. We combat this misconception with the dynamic of our own leadership and a full awareness that administration is not only a necessary task for the organization's functioning but also a glorious ministry to which God has called us. The creative administrator makes sure that all group members recognize that the administrative task is a supplement to, and not a substitute for, the supernatural working of the church as organism and organization.

## QUALITIES OF THE EFFECTIVE ADMINISTRATOR

From the many characteristics that could be named, Tead selects five which, in his opinion, most clearly define the necessary elements of administration as personal performance.

> My own studies of personal administrative qualities stress the need for (1) sheer physical and nervous vitality and drive, (2) ability to think logically, rationally, with problem-solving skill that "gets the point" more quickly than average, (3) willingness to take the burdens of responsibility for executive decisions and acts, (4) ability to get along with people in a sincerely friendly, affable, yet firm way, and (5) ability to communicate by voice and pen in effective ways.[2]

Notice how Tead's emphasis resurrects the significance of leadership qualities, focusing on the importance of the individual in the administrative process.

Along with those personal qualities, the team leader must recognize the enormous amounts of time that will be spent in what often appear to be the more mundane aspects of this task.

He must have time to talk to people about problems of great concern to them but which seem very small when compared to the big picture. She must be prepared to serve on and lead committees which play an important functioning role in the organization. Above all, administrative leaders must have time to think. The importance of initiation and ideation is foundational to creative leadership; and since the first law of brainstorming indicates that quantity of ideas breeds quality in ideas, we must have time to produce the quantity.

The emphasis on creativity suggests the value of listing some characteristics that can be developed by leaders seeking to be better administrators. The following ten are generally recognized qualities.

### 1. Sensitivity to One's Surroundings

The wise team leader notices people, places, events, and the little things that the average person will pass over.

### 2. Curiosity

The effective administrator was probably the kind of child who continually wanted to investigate a cave or take apart a machine. Curiosity is the handle on the pump of ideation.

### 3. Perspective

Unlike the child who draws a dog larger than the house in which its owners reside, the administrator sees things in proper relation to each other.

### 4. Mental Flexibility

The progressive leader is open-minded, listening carefully to other viewpoints and considering their value.

## 5. An Organized Mind

This is what Tead means by "ability to think logically and rationally." The organized mind can outline well. It sees things in symmetry and parallels.

## 6. Tolerance for Ambiguity

The untrained person in an organization can afford to jump to quick conclusions and be satisfied with simple answers. Leaders, however, must not view matters as categorical and concrete too soon. A willingness to let one's mind dwell on the abstract consideration of difficult problems is essential to satisfactory decision making.

## 7. Independent Judgment

The creative leader is willing to buck the crowd. Often she stands alone in her nonconformity, bolstered only by the dreams of what she believes can happen in the progress of the organization. Kouzes and Posner put it this way: "Leaders challenge the process."[3]

## 8. Pride of Workmanship

Willingness to assume responsibility carries with it willingness to tack one's own name to a job when it is completed. Pride of workmanship demands giving your best on any job simply because it will reflect upon you. In Christian leadership the further implications of this include a commitment to advance the name of Christ through the outcome of your work.

## 9. Ability to Synthesize

Because of mental flexibility and organizational ability,

good administrators can boil down and summarize problems and solutions. They then, of course, must be able to communicate the conclusions verbally to subordinates and peers in the organization.

### 10. Ability to Reason and Abstract

At heart administrative leaders are philosophers as well as pragmatists. Though often appearing to be caught up in the mechanical running of the organization, the administrator spends a great deal of time in abstract reasonings as preparation for the nitty-gritty decision making and supervision which are a part of her everyday task.

## FUNCTIONS OF ADMINISTRATION

Tead suggests ten elements of administration generally recognized by students in the field: (1) planning, (2) organizing, (3) staffing, (4) initiating, (5) delegating, (6) directing, (7) overseeing, (8) coordinating, (9) evaluating, and (10) motivating.[4] Let's back these elements with biblical examples. Consider their implementation in the administrative tasks of such God-used leaders as Joseph, involved in economic administration with the problems of the famine in Egypt; Moses, employing religious administration in the giving of Levitical laws and ordinances; Joshua, a general involved in military administration in the conquest of Canaan; and Solomon, called of God to the task of architectural administration in the building of the temple.

In an earlier version of this book, I diagrammed ten administrative functions in a stair-step pattern. But that gives the false impression of a neat progression from one function to another (e.g., organizing, then staffing, then delegating). Now, in the classroom, I describe a juggler keeping all the balls (duties) in the air at once.

ADMINISTRATIVE FUNCTIONS

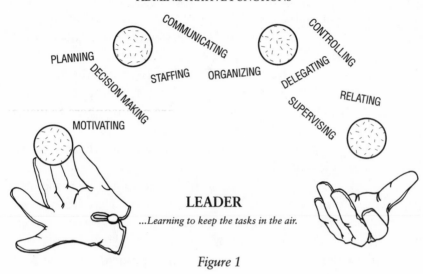

**LEADER**

*...Learning to keep the tasks in the air.*

*Figure 1*

Also, the "balls" are not always as clearly defined as they appear here. The motivation role may have to precede the change agent role, and recruiting and training may go hand in hand. Perhaps we can say that such categories provide a means of grasping the administrator's work. It becomes essential then to understand each of them and how they relate to a particular ministry.

## THE GIFT OF ADMINISTRATION

The New Testament church has two dimensions to its existence. As we have already seen, it is both *organization* and *organism*. Because of that dual nature, the church faces two kinds of problems—*organizational* and *spiritual*. Too frequently, church leaders attempt to give spiritual answers to organizational problems and organizational answers to spiritual problems. The difficulty is compounded by some confusion about the nature of administration. Consider, for example, the following three myths:

1. *Administration is nonessential.* Some think that the work of the Christian organizations will be carried on purely by an emphasis on pietistic endeavors with no concern for the dreary, paper-shuffling tasks frequently associated with the work of administration.

2. *Administration is uninteresting.* After all, the real glory of Christian leadership comes in preaching, teaching, counseling, and similar interpersonal ministries. Most people who hold this view would grudgingly agree that somebody has to handle the administration, but they have no inclination to offer an Isaiah-like "Here am I; send me" (Isa. 6:8 KJV).

3. *Administration is not spiritual.* Perhaps this is the most dangerous myth of all, for it attempts to drive a wedge between crucial ministries of the Christian leader. It suggests that some ministries are "sacred," and others are "secular." People who think this way tend to gravitate toward unbiblical views of leadership because they misunderstand the crucial, New Testament function of administration as a spiritual gift.

## Analysis of Biblical Backgrounds

As I noted in chapter 3, the word the New Testament uses to describe the gift of administration is _kubernetes,_ the noun form of *kubernao,* which literally means "to steer a ship." Although only one verse in the New Testament distinctively helps us understand the gift, other passages in both the New Testament and the Septuagint (the Greek version of the Old Testament) provide significant, parallel information. Since the word appears only three times in the New Testament, we can briefly examine each usage.

## New Testament Uses

_Acts 27:11._ The context of *kubernesis* here is Paul's trip across the Mediterranean Sea to Rome. Although Paul predicts danger from the coming storm, the centurion pays no attention to the words of the prisoner but listens instead to the suggestion of the master of the ship. Here the emphasis is clearly on the idea of a helmsman. It was the responsibility of this ship administrator to know times of the day, the nature and direction of storms, the habits of air currents, and the process of steering by the stars and sun; he was expected to use that knowledge to correctly direct the ship.

*Revelation 18:17.* I have deliberately skipped over the passage that would appear second in chronological order because the Revelation reference is so similar to the usage in Acts. Here, in a condemnatory poem spoken against historic and eschatological Babylon, John talks about the tremendous wealth of the city as viewed by tradesmen and "every sea captain."

*1 Corinthians 12:28.* This passage clearly marks administration as a spiritual gift. Although the word *governments* is used in the text of the Authorized Version, our understanding of "administration" (NIV) is the most fitting concept of the word in current vocabulary. Kittel has a most helpful, descriptive paragraph, which relates *kubernesis* to the other gifts that appear in the same passage.

> The importance of the helmsman increases in a time of storm. The office of directing the congregation may well have developed especially in emergencies both within and without. The proclamation of the Word was not originally one of its tasks. The apostles, prophets and teachers saw to this. . . . No society can exist without some order and direction. It is the grace of God to give gifts which equip for government. The striking point is that when in v. 29 Paul asks whether all are apostles, whether all are prophets or whether all have gifts of healing, there are no corresponding questions in respect of *antilenpseis* and *kubernēsis*. There is a natural reason for this. If necessary, any member of the congregation may step in to serve as deacon or ruler. Hence these offices, as distinct from those mentioned in v. 29, may be elective. But this does not alter the fact that for their proper discharge the *charisma* of God is indispensable.[5]

*Old Testament Uses (Septuagint)*

*Proverbs 1:5.* Most Old Testament uses of *kubernesis* appear in the book of Proverbs. The emphasis is closely related to the concept of wisdom and denotes the ability of the leader to offer proper direction to a group. In this passage, Solomon suggests that the wise person will increase knowledge, and one who has understanding will find proper direction to perceive the truth and act accordingly.

*Proverbs 11:14.* Where there is no proper administration, the people will fall. The dependence on clear-cut direction from a competent team leader is a frequent theme in Solomon's writings.

*Proverbs 24:6.* Only with wise administration can one win a war, for in the final analysis, wisdom rather than might prevails.

*Ezekiel 27:8.* Similar to the Revelation passage, this verse speaks of the helmsman, the administrator of a ship.

## SECULAR CONCEPTS OF ADMINISTRATION

All administrative situations yield at least three components, and some leaders in the field recognize four. There is, of course, <u>a person who brings to the administrative task his own personality and ability (or lack of it) as a decision maker, motivator, organizer, and leader of others.</u> Such an individual will have a distinctive self-concept that will greatly affect the work of administration she handles. The administrator's self-concept of leadership will significantly determine her approach to almost every duty.

There is also the *work group.* This term always refers to the people with whom the administrator interacts on a regular basis. It may be a congregation; it may be a professional staff; it may be a group of missionaries; it may be a faculty; or it may even be students over whom one has "helmsman" responsibility.

The third ingredient is generally described as the *situation* itself, but some writers derive a total of four components by dividing the situation into the *task* and the *organization*. Task refers to organizational goals established by others, usually a board of directors.

Interaction among the three (or four) elements forms a constant carrying out of administrative tasks in any ministry. We may be talking about a pastor, a Sunday school superintendent, a mission board executive, or a managerial consultant for General Motors. Since administration is a single science, each of these people faces similar tasks in attempting to achieve organizational goals by directing the activities of people. Obviously, such a conclusion holds some rather basic assumptions:

1. *The organization has goals.* These goals may not be written and may not even be clearly understood by the constituency. Many Christians have distorted concepts of what the church should be and do in contemporary society. If the administrator is really a helmsman, the way he perceives organizational goals dare not be fuzzy.

2. *The organization has some structure to facilitate goal achievement.* This issue of structure has become a battleground for the church in recent years. How much structure is really prescribed for a Christian organization? Where are the fences between form and freedom?

3. *The organization requires effective administration to reach its goals.* Effective administration is not simply an option for the church any more than it is for AT&T. The administrator's position as a decision maker and group leader will either facilitate or hinder institutional goal-achievement.

*How Leadership Differs from Management*

From James Lipham, who wrote more than thirty years ago, to John Kotter's 1990 book, *A Force for Change*,[6] management experts have emphasized that leadership is different from management. Lipham emphasized that leadership has to do with changing organization goals, but administration is concerned with maintaining established structures. Kotter suggests that the idea that management and leadership are the same is a major myth in administrative theory. He argues that we need to focus on discerning the differences in gifts and to develop those who have each without elevating either one.

But throughout this book I want to emphasize that we are looking for administrative leaders in various forms of Christian ministry. It is nearly impossible to be an effective leader in a ministry organization without carrying out high-quality administrative work. Likewise, it is difficult to be an administrator without having some leadership responsibilities. This is no new idea; in Lipham's words, "Leadership functions and administrative functions are usually combined in a single role incumbent."[7]

### Drawing Some Practical Implications

What help is there for harried administrators in an analysis of the relationship between secular research and biblical exegesis? Certainly, several themes emerge that properly fit both the biblical and secular patterns:

1. *The Christian leader's administrative style will depend upon what he considers administration to be.* If *kubernesis* is nothing more than paper shuffling, a necessary evil to the continuing existence of the organization, then administration will always appear unessential, uninteresting, and unspiritual. If, on the other hand, the leader can view herself as a biblical captain of the ship, handling its course and cargo in stewardship for the heavenly Owner, she certainly can approach the task with a dynamic and a spiritual enthusiasm not often attached to the role of administration.

2. *The blending of spiritual gifts and leadership roles has evolved considerably since the days of the New Testament.* Kittel notes that in the early church, administration was essential. But it was not usually the work of the apostles and prophets. Even by the time of Timothy and Titus, however, Paul was giving direc-

tion for activities that were basically administrative in function, such as widow rolls, leadership training responsibilities, and organization of congregational activities. Probably several people in any given congregation or organization will have the gift of administration. One of them may be the multi-gifted pastor who serves as main "helmsman." But the pastor who does not possess the gift of administration must seek out others who do and trust their judgment in matters of management.

3. *The gift of administration is a capacity for learning executive skills, not a package of already developed ability.* Of course, this describes any spiritual gift. No sensible person would argue that she has no need to study because she has the gift of teaching and that the Holy Spirit simply gives her things to say to her class. Yet, while many pastors and other Christian leaders train extensively for preaching, teaching, and counseling ministries, most of them spend very little time in formal training (or even informal reading) to develop the capacity for administrative oversight. The gift of administration suffers from neglect.

4. *The gift of administration is inseparably bound up with the process of working with people.* Team leaders must know how to get along with people. Developing and polishing human relations skills is a basic ingredient of successful administration. It will lead to understanding the innate conflict between individual personality and institutional role. It will recognize the necessity for matching personnel utilization with human interests and needs. Above all, it will emphasize a team leadership style and concept of administration which focuses on the community and *koinonia* of Christian groups, not merely as a desirable approach, but as the crucial guideline by which biblical administration can be effectively judged.

### FOR FURTHER READING

Anderson, Carl R. *Management*. Dubuque, Iowa: Wm. C. Brown, 1984.
Anderson, Leith, et al. *Mastering Church Management*. Portland, Oreg.: Multnomah, 1990.

Drucker, Peter F. *The Effective Executive*. New York: Harper & Row, 1967.

Engstrom, Ted W., and Edward R. Dayton. *The Christian Executive*. Waco, Tex.: Word, 1979.

Gangel, Kenneth O. *Feeding and Leading*. Wheaton, Ill.: Victor, 1989.

Johnson, James L. *The Nine-to-Five Complex, or the Christian Organization Man*. Grand Rapids: Zondervan, 1972.

Thompson, Robert R., and Gerald R. Thompson. *Organizing for Accountability*. Wheaton, Ill.: Harold Shaw, 1991.

Walton, Mary. *The Deming Management Method*. New York: Putnam, 1986.

## NOTES

1. Ordway Tead, *Administration* (New York: Harper, 1959), 2.

2. Ibid., 59.

3. James Kouzes and Barry Posner, *The Leadership Challenge* (San Francisco: Jossey-Bass, 1987), 8.

4. Tead, *Administration*, 30–42.

5. Gerhard Kittel, *Theological Dictionary of the New Testament*, s.v. "Kubern EQ kubernēsis," 1036.

6. John P. Kotter, *A Force for Change* (New York: Free Press, 1990).

7. James M. Lipham, "Leadership and Administration," in *Behavioral Science and Educational Administration*, ed. Daniel E. Griffiths (Chicago: Univ. of Chicago, 1964), 121–22.

# —7—

# THE TEAM LEADER
## AS ORGANIZER

W Edwards Deming shook the corporate world to its
very boardrooms a few years ago with his concept
of total quality management (TQM). A systematic approach to
analyzing the functions of any organization, TQM emphasizes
wide-angle thinking and decision making. Deming stressed that
we must view systems as wholes, since a piecemeal approach will
not produce. The only way to change an organization is to view it
as a whole and acknowledge the team leadership that collectively
determines its future.

But what kind of administrative structure facilitates cross-
communication and interchange among various sub-systems?
One reason many new organizations grow quickly may lie in the
sense of community that early participants build with each other.
A look at Acts 2 and again at Acts 4 shows a newly born church
spending time together, building a sense of unity, holding positions in common, meeting and eating together, enjoying corporate worship, and taking care of each other in times of need. As

the body of Christ they were organism, but they were also organization (see chapter 5).

Progressive administration depends upon effective organization. The organizing phase of the leader's work usually precedes other administrative duties such as staffing, supervising, and delegating. Proper organization facilitates all aspects of the ministry. Chaos and confusion have no place in Christian leadership; but without this crucial dimension, that's what we'll see.

## PRINCIPLES OF ORGANIZATION

Effective leaders recognize certain principles of organization which seem to characterize good work process. Though worded differently by different writers, the following generally appear. Organization:

### Should Never Be Viewed as an End in Itself

Developing organizational charts and planning programs just to look professional distorts the role of this leadership function. One of the stultifying diseases some leaders contract is "drawing-board-itis." We've all seen the symptoms. The patient spends a great deal of time in his office poring over books, charts, plans, and programs that have marvelous aesthetic value but never find their way into actual ministry with people.

### Should Always Grow Out of a Need

Both objectives and programs arise from our understanding of people's needs. Since organizational development is inseparably related to those needs, ministry structure should be designed to accomplish established objectives.

## *Should Contain Maximal Participation*

Ministry does not belong to the pastor, the field director, or the board. It is "of the people, by the people, and for the people." The wise Christian school principal, for example, will utilize department heads and curriculum directors by involving them in any planning sessions for the school. This philosophy of ministry relates specifically to effective team leadership.

## *Should Be Flexible*

Christian organizations should not encourage spiritual robots. Leaders do not lay down the mantle of creative thinking nor take off the shoes of individual initiative. Since most ministry programs set up just ten years ago will probably not meet the needs of this postmodern world, we must design organizational flexibility that can handle necessary changes to achieve the goals assigned them.

## *Should Be Participatory in Procedure*

All we have observed regarding leadership styles applies as well to the organization's participatory procedure. Autocracy hands down orders from the top and expects that they will be obeyed; team leaders encourage open discussion of the issues and a genuine choice by people involved.

## *Should Develop Creativity in People*

Far from stifling individual initiative, proper organization finds ways and means of drawing out new ideas. Leaders challenge the process, and most churches and Christian organizations need all the ideas they can get. When people feel genuine "ownership" of a ministry, they are much more likely to think through the best ways to do it.

## *Should Include Job Analysis and Description*

A job analysis asks the how, why, and what of all tasks in the organization. Good leaders use several methods of gathering information for a job description.

*Interviews.* The leader sits down with the person performing the job to discuss its various aspects and objectives.

*Questionnaires.* The questions must be designed to produce accurate information about how the job is performed.

*Observation.* Leaders watch people do their tasks and record their observations of job function.

*Job diary.* This is a daily, time-structured record of what the worker does, the process, and the results achieved.

*External research sources.* Job descriptions are so important that you can find various resources to assist you in their design.

In a helpful article Bob Welch reminds us,

> Job descriptions should be reviewed annually by the employee and by the church administration—perhaps the church administrator, personnel committee, or other similar group. Any changes in job descriptions should be done mutually by the employee and the administration. It is a good idea to make a notation with any changes, acknowledging that both parties agreed to them. This will diminish the possibility of future confusion and disagreement.
>
> Clearly written, up-to-date and effective job descriptions tell an applicant your church is both organized and efficient. They provide confidence, stability, and accountability related to employee actions and interactions. Finally, they facilitate positive staff relationships, making time spent on job descriptions time well spent.[1]

What Welch says about the church is true of every organization, Christian or secular. Job descriptions not only help us understand how a certain ministry is carried out, but provide useful information in creating effective evaluation procedures for that ministry.

## Should Emphasize Use of Records and Reports

A violation of organizational charts, line-staff relationships, and span of control can never produce ministry effectiveness. In order to utilize proper channels, all our people must be aware of their relationship with each other.

Leaders are always accountable for the actions of their subordinates, and each person should be responsible to only one boss. Good leaders secure from followers a written report of their achievements and activities. Such reports must be regular, complete, specific, and clearly related to the ministry mission.

## Should Include Clear Channels
## of Communication—Oral and Written

When communications in an organization function properly, all personnel receive the information they need in order to do their jobs. Effective communication provides not only for sending the message but also for the reception of feedback. Hrand Faxenian wrote an article several years ago in which he places the responsibility for such communication on the leader.

> You encourage your people to communicate effectively first by setting the example—by being a good communicator yourself. The second step is to set a *policy* which will draw attention to good communications. The third is to back up your policy with an *efficient management reporting system.*[2]

Kilinski and Wofford emphasize that objectives must be accomplished through the various organizational bodies that make up the structure of the congregation (or ministry).

These goals may be influenced in some degree by a formal, systematic approach, such as job descriptions and organizational charts. However, most of the activities of a dynamic organization cannot be programmed or even anticipated. They occur informally. Formal means of building the organization are important; however, they must be viewed as only a first step which inclines a person to fall flat on his face unless other steps keep him in balance.[3]

## ORGANIZING THE KEY RESOURCE—TIME

Every efficient leader has learned to invest time in order to save time. By organizing and planning our work, we give our goals much more chance of success than if we plunged ahead in a haphazard fashion, taking whichever task happened to pop up first. Christian leaders know that their work is never finished. They may have more or less productive days, but no day ever ends with the job completely finished. Selecting and achieving priorities should properly be scheduled before other tasks in the administrative process.

Why does time seem to be so scarce in leadership? One possibility is that we try to do too much. Or possibly we lack both efficiency and effectiveness; we must learn to work smarter, not just harder. Remember Parkinson's law: Work expands to fill the time available. But you can beat Parkinson—at least most of the time. Consider the following ten steps of time management:

1. *Understand how objectives and goals work.* I just dealt with this, but it's worth mentioning again. Unless we write achievable, realistic goals and identify how they fit the overall mission, time wasting will become a regular hobby.

2. *Clarify your lifetime objectives.* What has God called and gifted you to do? Certainly many Christian leaders change careers during their adult lives. But most do not; they simply change locations. Most pastors stay pastors; most college teachers hold that profession until retirement; most career missionaries remain on the field or in the mission organization somewhere. A clear grasp of gifting and calling can alleviate the painful deci-

sions we face every time somebody invites us to join a different organization or move to a different church.

3. *Analyze how you spend your time now.* Though some recommend using fifteen-minute increments, I find that a bit cumbersome. If you will study your time investment for one month in thirty-minute increments, you will have some reasonable idea how you spend your time now. Remember, you can't reorganize your time for the future until you know how you currently use it.

4. *Eliminate time-wasters that clutter up your life.* Attend fewer meetings; get rid of junk mail; stop micro-managing; control your telephone. Just practicing those four leadership behaviors could change your life.

5. *Analyze your activities to identify priorities.* I have dealt with this issue at length in chapter 4 of *Feeding and Leading* and refer readers to the "Activity Analysis Grid" contained in that chapter.

6. *Delegate wherever and whenever possible.* In chapter 23, I will talk more about this, but the principle is basic—effective leaders do not do everything they possibly can and delegate the rest; they delegate everything they can and do the rest.

7. *Practice effective self-discipline.* Notice how often church officers are called to self-controlled lives in 1 Timothy 3 and Titus 2. That may be as simple as excusing yourself from a useless (and seemingly endless) conversation with a drop-in visitor, or as complicated as forcing yourself to finish tasks you start if it has been your habit not to do so.

8. *Centralize your calendar and appointment information.* I struggled with this for years until I finally learned to delegate my calendars to my staff. My secretary handles on-campus appointments, meetings, consultations, etc., and my administrative assistant handles all off-campus meetings, speaking engagements, conferences, and travel. I keep duplicate calendars with both of them, and for off-campus ministry, we have duplicate folders for all correspondence and pertinent information. I carry a pocket calendar

in my briefcase and use desk calendars at my office and my home study. (Notice how principles 6 and 7 affect number 8.)

_9. Design work schedules and patterns that work for you._ Though I use a computer in my office, mainly for communication with other offices across campus, I do not get involved in word processing. For this choice I have been scoffed at, questioned, denigrated, and written off as a dinosaur by my Mac and PC friends. But a hand-held, portable audio dictation machine is infinitely faster for my purposes since all of my staff are completely computer literate. But don't miss the point. You have to find a system that _works for you._ The arrangement of your office, the makeup of your staff, the way you control your days and weeks will determine your effectiveness in leadership, and only you can make the right choices in these crucial areas.

_10. Make all research do double or triple duty._ I am amazed how pastors, professors, and other Christian leaders will spend twenty or thirty hours preparing a sermon or speech, yet use less than 50 percent of what they learned in that time, allowing the rest to lie on the cutting room floor or drift silently into cyberspace. When you study, try to think in advance of all the possible ways that you can put what you learn into practice in your ministry. For me it is simple—pulpit, radio, manuscript—in some order. You identify your own outlets.

## DEVELOPING AN ORGANIZATIONAL CHART

A perusal of books on leadership will uncover a variety of approaches to charting any organization. But the familiar pyramid of lines and boxes arranged in ascending or descending order of importance is the standard format of an organizational chart.

Some Christian leaders think the cold and empirical pyramid of boxes represents an unspiritual approach to spiritual issues. Nevertheless, order and proper function characterize the omnipotent God and therefore ought to mark His work and His people.

According to Donald Winks,

The true purpose of the Orgchart today is a reversal of the Bauhaus *obiter dictum* that form follows function; it is designed and distributed to induce function to follow form, being—in itself—an instrument of change. If this were not so, it would be no more worthy of study than the corporate telephone directory.[4]

I prepared the four charts on the following pages for various churches and present them here because each illustrates a different facet of charting a local church. Chart 1 is a simple four-function program in a church which operates with an official board as the ruling body. Chart 2 represents a congregationally governed church with seven functions all represented on the board of Christian education. Chart 3 demonstrates government through presbytery and session and also shows an emphasis on age-group committee organization rather than functional organization. Chart 4 is similar to 2 but includes a full-time director of Christian education.

Two major steps are important in the process of developing an organizational chart. The first charts the organization as it presently exists. On the basis of this information, knowledge can be brought to bear upon change (improvement). Winks notes:

> C. A. Efferson, an Orgplanner of national renown, has lucidly described the genesis of an Orgchart: "First," he said, "you study the work to be done, the functions, the long-range goals, and then draw the ideal organizational structure, forgetting personalities. The next step is to take the ideal structure to top management and determine what compromises have to be made—mainly because of personalities. However, the ideal structure is not thrown away when the official chart is published. It is kept and continually updated so the future planning does not run counter to the ideal structure, compounding mistakes and necessitating further compromises."[5]

Obviously Winks was talking about a business enterprise rather than a church; nevertheless, positively relating organization to personality requires our best efforts. A final note: The

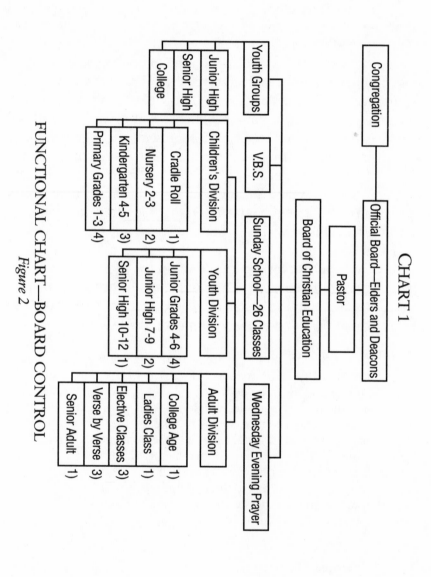

CHART 1

FUNCTIONAL CHART—BOARD CONTROL

*Figure 2*

## CHART 2

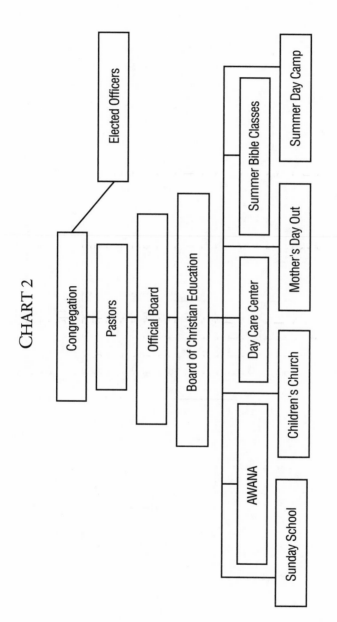

FUNCTIONAL CHART—CONGREGATIONAL CONTROL

*Figure 3*

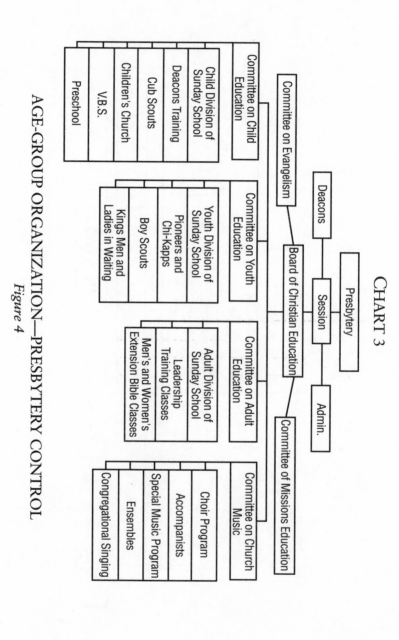

CHART 3

AGE-GROUP ORGANIZATION—PRESBYTERY CONTROL

Figure 4

120

CHART 4

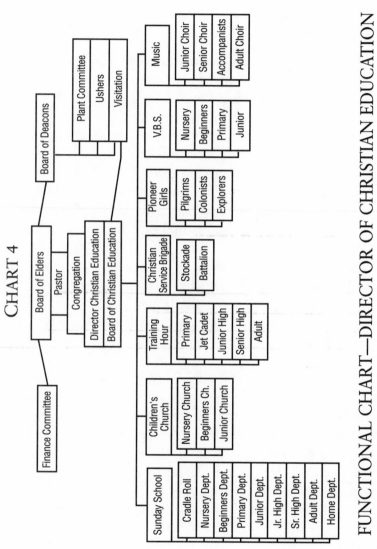

FUNCTIONAL CHART—DIRECTOR OF CHRISTIAN EDUCATION

*Figure 5*

final organizational chart should be circulated completely among all the personnel.

## A Word About Informal Organization

Everything we've talked about in this chapter deals with formal organization, and its importance cannot be overestimated. But every business, educational institution, church, or industry of any kind includes "informal organization." This term describes ways of doing things that have grown up through the years, yet cannot be found described in formal documents like job descriptions, bylaws, or organizational charts.

To function effectively as a leader in any organization, you must understand these informal processes. Since the very nature of informal organization makes it unique to each enterprise, perhaps the best help I can afford is to suggest how to study it. Try asking the following questions:
1. How are decisions made and communicated?
2. How are new people hired?
3. How are funds distributed for various projects?
4. How is information spread throughout the organization?

Let me illustrate that last point. In a college or seminary, formal organization calls for boards to inform presidents who inform vice presidents who inform deans who inform faculty who inform staff. And occasionally it actually happens that way.

But after thirty-five years in Christian higher education, I can assure you that the secretarial network on any campus is considerably more informed than the vice presidents. If a dean wants to get an urgent message to faculty, one that they will actually receive and read, he arranges for his secretary to contact their secretaries.

Don't think of informal organization as evil or distorted. It is a fact of life, and wise leaders learn to function where God places them. But you can't function in any system if you don't understand it, so watch out for that informal organization.

## JOB CONTROL

Participatory leaders don't control people, but they must learn to control their own jobs. The terminology "job control" indicates a level of confidence in managing a major leadership post, a happy condition one should not expect for at least a year. What does it take to attain job control?

1. _You must have adequate time to do the job._ Some ministry posts seem designed to drive good men and women to an early grave. A leader trying to carry out a ministry which consumes more time than she has is destined never to enjoy job control.

2. _You must have adequate staff._ For me, this is in first place. I mention it second here because many leaders will not have staff, and others, hopelessly lost in the time problem, never get around to considering the role of staff. I have often said I live and die by my staff, and that is no exaggeration. I select my staff carefully, train them vigorously, and depend upon them completely. The best image I can offer is the biblical picture of Moses holding up his hands over the battle of Rephidim, sustained in that posture by Aaron and Hur, without whose assistance the battle would have been immediately lost (Ex. 17:8–13).

3. _You must have adequate resources._ Money heads the list here, but other resources such as space must be considered too. One of the most frustrating experiences a leader can face is knowing how to direct the life of an organization but lacking adequate resources to do it.

4. _You must have adequate equipment._ This could be as massive as a $250,000 office building or as simple as $5,000 worth of computer equipment.

5. _You must have adequate grasp of objectives._ Job control can't be separated from what you are expected to do as a leader. If you have fuzzy perceptions of what the board requires

or what the Lord wants, job control will always seem somewhere beyond your grasp.

The key word in all the above items is *adequate*. You may never enjoy all the time, money, staff, equipment, and resources you would like to have, but that's not the point. The question is whether you can do your job to a point at which you feel confident you are doing it well. My advice to new leaders or leaders changing ministry positions is to concentrate immediately on job control by lining up these crucial items as quickly as possible. Remember—don't expect job control in any major leadership post in less than a year, and it may take longer.

Woodrow Wilson once said that efficiency in organization results from "the spontaneous cooperation of a free people." Now at the end of the twentieth century, leadership experts again emphasize this team orientation in leadership.

> Leadership is now understood by many to imply *collective* action, orchestrated in such a way as to bring about significant change while raising the competencies and motivation of all those involved—that is, action where more than one individual influences the process.[6]

These words echo the crucial role of process in leadership. They remind us how essential it is to balance process with person.

> We submit that leadership in the future will more closely reflect a process whereby a leader pursues his or her vision by intentionally seeking to influence others and the conditions in which they work, allowing them to perform to their full potential and thus both increasing the probability of realizing the vision and maximizing the organizational and personal development of all parties involved.[7]

The American Management Association clearly identifies the relationship of people to organizational planning in the following list of "ten commandments of good organization":

1. Definite and clear-cut responsibilities should be assigned to each executive.
2. Responsibility should always be coupled with corresponding authority.
3. No change should be made in the scope or responsibilities of a position without a definite understanding to that effect on the part of all persons concerned.
4. No executive or employee occupying a single position in the organization should be subject to definite orders from more than one source.
5. Orders should never be given to subordinates over the head of a responsible executive. Rather than do this, management should supplant the officer in question.
6. Criticisms of subordinates should, whenever possible, be made privately; and in no case should a subordinate be criticized in the presence of executives or employees of equal or lower rank.
7. No dispute or difference between executives or employees as to authorities or responsibilities should be considered too trivial for prompt and careful adjudication.
8. Promotions, wage changes, and disciplinary action should always be approved by the executive immediately superior to the one directly responsible.
9. No executive or employee should ever be required, or expected, to be at the same time an assistant to, and critic of, another.
10. Any executive whose work is subject to regular inspection should, whenever practical, be given the assistance and facilities necessary to enable him to maintain an independent check on that work.[8]

FOR FURTHER READING

Anderson, Carl R. *Management.* Dubuque, Iowa: Wm. C. Brown, 1984.

Hesselbein, Francis, Marshall Goldsmith, and Richard Beckhard, eds. *The Leader of the Future*. San Francisco: Jossey-Bass, 1996.

Rosenbach, Wm. E., and Robert L. Taylor, eds. *Contemporary Issues in Leadership*. Boulder, Colo.: Westview, 1984.

Schmuck, Richard A., and Philip J. Runkel. *The Handbook of Organization Development*, 4th ed. Prospect Heights, Ill.: Waveland, 1994.

Van Auken, Philip M. *The Well-Managed Ministry*. Wheaton, Ill.: Victor, 1989.

## NOTES

1. Robert H. Welch, "Job Descriptions That Work," *Your Church* (May/June 1995): 49.

2. Hrand Faxenian, "Effective Communication in Small Plants," *Management Aids* (April 1964).

3. Kenneth K. Kilinski and Jerry C. Wofford, *Organization and Leadership in the Local Church* (Grand Rapids: Zondervan, 1973), 151.

4. Donald Winks, "How to Read an Organizational Chart for Fun and Survival," *Harpers* (January 1967), 38.

5. Ibid., 39.

6. Stephen M. Bornstein and Anthony F. Smith, "The Puzzles of Leadership" in *The Leader of the Future*, ed. Francis Hesselbein, Marshall Goldsmith, and Richard Beckhard (San Francisco: Jossey-Bass, 1996), 282.

7. Ibid., 283.

8. American Management Association. Undated brochure.

# —8—
# THE TEAM LEADER
# AS DECISION MAKER

A s technology zooms in, the computer cable winds its octopus-like tentacles around every task. Teleconferencing proceeds; personal letters recede; multiethnic voices demand attention; and "business as usual" plans attract only derision. Meanwhile, baby boomers find their way back to the church, while baby busters fade away, and retirees, younger and healthier than ever, request a legitimate hearing for their concerns. One business writer describes the present corporate world "like the croquet game in *Alice in Wonderland*—a game that compels the player to deal with constant change. In that fictional game, nothing remains stable for very long, because everything is alive and changing around the player—an all-too-real condition for many managers."[1] How do Christian leaders respond? How do we flex with the constant change while remaining true to that which does not change? How can we design effective decision-making paradigms in such a volatile climate?

Can we possibly consider Jesus as the model decision

maker? Clearly He did not buy into accepted models of religious thought. First His life, coming to serve rather than be served, and then His death, destroying all hopes for a politically effective Messiah who would wrest Israel from her earthly oppressors—both denied accepted ways of thinking. After the Resurrection, He re-explained the Scriptures to two disciples on the road to Emmaus, a process that certainly crumbled the traditional framework of their understanding.

During His life, Jesus made no attempt to indoctrinate His disciples or cram them with knowledge. He encouraged them to draw their own conclusions from available evidence and trusted the Holy Spirit to provide all the further instruction they would need for the many things left untaught. Peter's vision, recorded in Acts 10, gave him freedom to share the gospel with Gentiles, which certainly challenged everything he had believed up to that point. God apparently has no fear of pushing our boundaries.

Christian maturity, then, not only permits but demands change, new ways of looking at the world, freedom to explore. Unfortunately, the Christian church has not built a reputation for encouraging such freedom—how many times have we seen the church's response to Galileo thrown in our collective face? Nonetheless, the necessity of using critical thinking skills in the decision-making process dare not annul the understanding of absolute truth upon which we must ultimately rest. We find ourselves faced with an interesting paradox: our desire to help people find Truth, contrasted with the knowledge that a truly mature person must question it first in order to fully own it.

## CAUSES OF INEFFECTIVE DECISION MAKING

Indecisiveness has ruined the effectiveness of many leaders. What produces it? What causes a person who seems to have the ability to perform a given task to stop short of shouldering the responsibility for making decisions? Ineffective decision making consists basically of two problems: the reluctance to make any kind of a decision, and the fear of making an inferior decision. Both negative results can be traced to several basic causes.

## Lack of Clear-Cut Objectives

Sometimes leaders don't act because they don't know what to do. Consider, for example, the case of a Sunday school superintendent faced with the responsibility of structuring a staff meeting for her volunteers. When should it be held? How often should the staff meet? What should be the focus of the meetings? Unless she determines in initial planning stages the kind of results she wishes to attain, such questions will be difficult to answer. When we clarify and specify objectives, we can make decisions in such a way as to achieve those objectives.

## Insecurity of Position or Authority

Sometimes leaders seem afraid to act for fear of the consequences. Perhaps a Christian college faculty member whose relationship with his department chairman is shaky doubts that others understand his field and at times gets the impression that some may even consider his scholarship inferior.

As a result, insecurity develops in that teacher's mind, and he has difficulty making decisions which might in any way demonstrate his authority in a manner distasteful to the chairman. This time bomb can explode when he does make decisions but they are set aside or criticized by the boss.

## Lack of Information

Decision making becomes more difficult when *no* alternative seems clear or when *all* alternatives seem equally clear. We must collect sufficient information about the problem in order to narrow the alternatives. Decision making commonly requires us to select among alternatives.

Cyert and March contend that in real life managers do not consider several possible courses of action, that their search ends
once they have found a satisfactory alternative. My sample of
good managers is not guilty of such myopic thinking. Unless
they were mulling the wide range of possibilities, they could
not come up with the imaginative combinations of ideas which
characterize their work.[2]

We limit information to demonstrate that some options
are less valid than others. Sometimes such information will
immediately focus on one course of action as the best. At other
times the limitations will chip away at the possibilities until only
one respectable alternative remains. Leaders who do not actively
seek all possible information before rendering decisions cripple
themselves in the decision-making process.

## Fear of Change

Whether or not they admit it, many leaders actually desire
to retain the status quo. Making a decision may represent a threat
to present modes of operation. The more radical the decision, the
more change will cause a fuss. What will people say? The attitudes and opinions of people are of great significance, particularly in Christian organizations. But when anticipated attitudes or
opinions impede effective decision making, they must be brought
into proper perspective.

### DECISION MAKING AND CRITICAL THINKING

Try this working definition for critical thinking skills: _the
ability to identify and challenge assumptions, to imagine and
explore alternatives, based on the understanding that absolute
truth does undergird our lives._ When defining absolutes, we
would do well to follow the model of Jesus and trust the Holy
Spirit to lead us into truth, giving people the freedom to discover
as much for themselves as possible. An environment like this can

provide the necessary atmosphere for the development of Spirit-generated creativity in decision making, the ultimate goal of critical thinking skills.

How, then, as administrators and teachers, do we foster the kind of atmosphere in which critical thinking skills flourish?

An article in *Business Week* magazine described the creative design process that led to the success of several particularly hot consumer items released in the last several years, many of them radically new in design and function.[3] Although the article is particularly concerned with product design and manufacture, it provides a workable paradigm for churches and Christian organizations seeking to provide an administrative structure that will encourage critical thinking and its resultant creativity.

We do have a product, so to speak, that will transform the world: the grace of God manifested in the cross of Christ. As first-century Christians had to cross barriers, both physical and psychological, to reach their world, so must we cross barriers to reach our own. While expressions like "marketing," "customer," or "designing for success" may seem crass, they need not secularize Christianity. Instead they provide impetus to recognize that our message deserves the best we can give to make it known. Products mentioned in the *Business Week* article found commercial success because they were *designed with the user in mind.* Is any message more uniquely tailored to the individuals of our world than that of forgiveness?

According to that article, <u>seven essentials mark the managing process that leads to design success</u>:

1. *Design from the outside in:* Make the customer's use of the product, not the technology, central to all product development.
2. *Partner deeply:* The only way to unleash the power of design is to team up with all the relevant business units within your company and help them define new prod-

ucts. Evangelize to make everybody aware of how design can help the business succeed.

3. *Partner widely:* Traditional businesses are deconstructing into virtual corporations, made up of internal and external departments. Designers must partner with all stakeholders—the in-house folks in marketing as well as the people outside, say, in manufacturing and distribution.

4. *Define product up front:* It's critical to get the right product for the right market before committing to tooling and manufacturing. Up-front designing helps screen out concepts that won't fly.

5. *Get physical fast:* Prototyping provides visualization of a concept. It offers quick feedback from both users and managers. Fast prototyping squeezes time out of the product development cycle.

6. *Design for manufacturability:* Always design within QCD parameters—quality, cost, and delivery. Manufacturing criteria are as important to product success as ergonomics, aesthetics, and function.

7. *Surprise the user:* Always build in something extra. Delivering more than the customer buys creates product loyalty and increases the chances of creating a truly "hot" product.

Not all of these seven steps relate to decision making, of course, but they do provide the framework of critical thinking essential to advancing the "products" and/or services of any Christian organization. And two, in particular, aim directly at decision making—partner deeply and partner widely. These concepts form the substance of our next section.

GROUP DECISION MAKING—THE NEW PARADIGM

Em Griffin emphasizes *five factors that mark a good decision:*

1. Quality—How good a decision is it?
2. Time—How long does it take to decide?
3. Commitment—Will all the committee members really support it?
4. Attractiveness—Did the process create an *esprit de corps* among committee members?
5. Learning—Did the committee learn during the process?

Then Griffin explores several different ways of making decisions and concludes that consensus best meets the demands of the five criteria. He suggests, "Consensus promises the wisdom of Solomon together with the kind of member commitment, attraction, and learning that a leader dreams of."[4]

*Group Consensus*

Teamwork—the synergy of many minds, the whole greater than the sum of the parts—has seized the corporate world. When a Christian organization pushes teamwork, does it buy into a secular business concept, or might it instead affirm a basic truth? From the very beginning, creation indicates the need for a team. How clear the Scriptures make this:

"It is not good for the man to be alone" (Gen. 2:18).

"Two are better than one, because they have a good return for their work: If one falls down, his friend can help him up. . . . A cord of three strands is not quickly broken" (Ecc. 4:9–12).

"So in Christ we who are many form one body, and each member belongs to all the others" (Rom. 12:5).

"From him [Christ] the whole body, joined and held together by every supporting ligament, grows and builds itself up in love, as each part does its work" (Eph. 4:16).

Even God is Three-in-One, each Person of the Trinity eternally in relationship with the others. Royce Gruenler writes concerning the Trinity, "One of the compelling characteristics of

God as he reveals himself in Scripture is that he speaks, converses, and is eminently social."[5]

And yet, we who should initiate partnership tend to reinforce just the opposite. We applaud the Lone Ranger pastor who builds a large church on the flimsy virtue of autocratic personality; we affirm the Christian "superstar" and ignore the millions who actually live out the faith; we accentuate competition in education, basing grades on individual effort rather than teamwork.

One parent yanked her children suddenly out of one school and enrolled them in another. When questioned about her decision, she responded, "The children had to work in groups and accept group grades. I think that is un-Christian." Actually, that practice may be *more* Christian. When people learn to help one another, to make up for one's weakness with another's strength, they reflect the body of Christ. Group decision making centers on that principle. Steven Sandvig makes the case with clarity:

> In light of strong biblical support for participatory methods, it is surprising that more churches are not using them. Fears and misconceptions about consensus are prevalent and need to be addressed adequately before a church can adopt participatory decision-making structures. Apart from this, most pastors and leaders have become comfortable with authoritarian and representative structures and attitudes, and change is just too difficult.[6]

### Group Unity

Partnering deeply implies an intense trust, a willingness to dispense with authoritarian rule so that all can function freely. Cooperation, not competition, becomes the key word in board and committee rooms. A cooperative environment encourages the whole body to move forward, not just one part to dominate the rest by claiming special insights about a decision affecting the entire group.

Partnering widely applies to communication process and

organizational support of integrated thinking. Just as an effective corporation will make sure that design engineers understand the frustrations of the sales force, a Christian organization will provide avenues for frontline people to express themselves honestly to support staff.

Keep in mind that we seek to build an environment that frees the depths of creativity in the human mind in order that through the wisdom God gives us we can discover new approaches and solutions to constantly changing problems and circumstances. Organizations whose departments or divisions work at cross-purposes drain incentive for fresh ideas. Such a climate promotes insularity rather than global or holistic thinking; each section seeks only turf protection and sloppy decisions result.

Churches and Christian organizations must provide vehicles to build oneness. Periodic retreats and meetings give participants a chance to see what part they play in the larger drama. However, large gatherings provide only a temporary emotional lift. Regularly conducted cross-departmental, cross-divisional, or cross-sectional meetings remain a necessity for healthy communication.

How many of us have agonized through boring, nonproductive, and poorly conducted meetings? The thought of more meetings may send us all scurrying to tightly compartmentalized cubbyholes, emerging only on payday. But meetings need not carry such a bad reputation. An effective meeting results in collective enlightenment, which is crucial since no one of us can comprehend all necessary information on our own. In such a context, group decision making by consensus can lead us to more effective ministry.

## DECISION MAKING AND
## THE PROBLEM-SOLVING PROCESS

Of course, not all decisions are problem-solving decisions. Some merely relate to selecting a course of action. But when we view decision making basically as a process of problem solving, certain steps can be delineated which describe how we solve the problem. The first three steps in the following structure represent the process of studying the decision; the next three relate to making the decision; the seventh and final step has to do with testing the decision.

## Step 1: Orientation to the Situation

How do leaders get familiar with the background problems and the context in which they arise? First of all, we might assume some general experience in the area. In fact, experience and knowledge are the very factors which elevated them to positions of leadership.

A Christian college department chair, for example, confronts a problem. "Prof. Smith is threatening to resign at the end of this year. Will you speak to him and see if you can talk him into keeping the position?" The professional leader brings to that problem an understanding of adult psychology, an appreciation of the factors that motivate Smith's action, and some notion of what she will do if Smith has to be replaced.

During the first step of problem solving/decision making, we practice deferred judgment. This is the study stage, not the acting stage. It is not necessary yet to know exactly what one will say to Smith or who will take his place if he leaves. First we attempt to understand why he is threatening to leave, why the informant happens to be the one telling the story, and what other variable factors may influence the climate of this problem.

## Step 2: Identification of the Key Facts

It is important to realize that we probably never have all the facts in any decision-making situation. We must all sift through the information we do receive in order to isolate and study key data. This particular step of the process requires acute observation of the problem and a careful sorting of available information.

One facet of this second step is asking effective questions. Such questions should be *open rather than closed;* in other words, they should allow the respondent to tell what he knows rather than answer yes or no as if he were in a witness box at a trial. They should be *leading rather than loaded* questions. Instead of "gunning" for answers we think we want, leaders should act as catalysts, hoping to stir up important facts in the responses.

Such questions must always be *cool rather than heated.* Some problem situations may aggravate the leader. Parents will often ask children, "Why did you do that?" using the question to scold rather than expecting a legitimate answer. Effective questions are *planned rather than impulsive.* It may be necessary for the leader to think by herself for a while before actually plunging into the problem. Whom should I ask? How should I approach him? When would be the best time to raise the issue?

We might add one additional criterion to our list of problem-solving questions. They must be *window questions rather than mirror questions.* That is, they should be geared to allow the leader to look through clear glass into the problem rather than reflecting any opinions or prejudices he may be tempted to bring to the situation (e.g., "Old Smith always has been a hard fellow to get along with, and I almost hope he really will quit this time").

## *Step 3: Identification of the Major Problem or Problems*

When an identifiable problem presents itself we must specify that problem before it can be solved. How does one go about such delineation?

*Look for causes rather than symptoms.* Wise leaders assume that all behavior is motivated. Sometimes the difficulty may be internal, such as sin in the life; sometimes it may be external, caused by friction with other people in the organization, difficulties and discomforts at home, or some physical malady. The need for counseling may enter the situation at this point.

*Isolate the sections through deductive reasoning.* Deductive reasoning proceeds from the general to the specific. General: Smith might leave the college; specific: he is not getting along with his wife and is therefore disgruntled about almost everything, or he dislikes fellow professors, or he has been unhappy with his salary for the past five years.

*Open-mindedly weigh all the evidence.* Do not assume that all evidence which presents itself in response to any given problem is accurate. Godly decision making combines knowledge, wisdom, leadership skill, and patience under the guiding hand of the Holy Spirit.

Haddon Robinson talks about "separating facts from problems" and observes, "I've discovered that often, as we look at problems and questions, we waste a great deal of emotional energy trying to change the facts of life. Even though it's not as easy as it seems, we need to separate the facts of life from the problems."[7]

## *Step 4: Proposal of Possible Causes*

Step 3 focused on identifying problems. Now we aim at the delineation and specification of causes. The leader should be able to verbalize the problem and the proposed causes at this point.

Sometimes a specific problem does not appear as the group works its way through steps 3 and 4 of the decision-making process. If so, it may proceed to generalize on past successes, apply the process of inductive reasoning, and reach consensus in light of the accepted principles of sound team leadership.[8]

Randy Hirokawa argues that there is a positive relationship between consensus and decision quality, but he reminds us that leadership groups must follow appropriate procedures.

When the group does not approach its task in a systematic and rational manner, there is no reason to believe that its members have considered all feasible alternatives. Therefore, there is no reason to believe that their agreement on a decision is the result of the fact that they have found all other alternatives to be less desirable or correct than the one agreed upon by the group. . . . The use of a "vigilant" decision-making strategy is likely to minimize the chances of a group's reaching consensus on an incorrect decision because it forces the group to consider the merits of alternative possibilities *before* reaching a final decision.[9]

## Step 5: Listing of Probable Solutions

The listing of probable solutions consists of engaging in creative brainstorming, the rules of which are simple and the rewards usually quite satisfactory if we carry out the process properly. Note the following guidelines:

*In brainstorming, quantity breeds quality.* This is another way of saying that the more ideas we have, the more likely we are to come up with some good ones. Ideation feeds the process of problem solving, and the leader must approach this task with an open mind to allow many and varied possibilities to present themselves.

*In brainstorming, one solicits as many ideas from others as possible.* This is not done merely to identify the facts involved, but to seek suggested solutions from people who may have something solid to offer. We continually ask the group, "What should we do in this situation?"

*Brainstorming does not allow for evaluation at this point.* When a member of the leadership team offers an idea during discussion and someone reacts by saying, "Well, that wouldn't work in this situation," she renders insignificant some information which may be of help in the next step, and may also stifle future contributions from that colleague. At this point in the process we assume that almost anything will work to solve the problem. Feasibility comes next.

## Step 6: Testing, Selecting, and Applying the Best Solution

In the testing of possible solutions, we ask such questions as, Will it work? Will it be accepted? Is cost a prohibiting factor? Is this solution permanent or merely a stopgap action? On the basis of the testing process, decision-making groups select the solution(s) that best seems to fit the case. As I have already said, they make this choice in the context of prayer, an understanding of biblical principles of Christian leadership and teamwork, and the sovereign leading of the Holy Spirit.

Wrapp suggests that deciding on solutions requires a high tolerance for ambiguity. Although he refers to one general manager in this section, the three evaluatory questions he proposes can be applied as a group tests and selects a solution.

> In considering each proposal, the general manager tests it against at least three criteria: First, will the total proposal, or more often will some part of the proposal, move the organization toward the objectives he has in mind? Second, how will the whole or parts of the proposal be received by the various groups and subgroups in the organization? Where will the strongest opposition come from, which group will furnish the strongest support, and which will be neutral or indifferent?
>
> Third, how does the proposal relate to programs already in process or currently proposed? Can some parts of the proposal now in front of him be added on to a program already under way or can they be combined with all or parts of other proposals in a package which can be steered through the organization?[10]

When a decision has been made to move in a certain direction, leaders must avoid vacillation or obvious apprehension about the decision. Also, all affected parties should be informed immediately.

## Step 7: Evaluation of the Decision

In the threefold process, the decision has been studied and

determined; now it must be tested. Did the problem disappear? If not, does failure lie in the decision itself or in some fault in the implementation? At what point did the flaw enter the application process ?

Should the leader or the group ever change a decision after it has been made and implemented? Yes and no.

*When the Decision Should Not Be Changed:*
1. Obstacles are blocking progress but it is possible that, in time, implementation will be successful and the problem will be solved.
2. Some people have reacted negatively, but there is no reason to believe that their behavior in any way represents error in the decision.
3. Implementation is difficult but possible. Experienced leaders expect difficulty; that is no reason for turning back.

*When the Decision Should Be Changed:*
1. New facts are available which alter the identification of causes or specification of solutions for the problem.
2. The situation has changed and the context in which we made it has been sufficiently altered to render it inadequate under the new conditions.
3. Faulty reasoning becomes apparent in the decision-making process. Leaders make mistakes; wise leaders recognize and correct them even if it means withdrawing a decision that has been publicly announced.

## EVALUATING ONESELF AS A DECISION MAKER

Like leaders, decision makers are made and not born. The process of leadership evolvement described elsewhere in this volume indicates that sometimes natural traits and gifts enable individuals to function effectively as leaders in certain situations, but most leadership behavior results from adequate training.

Use the following checklist to evaluate yourself and others in your organization relative to the adequacy they bring to the decision-making process. Questions may be answered "yes," "no," "most of the time," or "rarely."

1. Are the objectives of the organization clear to me?
2. Are the objectives of the organization clear to my leadership team?
3. Do we carefully consider the mission of our ministry when making decisions?
4. Are we able to specify individual goals for ourselves as well as general objectives for the organization?
5. Do we tend to shrink from decision making, or do we face each decision with the courage and conviction necessary to handle it competently?
6. Do we analyze our own problems clearly?
7. Do we generally have difficulty analyzing the problems of others for whom we are responsible?
8. Can we usually distinguish causes properly?
9. Can we verbalize clear statements about organizational and individual problems?
10. Do we have sufficient rapport with colleagues and subordinates to effectively work together in the decision-making process?
11. Does decision making occupy an inordinate amount of time; that is, do we spend too much time gathering information and procrastinating the actual decision itself?
12. Do we consistently regard the accuracy of the facts in every decision-making situation?
13. Do we face the issues open-mindedly, honestly considering the various alternatives?

14. Do we generally achieve good acceptance of our decisions by others in the organization?
15. Do people agree to implement decisions because of fear of authority or respect for judgment?
16. Do we tend to get unduly involved in decisions to the point that we react emotionally if someone challenges the wisdom of the decision?
17. Are we too unilateral or dictatorial in decision making (i.e., do we fail to allow the group to function)?
18. Do our decisions show a logical pattern of consistency over a period of time or does each one relate only to itself rather than to the whole?
19. Do we help other people make decisions as well as make them ourselves?
20. Can we effectively evaluate the wisdom and correctness of the decision?

Veteran leaders realize that decision making lacks permanence; that is, decisions made today which may be entirely correct and profitable for the improvement and progress of the organization may need to be rethought and revised within the next five years, if not sooner. So we build into the decision-making process a means for feedback that will provide a long-run, continuous testing with options for revision as the events brought about by the decisions fall into place.

Wayne Price summarizes the attitude essential for effective group decision making.

> Wherever possible, I try to allow [the] official group to carry the decision to its completion, maintaining my personal involvement by encouraging and helping those who are seeing it through. I have found myself changing my mind, modifying what I earlier thought best, and sometimes going ahead without any consensus except what I believed to be right. But when I have sought counsel and listened carefully and with an open mind, I have felt supported by the larger community.

A leader must lead, and leadership always implies some dis-agreement from some who follow. But when a leader has included many people in the decision-making process, the dissent will be diminished and participation in the issue will be substantially increased. Also, the pressures of decision making will be reduced.[11]

FOR FURTHER READING

Arnold, John, and Bert Tompkins. *How to Make the Right Decisions.* Milford, Mich.: Mott Media, 1982.

Kouzes, James M., and Barry Z. Posner. *The Leadership Challenge.* Rev. ed. San Francisco: Jossey-Bass, 1995.

Robinson, Haddon. *Decision-Making by the Book.* Wheaton, Ill.: Victor, 1991.

Schaller, Lyle E. *The Decision Makers.* Nashville: Abingdon, 1974.

Walton, Mary. *The Deming Management Method.* New York: Putnam, 1986.

NOTES

1. Rosabeth M. Kanter, *When Giants Learn to Dance: Mastering the Challenges of Strategy, Management, and Careers in the 1990's* (New York: Simon & Schuster, 1989), 19.

2. H. Edward Wrapp, "Good Managers Don't Make Policy Decisions," Selected Paper Number 26 (Chicago: Univ. of Chicago Graduate School of Business, 1967), 8.

3. "Hot Products: Smart Design Is the Common Thread," *Business Week* (June 7, 1993): 57.

4. Em Griffin, "Four Ways to Make Group Decisions," *Leadership* (Spring 1992): 82.

5. Royce G. Gruenler, *The Trinity in the Gospel of John: A Thematic Commentary of the Fourth Gospel* (Grand Rapids: Baker, 1986), 1.

6. Steven K. Sandvig, "Developing Church Leaders Through Participatory Decision Making," *Christian Education Journal* 16, no. 1 (Fall 1995): 109.

7. Haddon Robinson, *Decision-Making by the Book* (Wheaton, Ill.: Victor, 1991), 143.

8. For the actual procedures of effective team decision making, readers should con-

sult chapter 12 of *Feeding and Leading,* which also explains in greater detail the values of effective team decision making.

9. Randy Y. Hirokawa, "Consensus Group Decision-Making, Quality of Decision, and Group Satisfaction: An Attempt to Sort 'Fact' from 'Fiction,'" *Central States Speech Journal* 33, no. 2 (Summer 1982): 413–14.

10. Wrapp, "Good Managers Don't Make Policy Decisions," 8.

11. Wayne Price, "Encouraging Participation in Decision-Making," *Church Administration* (October 1989): 14.

# —9—
# The Team Leader
# as Group Facilitator

It doesn't take much of an analysis of the Synoptic Gospels to see how group-focused Jesus maintained His ministry. Certainly we find outstanding individual encounters (Zacchaeus, Nicodemus, Peter, the rich young ruler), but the broad-stroke picture of those three and a half years shows us Jesus with numerous small groups, prominent among which we find the disciples. Herein lies one of the major faults of the "lone wolf" theory of leadership which I have deliberately assaulted at every opportunity in this book. The autocratic leader removes himself from other people and then complains how lonely leadership has become.

The team leader, in contrast, always sees herself as a part of the team even though she may by reason of title or responsibility serve as the dominant player in some cases. The membership factor of Christian leadership shines brightest in group relationships, and we are reminded again of Paul's brilliant statement in Romans 12:4–5: "Just as each of us has one body with many members, and these members do not all have the same function, so in Christ we who are many form one body, and each member belongs to all the others."

Each member belongs to all the others! Some Christian organizations are run as though each member belonged to the leader. Others operate as though the leader belongs to the group, almost as a prized possession whose time and life they can control. But the mutuality of relationship so beautifully worded by the apostle is the foundation for a facilitating group ministry in churches and Christian organizations.

## THE ROLE OF GROUPS IN LEADERSHIP

Leaders must work with people, or their leadership will not be effective. They must meet people. They must learn from other people. They must help other people relate to each other as well as to their leaders. Christian leaders who develop group facilitation skills will be more effective, happier, and respected. But more important, they will be following the pattern of their Lord.

In a serious work like this, we must walk a tight line between becoming too technical and yet avoiding essential distinctions. Consequently, it seems useful at this point to stop and examine the definition of "group" lest we use it throughout the chapter without clearly agreeing on our meaning.

### Definition of a Group

According to management specialist Bernard Bass, "A group is a collection of individuals whose existence as a collection is rewarding to the individuals."[1] In other words, a collection of moths around a light bulb is not a group, for the plurality means nothing. On the other hand, the lamb and its mother, though only two, do represent a group, for the sucking of the lamb satisfies both.

This classic concept of group is shared by others. Cattell,

for example, defines group as "an aggregate of organisms in which the existence of all is utilized for the satisfaction of the needs of each."[2] And Gibb, like Cattell, views groups as mechanisms for achieving individual satisfaction through interaction.[3] Contemporary research shows that groups usually include such components as *perceived unity, common goals, and face-to-face interaction.*

People have worked in groups throughout the history of the world, but thorough studies of such collective behavior have only been conducted since the mid-twentieth century. Malcolm Knowles, once the executive director of the Adult Education Association, cooperated with his wife, Hulda, in a helpful book that introduced the concept of group dynamics.

Their book indicates that the phrase "group dynamics" can be used in four different ways: (1) it can refer to the complex forces at work in all groups at all times, consciously or unconsciously; (2) it can refer to a field of study and becomes then "a branch of the social sciences concerned with using scientific methods to determine why groups behave the way they do"; (3) it can refer to that body of basic knowledge about group behavior that has accumulated from past research; or (4) it can refer to that body of applied knowledge of technology that translates into practical methods of group work.[4] These distinctions are still generally accepted in the 1990s. In fact, the concept of a leader as group facilitator lies at the heart of andragogy, the modern understanding of adult education.

## Variables in Group Work

Among the minor variables relative to group work we can list *background of the members, life span of the group,* and whether *participation is required or voluntary.* The point here is that the leader, whether emerging from the group, elected by the group, or appointed by a higher authority, must constantly take into account these variables, which to a great extent condition the results of group activity.

One new variable has burst upon the scene in recent years —research regarding how followers form leaders. Litzinger and Schaefer went to West Point to study this effect, with interesting results:

> Not long ago, we posed a question to a group of officers, most of whom were on the West Point faculty, and many of whom were themselves graduates of the Academy. "Since developing leadership is what this place is all about," we ask, "how do you go about doing that task?" Their answer surprised us. "We begin by teaching them to be followers."
>
> This insight prompted us to undertake a study, not of the nature of leadership (a subject which has been widely discussed), but of the notion that leadership may be chiefly an achievement of followers—that able leaders may emerge only from the ranks of able followers. . . . Our concern is the developmental question of how leaders emerge and, particularly, how the mastery of followership may prepare and qualify one for leadership.[5]

Let's return a moment to the disciples. Not one of them could have been identified as a leader in his early days with the Lord. Jesus knew that; they knew that; and we should know it as well. They learned leadership because leadership is learned behavior, and they learned leadership through followership long before the founding of West Point.

## Components of Leadership Groups

As we have already noted, one of the basic functions of any group is *belonging.* The commitment of each group member, especially the leader, has a direct effect on the functioning effectiveness of the group.

Another component is *role taking.* Serious leadership teams allow for emergent leadership patterns and by design pass the ball around. Flexibility is the key here—even for the chairperson, senior pastor, president, CEO, or boss.

Groups provide *status and identity.* How do group members perceive each other? What kinds of interpersonal relationships have developed? What are the attitudes of group members toward one another?

Groups must also develop some form of *affection.* In his chapter entitled "One for All and All for One," Arlo Grenz urges Christian leadership groups to pray for each other, appreciate and encourage each other, show interest in each other, spend time together, and help one another.[6] Usually affection is the last phase to develop in interpersonal relationships, but leadership teams must work toward that goal.

Finally, a major component surfaces in the group's *sensitivity to process.* Give-and-take occurs with greater frequency in a group setting, and some understanding of how groups function is crucial if satisfaction, cohesiveness, and effectiveness are to result.

"Group effectiveness" describes the extent to which groups reward their members. "Group attractiveness," on the other hand, refers to the extent to which they are *expected* to reward their members. Research tells us that the "effects" of a group occur in direct relationship to interaction or non-interaction. In other words, interaction is an essential ingredient for effectiveness. Satisfactory interaction among the members of the group will result in behavior that changes both sooner and to a greater extent than if such interaction had not taken place.

If effectiveness is so important, leaders must recognize the obstacles to effectiveness and know how to combat them. We must also see that we do not build effectiveness as much as we *unleash* something already inherent in the group, the basic vitality of group dynamics.

## UNDERSTANDING GROUP BEHAVIOR

Business and industry have spent millions of dollars researching the dynamic factors of group behavior. More recently the church has become more interested in group study and wants to train its leadership (either professional or lay) in the principles of group work. Since we claim to operate from a high motivation —leading people to be more like Jesus Christ—our concern for "getting it right" ought to appear near the top of most ministry priority lists.

People behave differently at different times because their perception of situations differs. Changed perceptions lead to changed behavior. People feel satisfied when they realize that their perception and consequent behavior are considered correct in the eyes of the group. The following arrangement of forces that form group behavior is arbitrary at best but includes some crucial issues.

## Background

No group operates in a vacuum. Its members bring to it certain attitudes and patterns of behavior that they have cultivated as individuals and from their contact with other groups. Some may feel essentially involved in the success and future of the group (executives who have founded a corporation); others may be participating only because of compulsion (draftees in an army training camp). Some possess higher educational levels than others. Some may be wealthy, some almost poor.

## Participation Pattern

How does the group function? This depends largely on the style of the leaders involved. Is it basically dictatorial while one leader does all the talking and group members passively agree or silently disagree? Does it look like some adult Sunday school classes which proceed from week to week with a monologue unaccompanied by active participation or perhaps even interest on the part of the class members?

## Open Communication

In this context the word *communication* describes how group members relate to one another—how they transmit their ideas, values, feelings, and attitudes toward matters which the group decides. Of course, some communication patterns in a group will be nonverbal.

## Standards

Every group operates with some code of acceptable behavior. This could describe everything from being quiet in church to shouting and jumping as a member of a cheerleading team. The standards are not always written, and they may not always show high quality; but all groups embrace some mutually accepted determination of conduct.

## Sociometric Pattern

Every group contains formal or informal subgroups. Group members react differently to some members than they do to others. Any church committee meeting will demonstrate the fact that group members tend to identify with and support people whom they like, and disagree more frequently with people against whom they may have some prejudice or discrimination.

## Procedures

Formal groups may use formal procedures, and informal groups, informal procedures; but all groups operate with some pattern of function. The group and its leaders must select and follow the procedures that best facilitate the achievement of their objectives.

## Goals

The effectiveness of the group is linked to its goal achievement. In turn, goal achievement is affected by goal clarification. A group of women gathered on Tuesday morning for coffee has its goal. It may be only to share the latest information about their families, but their meeting reflects goal achievement. (See chapters 16 and 17 for more on goal clarification and achievement.)

### UNLEASHING GROUP DYNAMIC

After viewing leadership definitions by several experts, Clark and Clark conclude, "In almost every definition the process of leadership in organizations involves leaders, followers, members, subordinates, or constituents as they interact, create visions, become inspired, find meaning in their work and lives, and gain in trust and respect." They go on to talk about team leadership:

> Leadership is not the private domain of individuals who are highly visible in society. Many acts of superb leadership occur with small groups of followers or in obscure settings and can involve people who exercise little power and have few resources. Leadership acts are not always performed by only one leader; members of a group often take command and work collaboratively to produce astonishing effects.[7]

When Christians get together in groups, individuals must allow the Holy Spirit to control the activities of the group. This unleashes a spiritual dynamic. The question before us now, however, is whether there are aspects of team leadership which, by their presence or absence, facilitate the unleashing of that dynamic.

From a supernatural point of view, the spiritual level and maturity of group members determine the control of the Holy Spirit in the group itself. But within this context some natural (human) factors clamor for attention.

154

## Clarify the Group's Objectives

Once again we focus on this absolute essential of leadership effectiveness. The group must not only have objectives, but these objectives should be understood and subscribed to by all the members. Objectives influence the choice of leaders, and they are the most significant collective factor to guide the group through its procedures and functions.

A group unleashing its dynamic determines its own objectives. In a Christian group some absolute objectives may arise from the Word of God, but an understanding of the interpretation and application of the absolutes is developed through discussion among group members. Team leadership in this situation becomes the process of coordinating the group effort toward common goals.

In a stagnating group, objectives belong to the leader only. Having forced them onto the group, he or she is reduced to coercing members to conform to a behavior that will produce desired results.

## Consider the Group's Hedonic Tone

Hedonic tone describes the amount of pleasure members derive from their participation in the group. Is this a happy experience? Do the group members like one another and spend time with each other outside of group meetings? Is the atmosphere informal? Many factors determine whether a group will have hedonic tone, including how we select members, the attitude of the leaders, the conditions under which the group meets, the attractiveness and effectiveness of the group, and almost all of the properties described earlier in this chapter.

## Construct Patterns for Group Interaction

As people interact, behavior changes and groups achieve

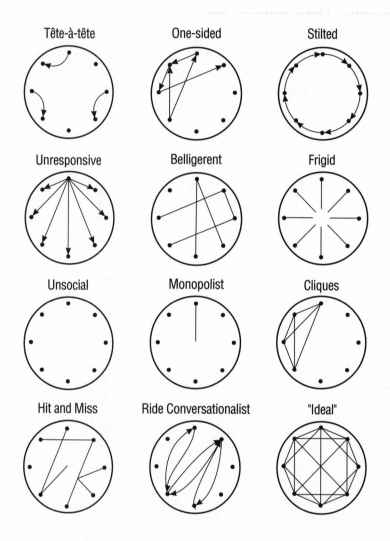

TYPES OF GROUP INTERACTION
*Figure 6*

*Grant Howard, "Group Dynamics," Christian Education Department Notes, Dallas Seminary, 12.*

goals. Effectiveness is inseparably linked to adequate interaction patterns. These patterns are never complete when any group minority (or even an individual in the group) does not effectively participate in group procedures. Though this is more easily achieved in small groups, it is no less important for larger groups. Grant Howard has visualized twelve different "types of group interaction" (see figure 6).[8]

## CRYSTALLIZE THE GROUP'S ACHIEVEMENT

Achievement is another word for effectiveness. The same quality might be described by the word *productivity*. Serving Christ in conformity to the Word of God is the ultimate objective of every Christian group. Its achievement is measured by its allegiance to biblical patterns of service.

### Create a Fair System of Evaluation

Evaluation should not only look at the past but plan the future on the basis of the past. Failures can be more helpful than successes. Creative groups try out new ideas and define a vision for the future.

Groups have been described as nomothetic or idiographic; dynamic unleashing or stagnating; power inhibiting or power releasing; and as healthy or sick. Paul Douglass offers a comparison of twenty characteristics of healthy versus sick groups:

| HEALTHY *A group is healthy when:* | SICK *A group is sick when:* |
|---|---|
| 1. All the members speak up about what they think. | 1. A few members do all the talking. |
| 2. Decisions are worked through until a general consensus of agreement is reached. | 2. Most members mumble assent. |

| HEALTHY | SICK |
|---------|------|
| *A group is healthy when:* | *A group is sick when:* |
| 3. Well-informed members contribute ideas in the area of their competence. | 3. Competent people sit silently by. |
| 4. A member's value is judged by the merit of his idea. | 4. New people with good ideas are not listened to. |
| 5. The whole group handles questions that concern the whole group. | 5. Decision making is quickly referred to committees. |
| 6. Major issues get major time. | 6. Minor issues consume the major time. |
| 7. Major issues evoke mature approaches to change and "working through." | 7. Minor and simple issues make people seethe or boil. |
| 8. Minor issues are settled with the attention they deserve. | 8. Major issues are passed over. |
| 9. Decisions reached by thorough participation are final and satisfactory. | 9. The same subjects, supposedly settled, keep coming up again. |
| 10. Members really understand one another's ideas, plans, and proposals. | 10. Quick judgments are passed on issues people do not understand. |
| 11. Members objectively center interest on goals and tasks. | 11. Members subjectively talk about people in scapegoating fashion. |
| 12. The group carries forward in the performance of tasks and the achievement of goals. | 12. The group accomplishes little in the absence of its chairperson. |
| 13. The group works goalwise toward change. | 13. The group is afraid to change. |
| 14. Rewards and criticism are shared. | 14. Rewards and criticism are concentrated on a few. |

| HEALTHY | SICK |
|---|---|
| *A group is healthy when:* | *A group is sick when:* |
| 15. Initiative and responsibility are encouraged by growth in a sense of personal confidence, competence, and worth. | 15. Initiative and responsibility are stifled by dependence. |
| 16. Search for help from all sources is continuous. | 16. No resources outside the group are drawn upon. |
| 17. Information is fed back into the group. | 17. Little is told to the group. |
| 18. The worth of persons is respected. | 18. The person is squelched in his expression and stunted in his growth. |
| 19. Experience is considered the occasion for growth in responsibility and love. | 19. Action lacks altitude and depth, remaining on the horizontal plane without the vertical relationships to God. |
| 20. Action is God-related. | 20. Action is self-centered.[9] |

## EXPECTATIONS OF GROUP MEMBERS

If followers create leaders and leaders come from the ranks of followers, it seems obvious that group members provide a major contribution toward group achievement. What can a missions committee chairman in a local church expect of her group members? What can a college president expect from his cabinet? Though the levels of intensity may vary, group expectations contain an amazing similarity regardless of size or setting.

### Attendance

If "each member belongs to all the others" (Rom. 12:5),

159

group members betray their commitment to the cause by repeated absence or tardiness. "Just do it," says Nike, and when it comes to being involved with group work in a Christian organization, just being there is a first and crucial step.

### Affirmation

Mature group members learn to disagree without being disagreeable, as the old line goes. They can express their opinions honestly, expecting that other colleagues will receive and consider them fairly.

### Confidentiality

We could call this loyalty. Group members, particularly Christian leaders, dare not appear vitally interested in the group only at its meetings while bad-mouthing it outside the conference room.

### Learning

Let's go back to that church missions committee. The chances are pretty good that members elected for a given year are not experts on global evangelization and the contextualization of the gospel. But they can learn through reading, through asking questions, and through making every attempt to understand what the group is supposed to achieve and how their contributions can make that achievement possible.

### Responsibility

This goes beyond attendance. Seriously committed group members find themselves saying with some frequency, "I'll take care of it." If you have chaired many committees, you silently or audibly pronounce that person blessed—thrice blessed when she actually does it.

## Avoid Defensiveness

Don't link your person to your ideas and don't link another member's ideas to his or her person. Be willing to critique and evaluate objectively without turf-guarding or, God forbid, serving some special interest like a pork barrel congressman.[10]

## ROADBLOCKS TO EFFECTIVE GROUP WORK

Research in group dynamics demonstrates that a number of dangers or difficulties can arise in group activity to stifle the dynamic that should provide the very lifeblood of the group's achievement. As we control and alleviate these problems, we raise the level of effectiveness.

## Forgetting the Individual

Old-style communism subordinated and sacrificed the individual to the interests of the group. We see this same mistake in simple group process, particularly when one or two individuals always find themselves in the minority. The leader and the group must safeguard and encourage recognition of each member's viewpoint.

## Expecting Too Much from Group Dynamics

Because of the emphasis that has been placed on group process in sociology, psychology, and education in the past two decades, some people tend to think of group work as a panacea for all of the problems an organization faces. Unreasonable expectations may later give birth to that death knell of traditionalism: "We tried it and it didn't work."

161

## Wasting Time in Group Work

If the group's objectives are not clear and the problem is not properly specified, group work itself may be quite unfruitful and unsatisfactory. The group fumbles around with various approaches to the problem and finally bogs down in its own discussion. Unless the leaders plan for productive group meetings through preparation of agendas and essential documents, the group will waste a great deal of time.

## Letting Group Dynamics Become an Activity of the Flesh

As in any ministry effort, dependence upon the Lord is essential. Just as the individual Christian yields to the control of God's Spirit, so the entire group yields its collective mind to that divine control.

## Handling Problem People

Calvin Miller talks about "six difficult souls—the chronically arrogant, the congenitally belligerent, the non-negotiator, the nit-picker, the wheedler (who needles leadership confidence), and the 'yes-butter.'" He notes, "Difficult people are those who stand between you and the realization of your objectives. They are a deterrent to the earliest possible achievement of your God-ordained dreams."[11]

Obviously, leaders deal with such people all the time, and team leaders sensitive to group process ask why people behave the way they do. Sometimes we find no answer, and we simply must move on without them. But often the sensitive leader can pick up strains of loneliness and longing that create negative attitudes that are unrelated to what the group is all about. To win over a difficult person is a significant leadership achievement.

The ultimate test of Jesus' discipling group ministry was the way the Twelve led the early church. Acts shows us how they

162

understood what He was trying to teach them about team leadership and group behavior. In any Christian organization (and especially in a local church), new people ought to feel the dynamic of those already working together in the bonds of Christ and the fellowship of the Holy Spirit. The mature group is no longer *centric* (focused on their own needs and goals rather than those of the wider group) but has become *radic* (demonstrating selflessness that fosters the achievement of group goals).

Let's remember, too, that Christian organizations of any size contain within them many subgroups. An analysis of group dynamics and behavior seems essential for any Christian leader who wants to serve God effectively.

## LEADER-GROUP RELATIONS

Earlier in the chapter I raised a question relative to the leader's position in group activity. Let's return to that question at this point. If leadership is not some kind of innate trait with which some people are born and some are not, but is rather a series of services which a group member performs for and in that group, many traditional concepts of leadership need to be reexamined. Traditional authoritarianism needs to be replaced by a move toward team leadership, which encourages member participation and responsibility.

Team leadership consists of coordinating efforts toward group goals rather than dominating group activities. If the leader acts as a boss, she plans, controls, directs, and decides. The group submits and conforms with some kind of passive assent. On the other hand, when the leader acts as a guide, he seeks to allow and to encourage the group to plan, control, direct, and decide. A guide leads or directs others in some path or direction, showing the way by accompanying or going on ahead.

STAGES OF GROUP GROWTH

The nature of a group largely determines the type of leader it needs. Groups are rarely static but rather possess changing needs and interests to which a leader must be sensitive. Let's review two phases or levels of group growth mentioned earlier.

### The Centric Group

Centricity marks a group at its immature or infancy stage. The individuals in the group are more concerned about their own needs and goals than those of the group. Group attractiveness may have been somewhat high, but effectiveness is often low because members of the group do not "pull together."

Such a group is characterized by wide heterogeneity in objectives and interests. Incompatibility with each other and sometimes with the leaders is quite obvious. We see a general resistance to authority, lack of uniformity, and minimal personal freedom. Such immaturity takes time to dissipate. Sometimes a group like this can pressure the transgressing individual out of his preoccupation with personal needs and goals.

### The Radic Group

"Radicity" marks a group concerned with more than just its own activities. Members exhibit a conscious altruism and receptive teamwork actually contagious to new members. There is some conformity in behavior in a radic group but certainly not in ideation. Members surrender selfishness to the achievement of group goals, but they do not sacrifice individuality on the altar of collectiveness.

A group progresses from centricity to radicity through careful team leadership that takes the emphasis off force and authoritarianism and extends the limits of freedom as the group is able to effectively use it. Sometimes self-inspection on the part of the group, and evaluation of its motives and objectives, are valid procedures.

Christian ministries ought to be radic groups. New members coming into a congregation ought to feel the dynamic of the people already working together there in the bonds of Christ and the fellowship of the Holy Spirit. Ministry groups ought to be both attractive and effective in carrying out their ministry.

## FOR FURTHER READING

Blumenthal, L. H. *How to Work with Your Board and Committees.* New York: Association, 1954.

Buchanan, Paul C. *The Leader and Individual Motivation.* New York: Association, 1964.

Gangel, Kenneth O., and James C. Wilhoit. *The Christian Educator's Handbook on Spiritual Formation.* Wheaton, Ill.: Victor, 1994.

Howard, J. Grant. *The Trauma of Transparency.* Portland, Oreg.: Multnomah, 1979.

Luft, Joseph. *Group Processes: An Introduction to Group Dynamics.* Palo Alto, Calif.: Mayfield, 1970.

## NOTES

1. Bernard M. Bass, *Leadership, Psychology, and Organizational Behavior* (New York: Harper & Row, 1960; rept. Greenwood, 1973), 39ff.

2. Ibid., 40–41.

3. Ibid., 41.

4. Malcolm Knowles and Hulda Knowles, *Introduction to Group Dynamics* (New York: Association, 1959), 11–13.

5. William Litzinger and Thomas Schaefer, "Leadership Through Followship" in *Contemporary Issues in Leadership,* ed. William E. Rosenbach and Robert L. Taylor (Boulder, Colo., 1984), 138.

6. Arlo Grenz, *The Confident Leader* (Nashville: Broadman & Holman, 1994), 147–59.

7. Kenneth E. Clark and Miriam B. Clark, *Choosing to Lead* (Charlotte, N.C.: Iron Gate, 1994), 20–22.

8. Grant Howard, unpublished class notes, Dallas Theological Seminary, 1963.

9. Paul F. Douglass, *The Group Workshop Way in the Church* (New York: Association, 1956).

10. Many of these concepts are adapted from *Getting Together,* by Em Griffin (Downers Grove, Ill.: InterVarsity, 1982), 35, 36.

11. Calvin Miller, *The Empowered Leader* (Nashville: Broadman & Holman, 1995), 140–41.

# — 10 —
# THE TEAM LEADER
# AS BOARD OR COMMITTEE CHAIR

A sea captain and his chief engineer were arguing over who was the most important to the ship. To prove their point to each other, they decided to swap places. The chief engineer ascended to the bridge, and the captain went to the engine room. Several hours later, covered with oil and dirt, the captain suddenly appeared on the deck. "Chief!" he yelled, waving aloft a monkey wrench. "You have to get down there; I can't make her go!" "Of course you can't," replied the chief. "She's aground!"[1]

That simple story illustrates a basic truth of ministry organizations: *members of a team don't excel over each other; we depend on each other.* Since this book is about team leadership, the reader should not be surprised at my emphasis on the leader's role as a team player on whatever board or committee he or she might chair. Indeed, that non-biblical adversarial aura we create between and among chairs and committee members makes this dimension of ministry difficult, even sometimes dreaded. As you

167

read this chapter, keep the team concept foremost in your mind. Michael Anthony puts it this way:

> Clearly, there are many benefits of operating a ministry as a team venture. . . . There is also a shared sense of ownership in the ministry, accountability and decision-making, and freedom for idea sharing, all of which provide the church with more creative approaches to programming. Team ministry also lightens the burden of overworked staff members, helps the average person in the pew understand the importance of serving the Lord by serving His people, and provides all members with a degree of recognition for their contribution and help.[2]

The values of committee work should be obvious. First, certainly group ideation is greater than the results of one person attempting to solve a problem alone. Second, in Christian circles the fellowship of God's people working together to accomplish God's work in God's way should make board or committee activity a highlight for leaders. Third, the presentation of joint thinking on a controversial issue has more authority and can evoke more respect than the attitude of one person, regardless of that person's title. Evangelicals should stop throwing stones at committees and recognize instead the great contribution they can make toward achieving the objectives of our organizations.

Perhaps it is necessary at this point to distinguish between a board and a committee. For purposes of this chapter, we will consider a board a higher-level, policy-making group; a committee we will view as a recommending group, usually appointed by and responsible to a board.

Though various structures appear in different types of Christian organizations, the actual function of boards and committees takes on a striking similarity. In a college, one generally finds a board of trustees or regents and administrative committees responsible to that board. In the church, a Christian education committee could have several subcommittees as in figure 7.

CHRISTIAN EDUCATION COMMITTEE
SUBCOMMITTEES

| Missions Education | Leadership Training | Music Education | Evangelism | Weekday Clubs |
|---|---|---|---|---|

SUBCOMMITTEE CHART
*Figure 7*

## VARIOUS FUNCTIONS OF BOARDS

The first step to proper functioning as a board or committee chairperson is to recognize the essential nature of the group and its objectives. Then team leaders convey this information accurately and adequately to all the members. A misconception of one's role on a board leads to inferior performance and possibly even to a distortion of the ministry that board or committee work should be.

No doubt the various functions of boards could be categorized in any number of ways, but one of the clearest would be to specify the board's relationship to the policies of the organization. In a church, the official board (deacons, elders, session, etc.) has the responsibility for total church policy. At the committee level, responsibility for policy narrows to authority over some specific aspects of ministry.

### Boards Determine Policy

This aspect of board work can be observed in the function of a school board. Operation of the school—its objectives and goals, enlistment of personnel, long-range planning for the institution, other aspects of policy making—are the board's responsibility. Recommendations may come to the board from faculty and administrative groups (through proper channels), but in the final analysis the board sets the policy.

169

In any organization, a number of steps should be followed in determining institutional policy. *A review of past policies and present procedures* helps analyze where the institution stands at any given time. *Confirmation of goals and objectives* and the gathering of information about various aspects of the program produce intelligent decisions regarding the direction the institution should take. This is one reason boards should receive thorough reports from all administrative officers in the organization.

When the board reaches a decision regarding policy, it communicates the decision to personnel in the organization. Generally speaking, it is not the role of the pastor to determine church policies any more than it is the college president's responsibility to determine the direction of an institution of higher education. Both are obviously influential on and to the board, but *the board itself is the policy-making body.*

You can see immediately why accrediting associations do not allow college presidents to chair the boards of their institutions. It destroys the balance of power and catapults one person into a frightening position. In my opinion, the same guidelines should prevail in churches and Christian organizations. In business and industry it is not unusual to find the CEO serving also as chairman of the board, but the entire scenario is different from nonprofit service organizations. In some situations, such as a church-planting ministry, it may be necessary for the pastor to chair the official board for a period of time. But he should always pursue the goal of passing that position to a lay leader as quickly as possible.

One further word on boards and policy. A major cause of distress between personnel in an organization and the members of its board stems from the idea that the few dictate work patterns for the many. Certainly the board should be sensitive to the needs and concerns of everyone in the organization, but it cannot abdicate its responsibility for setting policy and staying with it. DeKruyter puts it this way:

The board . . . must establish and stick to its policies. I believe this principle applies to the small church, as well. Yes, the small church usually is run by relationships rather than priorities, but certain policies ought to be adhered to nonetheless. If not, we risk the long-range trust and thus the financial health of the church.[3]

## Boards Implement Policy

Actually the board does not technically implement policy, since much of the policy set by boards is implemented by staff throughout the organization. Nevertheless, the necessity of setting in motion the wheels of implementation rests on the board. And sometimes the policies will actually be executed by the board. It is at least consistent to say that the board is responsible for seeing that the policies they have predetermined are satisfactorily implemented. Blumenthal comments on the improvements in the relationship between the board and staff:

> Considerable progress has been made by many organizations in achieving a satisfactory balance between board and staff functioning. We have come a long way from an earlier day when it could be said about boards that "they are usually the product of consistent effort of a well-entrenched secretary, to place about him a group of ornaments who will never fail to say yes"; that the "board runs the whole works. . . . This kind of a board, when conducting a case work agency, for instance, insists upon disposing of every individual or family by solemn vote"; or that boards have been preoccupied with drawing up by-laws "frequently so worded that the authority of the professional worker is carefully curtailed while the actual functioning of programs involved is delayed and hampered."[4]

## Boards Advise Policy

The board may, in effect, delegate its policy-making functions on occasion, passing to others in the organization the responsibility for deciding certain issues under study by the institution. In such a case the policy itself is formulated by a lesser body, but that formulation results from authority delegated by the board.

Consonant with transmitting the authority may very well be some counsel regarding how the authority should be used and how the decision should be made. The board then makes its own influence felt in the decision, while not exercising its policy-making function directly. The more a board trusts its administrative officers, the less it will get involved in implementation or advising policy.

I can recall many times as a college president being told by the board, "That's your area of responsibility, but we suggest that you keep in mind . . ." These were not directives but advice, and the wise leader (pastor, president, missions executive, etc.) gratefully accepts the collective wisdom of the board (Prov. 13:10).

In an outstanding book that should be on the shelves of all leaders who work with boards and committees, Robert and Gerald Thompson talk about what boards need from organizational leaders to do their jobs correctly.

> Effective directors receive needed *information* for weighing the pros and cons of alternative courses of action and making proper decisions. Effective directors are men and women of *integrity* who govern the organization's business, financial, and ministry affairs. They are *involved* in board and board committee responsibilities and committed to the organization's mission. They are *independent* from management and exercise their oversight responsibilities objectively. Decisions are based upon facts and information free of conflicts of interest and the pressure of other directors or the chief officer.[5]

## Boards Assume Legal Responsibility for Policy

Every organization exists as an entity that must be represented in some legal way. Generally such representatives take the form of some sort of board, such as a board of regents, elders, deacons, or trustees. Legal documents (e.g., land deeds, incorporation papers, etc.) are signed by the board members, who thereby assume legal responsibility for the organization's proper functioning. Should difficulties arise, the court cannot render judgment against the entire congregation, nor against the leader, but against those representatives whose names are affixed to legal documents.

For full details on legal and financial accountability, I refer readers again to Thompson and Thompson, who remind us that the central reason many businesses and nonprofit organizations are in trouble is that "management lacks accountability to an independent, informed, and involved board of directors."[6]

## BOARD AND COMMITTEE MEMBERSHIP

Although one can find innumerable technical differences in constitutions and bylaws, it is probably safe to say that boards recruit their membership in one of three basic ways:

1. *Self-perpetuation.* A self-perpetuating board may or may not have a limiting-tenure clause; that is, board members may hold office indefinitely, or the constitution may call for a limited stay on the board. When a vacancy occurs it is filled by election among the board members themselves. They add to their own ranks those they wish to serve. Many college boards operate in this way, as do some church boards, particularly in churches with a non-congregational polity.

2. *Popular election.* This is probably the most common approach and the one used by the Congress of the United States. Congress certainly is a policy-making body, and its members hold office by the choice of their constituents. Elected boards almost always place a tenure limit on board membership.

3. *Ex officio status.* Members who serve on a board by virtue of their office are neither appointed nor elected to that role. The pastor, for example, may be an ex officio member of every board and committee in the church. He holds that member-

ship because he is the pastor, not because any of the boards or even the congregation has invited him to do so. By the way, ex officio does not mean non-voting.

Limited tenure is certainly a valid and recommended procedure for almost all boards. Board members tend to become entrenched if no boundaries are placed on the time of service. Several obvious problems can occur when organizations practice lifetime board membership. Members tend to grow old together and a stagnancy in creative thinking and aggressive planning can develop at the highest level. People tend to adopt vested interests when they know they can protect them over a long period of time.

Still another problem, particularly for the church, is the dismissal of a board member when necessary. If a lifetime deacon falls into immorality, the church must exercise discipline and remove him from office. If he has held the office for some twenty or twenty-five years and has developed a following among the congregation, such action may split the church.

Unlike boards, most committee memberships are appointive in nature. It is not impossible to have a permanent committee, but most come up for review and change of personnel periodically. Appointments to committee membership are generally made by the board which the committee serves or perhaps by administrative selection. Membership may be approved at some other level, such as the entire board or even the congregation, but usually it is not elective. Committees study, discuss, and make recommendations, but they rarely operate in a policy-making role. Sometimes groups come together only for a specific short-term task. We call such a committee ad hoc or perhaps a "task force."

A competent board chairperson assesses the interests and abilities of various board members for strategic committees. Once a committee has been formed, it also needs a chairperson; and that position can be filled again by appointment from the board chairperson or by an election among the committee members themselves.

Productivity of any board or committee largely depends

upon the effectiveness and thoroughness of its chair. She bears the responsibility of calling the meetings, helping the board analyze the problems before it, motivating the members and drawing them into the ideation process, and assisting the committees in formulating an accurate and thorough report for the board. "The chair" is the strategic position on any board or committee, and most leaders will occupy that role many times through the years of their ministry.

Let me say again here that leaders in Christian organizations dare not let an adversarial attitude develop between executives and board members or the board as a whole. If we accept the concept of team leadership so carefully argued by Bruce Stabbert in *The Team Concept*,[7] we approach the board neither with intimidation nor manipulation. We serve together as one in the cause of God's kingdom, and anything less than team spirit denies the emphasis of Scripture. My friends and colleagues Mike Lawson and Bob Choun put it simply but clearly:

> The church board is, hopefully, the brains of the outfit. These are men, and perhaps women, who have been chosen by the congregation to use the resources of the church for the enlightenment of the people and the glory of God. The idea that godly men and women cannot be shrewd business people should be given the same credence as the myth that pretty girls are brainless. The authority and responsibility accorded to people in this position require a Christian lifestyle and administrative skills (1 Tim. 3; 2 Tim. 2; Titus 1).[8]

## THE CHAIRPERSON'S ROLE
## IN BOARD AND COMMITTEE WORK

About this point in the chapter some will wonder why we have not dealt with crucial specifics of board and committee work such as agenda preparation, handling of minutes, parliamentary procedure, and the like. Those issues are covered in my earlier book *Feeding and Leading* (chapter 18) and, as much as possible, I want this present volume to be a companion, not an echo, of that book.

Blumenthal writes about executives and subexecutives, pinpointing three different levels of authority in relation to the board's work: the executive or subexecutive, the president, and the chairman. For the sake of simplicity in the following paragraph, consider the pastor as the executive and an associate pastor as subexecutive:

> The subexecutive's relation to the committee at its meetings is generally similar to that of the agency executive to the board at its meetings. He is a partner with the committeemen in dealing with the business of the committee. There is mutual consultation, free and critical discussion, a wholesome process of give-and-take, and a recognition by the worker and the committeemen of their complementary roles. The subexecutive exercises indirect leadership: he too acts as stimulator, information giver, and interpreter. He also uses when necessary the direct approach: he is adviser, recommender, advocate, interpreter, and information giver. As in the relationship of the agency executive to the president, the subexecutive at committee meetings works primarily through the committee chairman, reinforcing the chairman where the need for so doing develops.[9]

Perhaps it would be helpful to delineate the chairperson's work in six major categories of function that would be applicable either to a board or a committee chair.

## _Planning_

The chair (in concert with the executive) is responsible for structuring board or committee meetings and gathering any necessary information to be disseminated there. The most strategic aspect of the planning function is the construction of the meeting agenda. This should be prepared and distributed in advance to committee members, and should contain sufficient information so that they know what they will face when they arrive.

Use action verbs that genuinely define what the commit-tee will do. Examples might include "discuss," "decide upon," "propose," and so forth. Ample announcement of the meeting should be given so that every member knows the details. Set time limits and keep them. Announce the next meeting either on the agenda or at the meeting itself and then include the date and time in the minutes.

Agendas should be firmly based on the mission of the organization and the vision for its future. Board or committee agendas which deal constantly with past problems and present struggles soon create discouragement and even defeat. As Leith Anderson puts it, "Every organization needs someone who looks out the window, outside the organization, to the world and to the future."[10] Surely that means the chairperson or executive officer, preferably both. Either way, a futuristic, purpose-driven agenda should result.

## Presiding

The board or committee chairperson does not dictate or dominate but rather catalyzes group discussion and action. Nor-mally he or she does not vote unless that vote is necessary to break a tie. The chair states the business clearly, keeps the discus-sion moving, secures necessary motions or consensus from the floor, and, as much as possible, refrains from influencing com-mittee members with his own opinion.

We may assume that the very role of chairperson indicates influence over the thinking of colleagues. Add a persuasive per-sonality to that authority and the influence can overwhelm the members. To do so is a perversion of the office.

In a thorough work on organization development, Schmuck and Runkel describe what your board or committee meetings should look like.

Effective meetings are characterized by at least four features:

177

(1) a balanced mixture of task and maintenance functions, with an edge given to sticking to the task; (2) many more group-oriented actions than self-oriented actions; (3) wide dispersal of leadership roles; and (4) adequate follow-through to permit decisions made at the meeting to result in the expected actions.[11]

## Appointing

Often chairpersons of boards or committees appoint other officers, committee members, or subcommittee members. This task must be carried out with the goals of the institution in mind. In Christian organizations it cannot become a political feather-bedding operation. Such appointments should generally be made publicly in the meeting and recorded accurately in the minutes.

In the seminary where I serve, one of my duties is to chair the Academic Affairs Committee, the central hub of faculty and curriculum decision making. Frequently I hear myself say something like, "Let's have the Systematic Theology Department discuss this matter further and report to the committee at its next meeting," or "We'll ask Dr. Malphurs to revise his proposal and submit it to the dean's office as quickly as possible." Such extramural appointment of work saves enormous blocks of committee time and generally produces an enhanced finished product.

## Representing

The board chair speaks for the entire board. In some situations this may require a great deal of public exposure, in others a certain amount of writing. Either way, the chairperson must accurately express the board's policies and attitudes to the organization's larger public.

My daughter serves as director of children's ministry in a Baptist church. Part of her task is to communicate all the ministries and functions of that age group. She represents every volunteer in the entire children's ministry program whether they serve in Sunday school classes, weekday club ministries, nursery duty, or in some other capacity. As chair of the children's ministry team, she communicates that crucial element of congregational life to the deacons, who will often be required to make decisions about time, space, and finances on the basis of information she provides.

## Counseling

The counseling role of a board or committee chairperson leans more toward the function of advising than personal counseling. She may (and should) on occasion attend meetings of those committees which she has appointed. On those occasions she may offer some words of counsel as to how the committee can best achieve its objectives and carry out its functions. She may meet personally with the chairs of the committees or subcommittees, encouraging them in their work and guiding them in the fulfillment of their tasks.

The chairperson is also responsible for spending some counseling time with officers of the board—the vice chairperson, secretary, treasurer, and others. Notice that knowledge of the total structure and function must be thorough and accurate.

> Finally, group members are often unaware of how they are influenced by group norms and processes. Members of a faculty, for example, may know that their meetings are going poorly but may not understand why. Some members may be upset because the group cannot work effectively on its agenda in a brief period of time; others may criticize meetings because they are all work and no fun. In such instances [chairpersons] acting as process consultants can collect and feed back data about meeting processes so that members can proceed, understand, and act in ways that will improve their meetings.[12]

## Reporting

Although committee reporting may not be done by the chairperson, she is nevertheless responsible for that report since the meeting minutes form the official record of what the board or committee does. When the secretary has been appointed or elected, the chairperson should give careful guidance to make sure that the minutes are recorded accurately and in proper style.

Since there is no virtue in spending a great deal of time in board or committee work just for the sake of having long meetings, a distribution of minutes in advance alleviates the drudgery of reading through them at the beginning of every meeting. Make sure you prepare the minutes in a concise fashion so that committee members do not need to wade through an enormous amount of material to find out what really went on in the last meeting.

Along with this oral reporting and the keeping of minutes, the chairperson may be responsible for the preparation of written reports describing the work of the group. These reports should pinpoint the policy issues and make them intelligible to all people served by the board or committee. The image of the board and its work is developed and maintained by the reports given to the public. The necessity for accuracy and clarity in such reporting is obvious.

## THE RESPONSIBILITY OF
## BOARD AND COMMITTEE MEMBERS

The chairperson should assume some responsibility for teaching the board how to function properly. This begins with *regular and faithful attendance* at all meetings. It continues with some kind of *preparation* for the meetings, which usually means studying the issues, perusing the agenda, or even preparing reports.

As the meeting progresses, the members should be *involved in asking discerning questions* about the policy issues on the floor. Constructive participation is essential on the part of every member. Of course, every committee has its negative members; they usually exhibit one or more of the following characteristics:

1. *Ability to see only one side of an issue.* This person makes sure that the committee realizes the dominant importance of her position. There may be several apparent views on the subject, but like a horse with blinders, the only direction this type can see is in the way that she is headed.

2. *An emotional fixation on some issue or side of an issue.* Some members throw aside an empirical approach to the committee's examination of problems and operate from an emotional rather than volitional concern for the issues at hand. This kind of member is likely to be offended and perhaps even walk out of a committee meeting if things do not go his way.

3. *The tendency always to vote with the chairperson or majority.* Even though the chair may exercise careful discretion in not offering his own opinion on the issues, this "rubber stamp" member will seize upon a position which he thinks the chair prefers and vote that way. On the other hand, if he sees the majority building up for a certain vote, he will immediately jump on the bandwagon and be counted with the larger group when the vote is taken.

4. *Nonparticipation in board or committee discussion.* This member may have a heart of gold and a head full of ideas regarding the issues that the committee faces, but she can't serve the committee in its work since her ideas and heart can't make an escape through a closed mouth. She may attend committee meetings regularly, listen carefully on all issues, and vote diligently. But in the very necessary dissection of issues and review of various options she is of no value simply because she does not contribute.

5. *A tendency to monopolize the conversation.* The opposite problem from that described above, loquaciousness can reap one of two possible results for this committee member. Either his arguments are persuasive and he draws support from the rest of

the group, or his much talking builds enmity among other committee members. Even if they favor a given issue, they might vote against it because of his enthusiastic support. In the final analysis, he may be easier to deal with than the person who never says anything, but when you chair, be careful not to allow such a member to dominate meetings.

6. *A begrudging expenditure of time.* Every committee has clock watchers who are more interested in a motion to adjourn than they are in the business at hand. They probably serve on the committee for the prestige it may afford, little concerned with genuinely effective participation. If we see this attitude only once or twice in a year of committee work, it can be quickly excused; all members of boards and committees have occasions to watch a time schedule carefully. If, however, this characterizes a member's attitude at every meeting, she probably should not be asked to serve again.

Certainly voting on issues forms a significant part of the responsibility of board and committee members. That voting must not be a careless affirmative, nor should it be a constant negative (just to make sure that nothing passes unanimously). Serious members vote according to conviction based upon a thorough understanding of issues. Anything less perverts the significance of committee membership.

Perhaps, in closing this chapter, I should call attention to the fact that participation in a board or committee provides not only for contribution of the individual to the work of the group but also for the influence of the group on the member. Blumenthal suggests that

> the behavior of the board member is influenced not only by his own background, motivations, and attitudes. It is influenced also by the behavior of the board as a group. As has been indicated, man—by his very nature—is a social being; he is not independent of his environment. The attitudes of the group tend to modify his behavior, and few persons will behave in ways contrary to that of their group. (It is not implied that the

board member's behavior is entirely controlled by the board group.)[13]

The hedonic tone of the group is largely set by its chairperson. He is responsible for developing a satisfactory climate in which a free and open discussion of controversial issues can be carried out without any loss of love among members. The chair must attend to the attractiveness of the group as well as its effectiveness. Far from a pedantic, mechanical vestige of bureaucracy, board and committee work challenges group dynamics at the highest level.

### FOR FURTHER READING

Anthony, Michael J. *The Effective Church Board*. Grand Rapids: Baker, 1993.

DeKruyter, Arthur, et al. *Mastering Church Management*. Portland, Oreg.: Multnomah, 1990.

Hesselbein, Francis, Marshall Goldsmith, and Richard Beckhard, eds. *The Leader of the Future*. San Francisco: Jossey-Bass, 1996.

Schmuck, Richard A., and Philip J. Runkel. *The Handbook of Organization Development in Schools and Colleges*. Prospect Heights, Ill.: Waveland, 1994.

Thompson, Robert R., and Gerald R. Thompson. *Organizing for Accountability*. Wheaton, Ill.: Harold Shaw, 1991.

### NOTES

1. *Leadership* 12, no. 4 (Fall 1991): 44.

2. Michael J. Anthony, *The Effective Church Board* (Grand Rapids: Baker, 1993), 124.

3. Arthur DeKruyter, *Mastering Church Management* (Portland, Oreg.: Multnomah, 1990), 92.

4. L. H. Blumenthal, *How to Work with Your Board and Committees* (New York: Association, 1954), 60.

5. Robert R. Thompson and Gerald R. Thompson, *Organizing for Accountability* (Wheaton, Ill.: Harold Shaw, 1991), 74.

6. Ibid., 43.

7. Bruce Stabbert, *The Team Concept* (Tacoma, Wash.: Hegg Bros., 1982).

8. Michael S. Lawson and Robert J. Choun, Jr., *Directing Christian Education* (Chicago: Moody, 1992), 81.

9. Blumenthal, *How to Work with Your Board,* 36.

10. Leith Anderson, *Mastering Church Management* (Portland, Oreg.: Multnomah, 1990), 69.

11. Richard A. Schmuck and Philip J. Runkel, *The Handbook of Organization Development in Schools and Colleges* (Prospect Heights, Ill.: Waveland, 1994), 187.

12. Ibid., 190.

13. Blumenthal, *How to Work with Your Board,* 60.

# –11–

# THE TEAM LEADER

## AS CONFLICT MANAGER

W e should not have been surprised—he had done it several times before. Less than forty-eight hours before, at a church elders' meeting on Saturday night, Stan had been on the losing side of a vote that seemed clear to the rest of us. He was not the type to shout, kick over a chair, or slam the door while leaving. Stan used a more effective tactic. He merely dropped into deadpan silence for the rest of the meeting, leaving us to guess what would happen next.

By this time all the guesswork was gone; as expected, Stan delivered his written resignation from the board to the church office first thing Monday morning. Terse, cold, and with just the right touch of self-pity for so frequently finding himself in the minority, the document found its way into the file with those that had come before it.

Of course it was my duty as pastor to follow through, invent some redemptive solution to keep Stan in the family, and convince him to retract his resignation. This went on for several years until finally, when Stan's name would have been scheduled to appear on a congregational ballot to continue his seat as elder, the nominating committee, quite aware of the problem, prayerfully deleted his name.

At the congregational meeting someone offered the nomination from the floor, and Stan was back on the ballot. But he was not elected and when the secretary announced the results, he and his wife quietly got up, left the building and left the church.

This vignette hardly describes what we commonly think of when we hear the word "conflict." We see two faces scarcely twelve inches apart, simultaneously shouting at the top of their lungs, neither listening to the other. Or perhaps we see church members at a congregational meeting rising to threaten some kind of "pull-out" if a certain pastor isn't hired, fired, or in some other way dealt with.

Paul said it well: "I hear that when you come together as a church, there are divisions among you, and to some extent I believe it" (1 Cor. 11:18). William Willimon, now dean of the chapel at Duke University, reminds us that

> The word "conflict" comes from the Latin *fligere*, meaning literally "to strike together." Whenever two or more people pursue mutually exclusive goals, or whenever one person's needs collide with another's, conflict results. If there were no effort among humans to fulfill ideas, goals, or desires, there would be no conflict.[1]

Let's recognize that conflict and disagreement are not the same. Indeed, Stan did disagree with the other members of the board, but the situation could easily have been handled without any degree of conflict. Yet in the American Civil War, teenage farm boys on both sides killed each other without any personal disagreement and probably very little understanding of the issues at stake.

Conflict is perhaps better described than defined. Usually it includes a struggle over values and ideas, or perhaps power and resources. One thing is clear in Willimon's description: "Two or more people" must be involved to have conflict (we are not dealing here with one's intrapersonal conflicts). Mike Anthony identifies four causes of church conflict:

> In the eyes of most pastors and board members, there seem to be as many sources of church conflict as there are people in the congregation. The longer I am in the ministry, the more I discover! In speaking with pastors and board members over the years, I have identified a few causes of strife common in most churches: personalities, power plays, perspective, and purpose.[2]

### LEADERSHIP ASSUMPTIONS ABOUT CONFLICT

My research for this chapter surfaced an amazing discovery—very few leadership books, secular or Christian, have adequately dealt with the subject of conflict management. Much to my shame, *Feeding and Leading,* to which I refer frequently in this volume, leaves the subject virtually untouched. I attempted to atone for that, however, by collaborating with a friend and colleague, Sam Canine, in producing *Communication and Conflict Management.* That volume vastly expands the limited treatment of the subject readers will find in this chapter.

As our title indicates, Sam and I see the issues of communication and conflict management as inseparably related. Conflicts are rarely isolated—they arise from some kind of previous episode that may or may not have been connected with the same person or issue. Furthermore, the "conflict episode" includes at least three dimensions which form a grid or process for understanding the conflict—input, through-put, and output.[3]

So the context of communication forms an assumption regarding conflict management. Indeed, a survey of available materials indicates a multitude of assumptions, but I want to narrow our focus in this chapter to five.

## Conflict Is Inevitable Where People Are Interested and Involved

If you asked a Young Life staff member whether she wants teen leaders in her arena of ministry to be "interested and involved," she would probably doubt the sincerity of your question. Of course! Every Christian leader wants people to be interested and involved. Yet many Christian leaders fear conflict because they view it from a negative perspective.

To turn this axiom around, one might say, "When leaders do not see conflict in an organization, they have reason to doubt that people are seriously concerned about the organization's effectiveness, progress, and goal achievement." In my leadership classes some students are astounded when I tell them they need not fear conflict because it is inevitable. In other words, fearing it won't help a bit because it will come one way or the other. To borrow from Mike Anthony again,

> The biblical record is permeated with stories of discord and strife among God's people. Conflict is as old as the Garden of Eden. The Old Testament religious establishment was riddled with factional disputes, and the New Testament church has not done much better. Even a casual glance at the history of Christianity reveals the perennial nature of human conflict. . . . Conflict will come, and there is seldom anything you can do about it except keep it from catching you unprepared.[4]

## Conflict Accelerates as Change Accelerates

Change throws people off balance and makes them wonder whether the organization is headed in the right direction. In a day when institutional loyalty flows at a very low ebb, many organizational members are suspicious under normal circumstances and get really jumpy when change accelerates. In a helpful booklet Philip Van Auken points out the causes of team conflict.

One primary source of interpersonal, or team, conflict is *lack of goal assimilation.* The seeds of conflict are sown whenever team members fail to internalize ministry goals and "own" them. In the absence of shared goals, team members have little basis for consensus and compromise, so essential for conflict avoidance.

The second major source of team conflict stems from *lack of "suboptimization"*—the team's unwillingness to make sacrifices on behalf of the larger organization. When team members are willing to put the organization's needs ahead of team needs, most conflicts can be diffused.[5]

## Conflict Is Not Inherently Destructive or Constructive

Sometimes leaders label people unspiritual or even abnormal when conflict occurs. And, on the rare occasion, that may be true. Nevertheless, when such an attitude prevails in leadership, people in conflict tend to perceive themselves as abnormal or "out of order," a posture which does not lend itself toward conflict resolution. Since we know that conflict is inevitable and that it may well be linked to some recent announcement of change (either personal or organizational), we should be prepared to recognize that positive results can occur when two people who are interested in the ministry have strongly differing viewpoints on an important issue. Bennis claims it often results from varying perceptions.

> People simply see things differently. For example, marketing sees products differently from the way their designers do, or a Princeton graduate has a different perception of life from a retired army colonel. Where one sits determines where one stands. In these general areas, the manager is apt to rush about, trying to encourage workers to learn, insisting that they be honest, and literally intervening in conflicts. The leader, on the other hand, has already created an environment in which opportunity, honesty, and a kind of automatic mediation device exist.[6]

Bennis gets just a bit ahead of where we are at this point in the chapter, but he's right on target. The climate of the organization, established well before specific conflicts emerge, makes possible or impossible, facilitates or hinders, the resolution of conflict. If Stan had a less dismal history of interacting negatively and reacting badly, his disagreements in the elder board could have had a constructive result. Even now, it is possible to observe that we learned a great deal about how to handle disgruntled church leaders, and (though we couldn't see it then) that is a positive outcome.

## Conflict Is Best Handled by Diplomacy and Negotiation

Here we must bring up the term *confrontation*. In almost any conflict resolution model, it should be obvious that neither diplomacy nor negotiation implies walking away from the problem or pretending that it doesn't exist.

Conflict resolution experts have come up with the least effective and most effective patterns for handling conflict; note where negotiation falls in each process.

Least effective: confronting—forcing—withdrawal—smoothing—compromise.

Most effective: confronting—smoothing—compromise—forcing—withdrawal.

One thing seems clear—confrontation must take place early in the game. We affirm the person but confront the issue.

## Conflict Resolution Can Be Taught

Leadership is learned behavior. Creativity is learned behavior. And conflict resolution is also learned behavior. The second two are subcategories of the first, but no less important. Henry Kissinger offers us an international model. Sent by several presidents to several countries of the world over the past twenty-five years, Kissinger employed processes of diplomacy and mediation to resolve conflicts. Whether he learned this from books or in the faculty meetings at Harvard, I can only guess. But learn it he did.

Chip Zimmer notes the importance of the word "mediation" in the learning process.

Mediators don't judge conflicts. They simply try to facilitate negotiation, helping people examine issues from a Christian perspective and work toward a resolution pleasing to God. Mediators must remain neutral and can't be advocates for one side or the other. On biblical matters, however, Christian mediators must be advocates for the truth. They can't be neutral regarding the basic principles of Christian living.[7]

## LEADERSHIP STRATEGIES FOR HANDLING CONFLICT

Let's go back to Monday morning, the day my secretary called (again) about Stan's resignation. As I face this conflict situation and remember my basic assumptions, I must employ a leadership strategy that diffuses the current crisis and mediates a satisfactory solution. One thing I know for sure—I must do nothing that will escalate the problem. How might I do that? By labeling Stan a quitter or a loser, stubborn or inflexible, either to his face or, worse, behind his back. I could dump the problem since I'm not the chairman of the board (see chapter 10), but I know full well the elders expect me to handle this as I have each previous episode.

I know what you're thinking. If Stan is so much trouble, why not just accept his resignation this time and forget it? Believe me, I was tempted. But I try to practice a team leadership style that is constantly redemptive whenever possible. As I have already indicated, the time eventually arrived when we had to think more of the congregation than of Stan, but he desperately needed to learn how to work with colleagues in groups, and I wanted to give him every opportunity to mature toward that level.

Gary McIntosh talks about three types of conflict: interpersonal—conflict with people; intrapersonal—conflict with ourselves; and substantive—conflict over issues. He goes on to observe that "substantive conflict generates interpersonal and intrapersonal conflict. Disagreement on issues quite often degenerates into conflict between people."[8]

I have already indicated we will not deal with intrapersonal conflict in this chapter, but interpersonal and substantive conflict do often flow together. Separating them, as essential as that is, sometimes feels like sorting out oil from water.

## _Confrontation_

Yes, we have mentioned this earlier; but it needs expansion here as an actual strategy. If we fail to confront either issues or people in conflict situations, we face three major dangers in Christian organizations: disintegration of resources, dysfunction of objectives, and disassociation of relationships. Leaders utilize confrontation strategy not because they enjoy it (though perhaps some actually do) but to avoid these three negative outcomes.

When we confront in the spirit of Matthew 18:15–20, it can begin to alleviate conflict. The book of Philemon shows us that confrontation is a biblical behavior, though notice how gently Paul makes his case (vv. 8–11). Habecker claims,

> Confrontation is one of the least glamorous and most difficult facets of leadership. It is, however, one of leadership's most necessary and important responsibilities. Failure to confront produces negative results for both persons and the organization. Only as the art of confrontation is carried out under the divine leadership of the Holy Spirit will the kind of personal and organizational results desired by leaders be accomplished.[9]

## _Compromise_

I remember the day I engaged in a minor public confrontation with a student in a classroom after suggesting that compromise is often a positive concept. His background had led him to conclude that compromise was a dirty word indicating weakness, vacillation, and a surrender of one's convictions.

To be sure, there are times one should not compromise— in debates surrounding basic orthodox theology such as the deity of Christ, the Resurrection, and the reality of Christ's second coming. But in conflict resolution compromise is a good tactic. Schmuck and Runkel talk about the shortage of money in a secondary school that leads to inadequate resources for two teachers. They describe the compromise this way: "Sometimes both parties can agree to give up a little. The English teacher could agree to get new books for only one course, and the science teacher could agree to get new equipment for only one course."[10]

## Working Through

The concept of *process* is essential to every aspect of leadership. Rarely do leaders deal with events that come and go in a flash. Certainly conflict resolution requires working through the issues or personality differences, and leaders must solicit the cooperation of both parties in joint solution seeking. When the leader is one of the parties, as in the case study with Stan, he must throw off dogmatism and approach the conflict with a commitment to finding a solution. We waste a great deal of kingdom-building time and energy by insisting on the correctness of our own opinions, a posture which rarely leads to conflict resolution.

Furthermore, notice how working through the issue is vastly different from either attacking or withdrawing. When we attack we punish people and hurt them for their role in the conflict; the result is often one or both parties being diminished or overpowered (more on this in the next section). Interestingly, the same result comes from withdrawal, when we let the other party take whatever he or she wants. In a very real sense, both parties are still diminished or overpowered, even though it may seem like a victory for the taker.

## Teaching

Experienced managers may be surprised by the inclusion of this concept as a tactic for handling conflict, but follow the

193

logic. If conflict resolution is learned behavior; if conflict resolution requires the cooperative efforts of both parties; if conflict resolution demands a process in which two or more people must cooperate; surely it stands to reason that in any organization people must be taught how to handle conflict.

Now one could do that in seminars during periods of peace and harmony, and that's probably a good idea. But an actual conflict situation provides a glorious "teachable moment" as the leader wears the hats of both conflict manager and instructor. Gently, lovingly, patiently, we explain to people what is happening and why. We warn how they can inflame the conflict rather than resolve it. For example, Calvin Miller talks about "the non-negotiator":

> The difficulty in dealing with this type of person is that they really seem to be in pain. Their aim is to make you feel especially heartless if you confront them. But make no mistake about it, manipulating your feelings is their intentional ploy. Even though they appear Christlike and needy, they must not be allowed to delay the objectives of the leadership team.[11]

He goes on to observe,

> Everyone has a right to dignity. So the key issue in coping with difficult people is to handle them without belittling them before others. Love is a key ingredient of leadership. Even in the direst circumstances, any sort of rebuke should be as private as possible. Leaders must honestly determine if a person causing trouble is really difficult. They may only be trying to express a difficulty with some issue at hand. Difficult people and people with difficulties are two different things. Great leaders study and understand both.[12]

The variety of strategies takes shape in a model that often provides the quickest and easiest way to grasp a concept. Let's move immediately to that level.

## LEADERSHIP MODEL FOR CONFLICT RESOLUTION

In several of my leadership books I have used quadrant models to reflect a singular but complicated concept. The model on the next page represents that same pattern and, as in many such diagrams, urges the leader to move in a constant northeasterly direction to achieve the best results.

Although the model should largely speak for itself in light of our earlier discussion, perhaps a brief explanation of segments might be useful.

### *Withdrawing*

Withdrawing is a 1–1 level, lose/lose position. People in conflict just walk away from each other, either hoping the issues will sort themselves out or assuming that agreement is impossible. The most obvious example of this is divorce in which terminology such as "irreconcilable differences" indicates a willingness on the part of one or both to withdraw. Withdrawing denies confrontation and can never solve the problem.

### *Taking*

In this 10–1, win/lose position, some person or group achieves personal goals while the rest get nothing. The competition element in virtually every athletic event demonstrates this. Just a few days before I wrote this chapter the Detroit Lions scored a last-minute surprise upset over the San Francisco 49ers at the Silverdome. The ecstasy and exuberance of the hometown crowd must have been matched by the agony and deflation of 49er fans around the country. That's the way it is in competition—somebody wins and somebody loses. But team ministry in Christian organizations is not competition, neither intramural nor inter-organizational.

## CONFLICT RESOLUTION MODEL

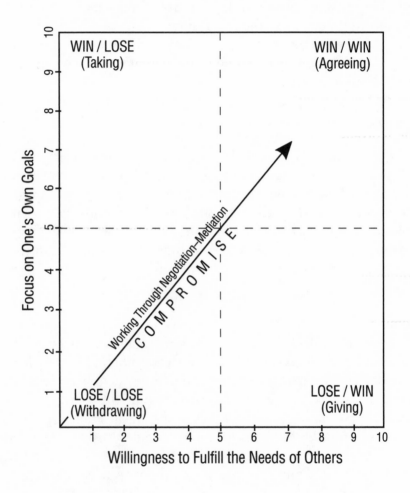

*Figure 8*

## Giving

The 1–10, lose/win pattern of giving looks like the biblical pattern. Are we not to turn the other cheek? If someone asks for a jacket, are we not to give him our shirts as well? To be sure, the spirit of biblical humility certainly favors 1–10 over 10–1, but this posture does not facilitate team ministry. _People still lose even when they choose to lose._

My example here would be the battered wife. Her attitude is, "Anything to keep peace." Anything to keep him from hitting her or the kids again. She refuses to leave. She refuses to press charges. She suffers in silence. Meanwhile, the husband's behavior worsens, and ultimately everybody in the family pays the price for her willingness to give in.

Please notice that leaders must accept the responsibility to protect people from themselves. A conflict manager pushes people away from a 1–10 stance because by doing so she facilitates and enhances the life of both the individuals and the organization.

## Agreeing

How do we get to a 10–10, win/win position? Well, let's admit that we rarely ring the bell at that level. The process is clear—work through the issues, negotiate, and mediate. The point is that a 5–5 or an 8–8 is considerably better than a 5–1 or a 1–8, and again the word _compromise_ arises. I like what Van Auken says:

> Circumstances for constructive compromise are ripe when team members are so "sold out" to ministry goals that they are willing to make implementation concessions to achieve these goals. Goal-driven team members are usually open to changes or concessions that facilitate progress. Compromise that does not jeopardize the ultimate ministry mission will actually be welcomed under these circumstances.[13]

## LEADERSHIP BEHAVIOR THAT REDUCES CONFLICT

Perhaps we should examine the other side of the coin. How do leaders exacerbate conflict? Sometimes through insecurity that demonstrates itself in the inability to make decisions, an eagerness to please everybody, or an unwillingness to acknowledge conflict, i.e., withdrawing. Sometimes by hiding behind a framework of the bureaucracy, inviting anyone who doesn't fit into the system to leave. In an organization that practices administrative dominance over decision making (a characteristic of unhealthy bureaucracy), leaders at lower levels may not have opportunity to practice conflict resolution simply because they do not have the authority to negotiate compromise. But enough on the negative side; what leadership behaviors serve the reduction of conflict?

### *Participatory Leadership*

I have written so much on this subject and introduce it again here with reluctance. Nevertheless, it is an absolutely essential ingredient in the overall environment that lends itself to conflict reduction and resolution. Part of it has to do with the way we use the authority of leadership. Listen to Larry Richards:

> Essentially, the authority of leaders today is a moral authority, a freedom of action extended to them by God, to influence the people of God to respond to Christ's moral authority. Since even Jesus was careful never to claim a coercive authority over persons who are free moral agents, mere humans in spiritual leadership must be even more careful not to claim such an authority. It is right and proper for secular governments to demand, and compel, obedience. But it is not now and never has been right for those in spiritual leadership to attempt to compel a response which, to be meaningful, must be free.[14]

## Effective Leadership

Make no mistake about it; many people holding leadership positions are ill-qualified for those positions and are more likely to create conflict than resolve it. In one sense we define leaders by who they are as we focus on spiritual character, God's call, and the gifting of the Holy Spirit. In another sense we define them by what they do, which brings to mind the now-famous "five fundamental leadership practices" introduced by Kouzes and Posner some years ago.[15]

1. *Leaders challenge the process.* Not in rebellion, but in a genuine effort to find a better way. Effective leaders constantly ask how organizational practices, including conflict resolution, can be improved.

2. *Leaders inspire a shared vision.* The key word here is "shared." The vision does not have to be vertical and downward. Modern Christian organizations do not need another Moses to come down the mountain with tablets of stone and tell everybody what to do. They need team facilitators who know how to get people involved in shared goals, who are dedicated to a shared vision.

3. *Leaders enable others to act.* Often we call this "empowering," but it means the same thing. And one can only empower by giving away portions of his own authority and influence to subordinates, enabling them to take greater responsibility and greater authority in the organization. Such people rarely cause conflict.

4. *Leaders model the way.* We'll deal with this in a later chapter, but one can see immediately how the modeling role of peacemaker sets the stage for conflict resolution process.

5. *Leaders encourage the heart.* All truly Christian leadership begins with heart attitude. Team leaders who invest time encouraging the hearts of people will face conflict episodes with much more credibility as negotiators.

## Celebrative Leadership

Conflict often surfaces in the dark and dreary failure of an organization. Discouraged people will more likely be drawn into conflict episodes than encouraged people, and we encourage people by rewarding their individual achievements and celebrating team accomplishments. This is precisely what Nehemiah did after the building of the wall (Neh. 12:27–47). Aubrey Malphurs describes it this way:

> Some ministry organizations celebrate important events. For example, schools have graduations and founder's day banquets. Churches celebrate the purchase or completion of new facilities, the accomplishment of a critical growth goal, or the addition of new staff. Some create special events for the purpose of celebration, such as a Celebration of Friendship Sunday. These celebrations also provide good opportunities for enhancing team relationships, the communication of ideas, good fellowship, and stress relief.[16]

## Vulnerable Leadership

In the process of conflict resolution we will make mistakes. Particularly leaders who have little experience or training in this process will stumble and face the potential of a worsening situation. This is especially poignant when you are one of the parties in the dispute. Anthony states it well:

> If you, as a church leader, make a mistake that causes hurt feelings, embarrassment, or pain in the life of someone in the congregation, admit it and confront the aftereffects head on. If you run and hide, or pretend it didn't happen, you will only intensify the conflict. . . . A high degree of transparency can be an asset in times of conflict.[17]

200

## Communicative Leadership

I have often been accused of erring on the side of saying too much to my staff and others in the organization, and quite frankly, I plead guilty. Having served in organizations which operated on that CIA "need to know" principle, I determined that my leadership style would look neither bureaucratic, secretive, nor military. Kathleen Edwards engaged in a massive study that investigated factors that affect the quality of board-executive relationships in nonprofit organizations. Her findings should make us all sit up and take notice. She concludes that successful, non-adversarial relationships are found in the following situations:

1. Chief executives were skilled at educating and developing their boards, and assumed responsibility for doing so.
2. Chief executives understood the importance of cultivating directors as a means of developing personal relationships with them.
3. Board members provided chief executives with strong and consistent support.
4. Board chairs understood their own roles.
5. Communication systems were open, candid, and free-flowing.
6. There were high levels of trust, respect, and positive regard among all the participants.[18]

What should we conclude? That the potential for conflict resolution resides squarely in the quality of the leader and the environment of the organization he or she directs.

### FOR FURTHER READING

Gangel, Kenneth O., and Samuel L. Canine. *Communication and Conflict Management*. Nashville: Broadman, 1992.

Hesselbein, Francis, Marshall Goldsmith, and Richard Beckhard, eds. *The Leader of the Future*. San Francisco: Jossey-Bass, 1996.

Kouzes, James M., and Barry Z. Posner. *The Leadership Challenge.* Rev. ed. San Francisco: Jossey-Bass, 1995.

Leas, Speed. *Leadership and Conflict.* Nashville: Abingdon, 1982.

Wilson, Gerald L., et al. *Interpersonal Growth for Communication.* Dubuque, Iowa: Wm. C. Brown, 1985.

## NOTES

1. William Willimon, "Crisis and Conflict," in *Leadership Handbooks of Practical Theology,* vol. 3, ed. James D. Berkley (Grand Rapids: Baker, 1994), 187.

2. Michael J. Anthony, *The Effective Church Board* (Grand Rapids: Baker, 1993), 158.

3. Kenneth O. Gangel and Samuel L. Canine, *Communication and Conflict Management* (Nashville: Broadman, 1992), 133.

4. Anthony, *The Effective Church Board,* 160–61.

5. Philip M. Van Auken, *The Well-Managed Ministry* (Wheaton, Ill.: Victor, 1989), 172.

6. Warren Bennis, *Why Leaders Can't Lead* (San Francisco: Jossey-Bass, 1990), 158.

7. Chip Zimmer, "Mediation and Arbitration," in *Leadership Handbooks of Practical Theology.* vol. 3, ed. James D. Berkeley (Grand Rapids: Baker, 1994), 197.

8. Gary L. McIntosh, "Managing Conflict," *Church Growth Network* 7, no. 5 (May 1995): 1.

9. Eugene B. Habecker, *The Other Side of Leadership* (Wheaton, Ill.: Victor, 1987), 102.

10. Richard A. Schmuck and Philip J. Runkel, *The Handbook of Organization Development* 4th ed. (Prospect Heights, Ill.: Waveland, 1994), 341.

11. Calvin Miller, *The Empowered Leader* (Nashville: Broadman & Holman, 1995), 147.

12. Ibid., 152.

13. Van Auken, *Well-Managed Ministry,* 179.

14. Lawrence O. Richards, "Theology of Servant Leadership—A Response," *Christian Education Journal* 9, no. 2 (Winter 1989): 69.

15. James M. Kouzes and Barry Z. Posner, *The Leadership Challenge,* rev. ed. (San Francisco: Jossey-Bass, 1995), 14.

16. Aubrey Malphurs, *Developing a Vision for Ministry* (Grand Rapids: Baker, 1992), 195.

17. Anthony, *The Effective Church Board,* 163.

18. Kathleen Edwards, "Six Characteristics of Successful Board-Chief Executive Relationships," *Board Member* 4, no. 3 (May/June 1995): 3.

# –12–

# The Team Leader

## as Change Agent

A professor once told his class that he would place on the board the most important principle relative to the process of change. Thereupon he turned and spent the next fifteen minutes etching out two words: GO SLOWLY. Good team leaders know and consistently practice this crucial axiom.

Sometimes leaders are hired specifically as change agents. Organizations fall into disarray and perhaps even face questionable survival. Boards conclude that anything must be better than the present, so they bring in someone with a mandate to overhaul the organization.

But remember—that is the exception. One would not want to develop a leadership strategy for change on the basis of overnight renewal. Under normal conditions team leaders ought to follow a simple guideline: _change nothing major the first year._

Some people fear innovation. They closely watch the young aggressive leader who comes dashing out of college or seminary with a briefcase full of ideas, casting about for a group of people on whom to experiment his theories. Phrases such as "We've never done it that way before," "It will never work here," or "We tried it that way and it didn't work" characterize almost every organization, and such thinking throws up roadblocks to the process of change.

Yet change plays such a significant role in leadership that it has coined its own distinctive vocabulary: "sacred cow," "trial balloon," "innovation," "experimental design" and, of course, "it's not in the budget." One pastor keeps a motto on his desk that reads, "Come weal or come woe, my status is quo."

## KINDS OF CHANGE

Thomas Bennett once identified four kinds of change that confront leaders. The first is change in _structure._ This has to do with the changing of the organizational chart, the shuffling of positions in personnel, and the reworking of the organization itself. "Such a reorganization of a company or a committee is intended to change the relationship of persons so that work is done more effectively and efficiently."[1]

The second kind of change comes in _technology._ The introduction of electronic processes—e-mail, Internet, telemarketing, laptops—all can be classed as technological change.

A third type has to do with the _behavior_ of people. Bennett points out a crucial question: "How can people be helped in the present to develop behavior which will enable them to be more effective and creative persons?"[2]

The final type deals with _assumptions_ and _values._ People's assumptions and values determine their behavior, so leaders must understand why people behave as they do before they can help them change. Indeed, the leader must have this information for himself. Bennett says, "The leader needs real insight into the assumptions and values guiding his behavior, and why he has made his judgments about the importance of the change he is seeking."[3]

## PRINCIPLES OF THE CHANGE PROCESS

### *Changing People Is More Important than Changing Things*

I have long appreciated Abraham Zaleznik's classic book, *Human Dilemmas of Leadership,* in which he deals with the relation of an individual to an organization.[4] Perhaps the book's key concept is Zaleznik's acceptance of human tension and conflict as a condition of existence and an opportunity for change and progress. He identifies four polarities of human existence relative to one's individual development: giving and getting, controlling and being controlled, competing and cooperating, and producing and facilitating.

Personal development emphasizes how the individual learns to assume responsibility and to exercise choice. Zaleznik complains that the unsolved problem in understanding people and organizations revolves around the inability of existing theory to grasp the essential dynamics of the individual.

Zaleznik claims that the act of choice, whether through conscious or unconscious mechanisms, places the individual in the forefront of organizational behavior. In the final analysis, people think, feel, choose, and act.

If there is any organization in which an emphasis on changing people ought to be basic, it is the local church! General Motors and AT&T may want to change the attitudes and behavior of their employees, but they are limited to natural means. Leaders in Christian organizations can depend upon a supernatural force who changes human behavior from the inside.

### *Change Begins Where the Leader Has the Most Control*

Nothing is too hard for God; therefore, any change is possible within a Christian organization. But on the human level, leaders must operate within their own span of control and must be able to make reliable predictions about the consequences of their actions. Bennett speaks to this issue:

> For most of us, this point is within a day-by-day relationship in which we function. In these daily relationships with superiors, colleagues, and subordinates, a leader is likely to know more accurately what can be expected of other persons and what is expected of him. This is also the network of relationships in which he has the most self-control. He can do more about his own attitudes and actions to be of help to the person who will be directly affected by the change. A supervisor may expect to have little success in changing the behavior of the president of the company, but he can expect to have considerable influence in bringing about change among subordinates.[5]

You should probably not innovate unless you have clear-cut goals relative to the direction that innovation will take and the ultimate results of the change. Since some resistance to change comes from fear of the unknown, provide as much information as possible about what will happen next.

### Change Runs More Smoothly When People Participate in Its Planning

If leaders develop and hand down a report of what they want to see changed, the change will be much more difficult to implement than if the people themselves (or at least their representatives) have a voice in planning the change. Involvement in the planning process tends to generate the necessary force for the change itself. Facts personally researched are better understood, more emotionally acceptable, and more likely to be utilized than those passed down by someone else. Participation in analysis and planning helps overcome resistance, which arises from proceeding too rapidly or too slowly.

By definition, change is dynamic, not static. Consequently, the very involvement of the leadership team, the staff, and as many people as possible feeds that dynamic, helping to counter the following axioms of the change process.

1. People naturally feel somewhat awkward and self-conscious in a period of change, particularly if it affects their specific areas of responsibility.
2. People first focus on what they will lose and feel a need to express this, perhaps to others, perhaps to top leadership.
3. People believe others can handle change better than they can, so the idea that everyone in the organization is involved doesn't help much.
4. People can handle change in direct proportion to their experience at handling change.
5. People tend to immediately turn to the argument of insufficient resources to thwart change that they find distasteful.

Lyle Schaller ascribes a three-phase theory of innovation introduced by Rosabeth Moss Kanter:

> She states the prototypical innovation goes through three phases. First, the project has to be defined. . . . Kanter identifies the second state of innovation as building a coalition. Too often that second step consists of going around and seeking the approval of every potential veto group. This creates a situation that invites opponents to register their negative votes. . . . The third stage is the action phase or implementation.[6]

## Change Includes Overcoming Resistance

Any leader who suggests change implies that the organization is not functioning satisfactorily. At that point some people become uncomfortable.

Vested interest and/or conflict of interest are both detriments in the process of change. People feel threatened by the thought of innovation in something of which they have long been a part. We now call people like this "stakeholders." People on the periphery of ministry in any Christian organization may not even know change has taken place for weeks or months. But the stakeholders, people who have clear-cut involvement in what is changing, make up the key participants in the change process because their lives have been directly affected.

An example in church education is the difficulty that confronts some church leaders in moving adults from one class to another in an age-group Sunday school organization. Cliques have entangled themselves around the roots of the class, and people want to stay with "their group" and "their teacher," fighting the change of atmosphere.

## Change Success Directly Relates to the Group's Maturity

Mature groups tend to change more quickly and more thoroughly than immature groups. Maturity, of course, does not describe the group members' ages or how long they've been together but rather analyzes group dynamics.

Since progress requires change, Christian leaders must learn how to bring it about with the least amount of difficulty. Team leadership that depends upon the development of spiritual motivation seems the best route toward achieving satisfactory change. This will involve meeting and overcoming opposition, and providing accurate and adequate information to all persons involved.

The concept of changing people especially relates to their growing maturity. Leighton Ford illustrates the idea of "the leader as strategist."

Alexander Solzhenitsyn, the Russian novelist, said in his Harvard University address, "A World Split Apart," that the most significant lines of division in our world today are not those which run *between* nations, but the line which runs *through* East and West, which separates all of us from our spiritual nature. The mayor of Timisoara, Romania, when the December 1989 Romanian uprising began, spoke after the revolution about the social problems that came from bad working habits and massive alcoholism. "We have accomplished only 20 percent of the revolution by changing the old system," he said. "Now, the new system has to change the people." On the Capitalist side of the world, Michael Maccoby, a management consultant, writes of interviewing many engineers and executives who have "over-developed heads and under-developed hearts."[7]

## POSITIVE APPROACHES TO LEADING CHANGE

Strain and conflict arise between people and organizations when expectations and needs are not properly harmonized. Some folks begin to feel like hired hands rather than members of the team. We do well to remember our Lord's words to His disciples just before the Crucifixion: "I no longer call you servants, because a servant does not know his master's business. Instead, I have called you friends, for everything that I learned from my Father I have made known to you" (John 15:15). Christians must have unyielding commitment in service. But that commitment is to the person of Jesus Christ and the universal church, not necessarily to a given local representation of that church. So how do you and I as finite, failing human beings lead others in change?

### Resist Beginning a New Ministry with a Preconceived Plan

Occasionally a student will come back from a weekend interview for a new ministry position and rush to my office for advice. "Help! I'm being interviewed for a church staff position and they asked me what kinds of programs I would design for their church over the next five years. What should I tell them?" The answer, of course, is simple: "I don't have any idea." Certainly every candidate for a church leadership position needs to know the status of the evangelical church as we approach a new century, and the general layout of what effective ministry might look like. But to suggest that a candidate can correctly assess the needs of a local congregation and map out solutions during an interview is ludicrous.

In fact, since pastors, presidents, directors, and other types of leaders tend to come and go, the interviewing body must have a strong grasp of both mission and vision to determine whether any new leadership candidate might fit. Without clear objectives and a sharp "job profile," a congregational search committee could spin its wheels for months and then make a poor choice.

Whenever an interviewing group pushes you to design hypothetical ideas of what might happen in the future, two inevitable traps await: (1) you will suggest ideas and programs that have worked in your last ministry; or (2) your guesswork will be so sketchy that it will be virtually impossible to follow through when reality hits. Ministry in churches or para-church organizations is no longer "universal" within denominational or geographical boundaries. *In this decade and the next, ministries need to be tailored to specific situations and fitted to each organization's distinctive call and mission from God.* It's time to stop mimicking what other ministries do well.

## *Lead with a Flexible Agenda*

Leadership is always situational (relative) because it always relates to the task, the group, and the environment. Any one of those three factors could upset your leadership cart very quickly if you approach leadership with an inflexible posture. Obviously, the most likely trouble spots rest with the group. As change continues to accelerate every year, the ministries we begin working with now will look very different five or ten years in the future.

## *Move Slowly into Change*

Inexperienced leaders believe organizations are waiting for them to take charge and act boldly. So they start new programs, hire and fire people, rearrange the furniture, and change the logo.

Some writers on this subject actually advocate rushing through as many changes as possible in the first year, "before the congregation catches on to you." That behavior, of course, defies everything we have learned in the research of how change takes place.

Experienced leaders make changes slowly by working through existing structures if they can. In *Christian Education Journal,* Perry Downs described "baby boomers' ministry needs."[8] The thesis of that article argues that ministry needs of baby boomers are rooted in the philosophies of the eighties and nineties, and our response must first of all be theological. Indeed, most church leadership problems are primarily theological, not sociological. Anderson, Gallup, and Barna will help us immensely in generalizing about the kind of people we serve, but only we can define biblical answers for their specific life needs.

Downs suggests that the end of the twentieth century is marked by a spirit of despair and futility, with people's lives being controlled by a quest for dignity and worth. He sees this loss of meaning as the primary cause for the frenetic activity that makes it even more difficult to involve people in learning programs and ministry opportunities in evangelical churches. Rearranging the furniture and changing the logo will solve none of those problems.

One dangerous temptation facing congregational leaders as we approach the next century is the radical restructuring of programs and services to accommodate the external sociological preferences of baby boomers. Trading in hymnals for worship chorus slides; exchanging organs and pianos for rock combos; offering a message of languorous goodwill—these Band-Aid solutions may draw people into public meetings but may not meet their inner spiritual needs.

Effective leadership for the long term demands that we understand the surrounding situation, cope with collective needs, and develop a climate of trust that makes it possible for us to stay and serve.

## See Yourself as a Joiner, Not Always an Impactor

The trend in leadership literature, both secular and Christian, leans toward a more aggressive, "take charge" posture. We challenge seminary students to "impact" a church with aggressive visionary leadership. Yet, as we read the New Testament, we get a firm sense that change takes place through joining. The apostle Paul and the missionary team involved themselves in the lives of people in various places, and churches were born or they grew and developed. Paul's letters carefully explain that he did not move into town as a thunderous and dynamic personality but boasted in only two qualities he could truly call his own—weakness and suffering (2 Cor. 11:16–12:10).

A transactional leader develops ministry teams by "joining" the troops as a servant. The joiner becomes the affirming leader because affirmation is a servant's way of securing the importance of other people and their ministries. The servant leader provides needed endorsement and support; she leads the parade of celebration when a follower's ministry succeeds.

## Make Sure People Understand Goals

There may be honest differences of opinion among the members of any group as to what they are supposed to do. One Christian worker often caught in this dilemma is the Christian education specialist. Perhaps she has been called to a church that has never before employed a person of her skill and training. Fifteen different church leaders expect her to focus on fifteen different aspects of the task. To some, she is really a youth director; to others, administrator of the Sunday school; to still others, a children's worker. Such multiple expectations greatly contribute to the short tenure of ministry associates during the last thirty years.

In fact, W. Edwards Deming identifies "lack of constancy of purpose" as the first of his "seven deadly diseases" that paralyze business and industry.

Employees in many companies have been exposed to a succession of plans for improvement. They have seen programs come and go, often coinciding with the term of the chief executive officer. A new president, a new program. Disenchanted and disillusioned, they require proof that the company is serious this time.[9]

## Don't Be Afraid to Fail

An old cliché in leadership studies states that "success breeds success." Those in touch with the realities of experience, however, understand that success does not breed success—failure breeds success. Al Neuharth, founder of *USA Today,* warns, "If you are over 30 and haven't had a major failure in your business or professional career, time is running out on you. . . . It needs to be a big failure. You can only fail big if you take a big risk. The bigger you fail, the bigger you are likely to succeed later."

Kouzes and Posner devote an entire chapter of *The Leadership Challenge* to learning from mistakes. They include this example: "At precisely 8:01 P.M. on September 11, 1985, baseball star Pete Rose smacked his 4,192nd career hit. That was good enough to surpass Ty Cobb and put Rose in the record books for 'most hits, career.' But Rose also deserves another baseball record: 'most outs—9,518 of them.'"[10]

The sin lies not in failure; the sin lies in refusing to learn from your failure, in not picking yourself up and going at the task from a different direction.

## Don't Take Yourself or Your Leadership Too Seriously

James T. Murphy is associate dean of the Graduate School of Education at Harvard University. He recalls assuming that role with a great vision for leading Harvard into a clearly focused organizational mission and fiscal stability. His first challenge came from a faculty member who asked, "By the way, what are you going to do about the odor strips?" Sensing Murphy's puzzlement, he pressed on. "I'm allergic to the new odor strips in the fourth floor bathroom, and something needs to be done."

Murphy refers to these moments as "The Unheroic Side of Leadership: Notes from the Swamp." He goes on to say, "Those who lionize leadership miss important behind-the-scenes aspects of day-to-day leadership. They depict the grand designs without the niggling problems. They assume that leadership is the exclusive preserve of the heroic boss."[11]

This image of the leader as hero can undermine Christian servants who think they need to live up to such expectations. In fact, such an idealistic posture is precisely what identifies the amateurs! Swamp veterans understand how unheroic they and their tasks really are. If the truth were known, most of us holding leadership positions are just faithful plodders who owe every achievement to the grace of a patient God.

## *Pray More, Say Less*

I have frequently been asked what I would do differently if I chose to return again to a college presidency. I would do many things differently; but the most important is that I would pray more and say less. I would also pray more and worry less. My problem is not that I do not believe in prayer nor that my theology of prayer is somehow defective. My dilemma arises from the convoluted thinking that leads me to genuinely believe in prayer but not make time for it in my busy life. This kind of crazy human behavior must drive the angels berserk.

In the twenty-first century Christian leadership may be more difficult than ever before. Yet God still calls men and women to assume more responsibilities than others, to model courage and initiative, to respond joyfully to that sometime unexpected tap on the shoulder, and to lead God's people effectively in creative, positive innovation.

## ORGANIZATION OR INDIVIDUAL:
## WHO NEEDS TO CHANGE?

Is it possible to be both spiritual and competent? Can the Christian leader be biblical as well as tuned in to contemporary thinking of administrative science? It is my contention that he can and that administrative science has, in fact, spent millions of dollars only to discover that *the biblical pattern of balance between task and individual is the best approach to leadership.*

Although in management science there is still a great deal of research with respect to changing either the person or the organization, many experts have decided upon the transactional approach between the nomothetic (abstract) and the idiographic (concrete) dimensions. In reality, these dimensions exist in constant relationship to and interaction with one another rather than in separate spheres. Individual values will ultimately determine behavior unless people compromise their values for some item of secondary importance, such as salary or position. Therefore organizational values must somehow be integrated with those of the individual.

The model on the next page was developed by Getzels and Guba and clarifies the kind of difficulties that arise in institution/individual balance.[12] The top line indicates institutional plans and roles. The bottom line focuses on the individual. The vertical arrows show the necessity of bringing the conflicts into creative tension to achieve harmony in the organization.

Without reference to the model or its components, Bennis picks up the basic idea of transactionalism dealing with what he calls "the new metaphysics of our age."

> Organizations, by definition, are social systems in which people have norms, values, shared beliefs, and paradigms of what is right and what is wrong, what is legitimate and what is not, and how things are done. One gains status and power through agreement, concurrence, and conformity with these paradigms. Therefore, both dissent and innovation are discouraged. Every

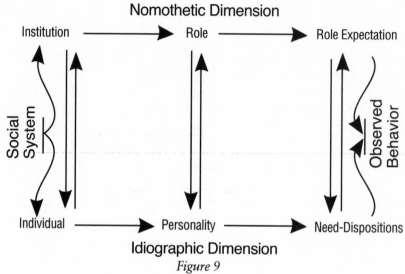

Nomothetic Dimension

Idiographic Dimension

*Figure 9*

(Getzels and Guba p. 217)

Therefore, both dissent and innovation are discouraged. Every social system contains these forces for conservatism, for maintaining the status quo at any cost, but it must also contain means for movement, or it will eventually become paralyzed. Basic changes take place very slowly, if at all, because those with the power generally have no knowledge, and those with the knowledge have no power. Anyone with real knowledge of history and the world as it is today could redesign society, develop a new paradigm in an afternoon, but turning theory into fact could take a lifetime—unless the person happened to be president of the United States.[13]

A Christian position agrees that both the organization and the individual can change, but an emphasis on changing either one to the sacrifice of the other will lead to confusion and turmoil.

## SHAPING AN IDIOGRAPHIC MINISTRY

The Scripture speaks frequently of the church as a building and of its members as various blocks of stone in the framework. Just as the architects of a physical building take into account the qualities of the material with which they work, so must the architects of the Christian organization consider the characteristics of the people who make up the structure of their institutions.

The tasks of the human architect are considerably more complex. Qualities of human materials, only partially known, are notoriously changeable. Some people reject the organization because they think they give without receiving. Others do the opposite: they take without giving anything in return. Both result in a sterile organization which becomes a liability rather than an asset to the ongoing ministry of God's work in the world.

Another problem lies in mobilizing the great amount of human resources we have but do not use. The organization can become a deep freeze in which we store human resources, rather than an educational experience where the immature become mature; the undeveloped, developed; and the small, increasingly large in outlook and perspective. Douglas McGregor says,

> We have not learned enough about the utilization of talent, about the creation of an organizational climate conducive to human growth. The blunt fact is that we are a long way from realizing the potential represented by the human resources we now recruit into industry. We have much to accomplish with respect to utilization before further improvements and selection will become important.[14]

We can substitute the word "ministry" for "industry" in the above quotation, and nod to the truth of McGregor's words. The organization is not an end in itself, but rather a means to accomplish the tasks of the worldwide program of Christ.

In the process of change, we move forward with small steps. Gilmore elaborates on the research of Weick in explaining this crucial strategy:

Small wins are defined as concrete, complete, implemented outcomes of moderate importance. . . . They can be either important changes in unimportant variables or unimportant changes
in important variables. Weick argues that the overwhelming
feelings of helplessness, frustration, and anxiety associated
with the complexity and interdependence of today's problems
have the effect of reducing our creativity. He suggests framing
problems in focused ways that make us better able to achieve
creative responses. The satisfaction gained from real progress
early on, Weick says, can provide the momentum for tackling
further problems down the line.[15]

A focus on *program* instead of on *people* is another alba-
tross of earlier years. In our success-oriented society, we tend to
see a large church with a large program as the model, with small
churches running along as fast as their tiny, organizational legs
can carry them, trying to match the big one. The result is frequently fatigue, disinterest, and rank disillusionment.

In the old days, before the pyramid began to crumble,
organizational problems were successfully solved by generous
applications of "techniques of management." But the current
stress calls for flexibility rather than rigidity in coping with institutional tensions. Spontaneity and openness provide the raw
materials out of which creative energy can come to recharge the
batteries of Christian organizations in these days of opportunity.

All the information we can gather about restructuring,
administrative forms, leadership styles, and human relations
ought to be gathered. Then it should be carefully compared with
and run through the grid of special revelation. Perhaps what we
have left will be a desirable integration of God's truth revealed in
natural forms of order and design, based on God's truth in special revelation.

We dare not baptize secular research and stuff it, still
damp, into the organizational potholes on the road the church
must travel. Rather, we apply biblical principles of leadership,
better understood because we have taken the time to grapple
with the secular research.

And the secular research now emphasizes team leadership in a dominant way. In *The Leader of the Future,* published early in 1996, Charles Handy talks about "distributed leadership" and the role of teams.

> The leadership of these groups is not of the old-fashioned "follow me" type. You could call it a distributed leadership. I inadvertently got a glimpse of what this might look like when I facetiously compared an English team to a rowing crew on the river: "Eight people going backward as fast as they can, without speaking to each other, steered by the one person who can't row." I thought it rather witty, but an oarsmen in the audience corrected me: "How do you think," he said, "that we could go backwards so fast, without communicating, if we were not completely confident in each other's competence, committed to the same goal, and determined to do our best to reach it? It's the perfect prescription for a team."[16]

We lead institutions made up of people. Our needs are both similar to and diverse from those of secular organizations. But one thing seems clear: unless we learn how to be laborers together with each other and with God, the complexities of change will trip us up. And that could happen now—just when the world is beginning to see the supernatural dynamic of the Lord's body in the darkness of our contemporary pagan culture.

FOR FURTHER READING

Bennis, Warren. *Why Leaders Can't Lead.* San Francisco: Jossey-Bass, 1990.

Ford, Leighton. *Transforming Leadership.* Downers Grove, Ill.: Inter-Varsity, 1991.

Gangel, Kenneth O. *Feeding and Leading.* Wheaton, Ill.: Victor, 1989.

Hesselbein, Francis, Marshall Goldsmith, and Richard Beckhard, eds. *The Leader of the Future.* San Francisco: Jossey-Bass, 1996.

Nanus, Burt. *Visionary Leadership.* San Francisco: Jossey-Bass, 1992.

Schaller, Lyle E. *Getting Things Done.* Nashville: Abingdon, 1986.

Walton, Mary. *The Deming Management Method*. New York: Putnam, 1986.

## NOTES

1. Thomas R. Bennett, *The Leader and the Process of Change* (New York: Association, 1962), 23.

2. Ibid., 25.

3. Ibid., 27.

4. Abraham Zaleznik, *Human Dilemmas of Leadership* (New York: Harper & Row, 1966).

5. Bennett, *Leader and the Process of Change*, 27.

6. Lyle E. Schaller, *Getting Things Done* (Nashville: Abingdon, 1986), 216.

7. Leighton Ford, *Transforming Leadership* (Downers Grove, Ill.: InterVarsity, 1991), 63.

8. Perry Downs, "Baby Boomers' Ministry Needs," *Christian Education Journal* (Autumn 1990): 25–32.

9. Mary Walton, *The Deming Management Method* (New York: Putnam, 1986), 89.

10. James Kouzes and Barry Posner, *The Leadership Challenge*, rev. ed. (San Francisco: Jossey-Bass, 1995), 63.

11. James T. Murphy, "The Unheroic Side of Leadership: Notes from the Swamp," *Phi Delta Kappan* (May 1988), 654.

12. J. W. Getzels and E. G. Guba, "Social Behavior and the Administrative Process," *School Review* 65 (Winter 1957): 423–41.

13. Warren Bennis, *Why Leaders Can't Lead* (San Francisco: Jossey-Bass, 1990), 30.

14. Douglas McGregor, *The Human Side of Enterprise* (New York: McGraw-Hill, 1960), vi.

15. Thomas N. Gilmore, *Making a Leadership Change* (San Francisco: Jossey-Bass, 1988), 243–44.

16. Charles Handy, "The New Language of Organizing and Its Implications for Leaders," in *The Leader of the Future*, ed. Francis Hesselbein, Marshall Goldsmith, and Richard Beckhard (San Francisco: Jossey-Bass, 1996), 7.

222

# –13–

# THE TEAM LEADER
# AS MOTIVATOR

Effective Christian leaders work hard to stimulate spiritual growth in people's lives individually and collectively. Obviously, such a process is intensely relational. The productivity and effectiveness of the team directly relates to the kind of leadership we provide. Authoritarian leaders press on with ideas and concepts regardless of what the group thinks or feels. Dissatisfied minority members either cause trouble in the group or leave it.

The free-rein leader, on the other hand, can allow the pendulum to swing too far to the other side. She sees herself only as a catalyst and can allow the group to wander aimlessly up and down the bypaths of their own discretion, sometimes with minimal productivity as the result. Group members may blame the leader for this lack of productivity, as well as becoming discontented with the group and with their own positions.

Perhaps the most crucial concept of motivation, one we abuse with regularity, is that motivation springs from the inside, and is not created externally. We always talk about "motivating people" when what we really do is facilitate their own motivation, or put them in touch with things that capture their attention and interest. Part of our problem here stems from our failure to understand the difference between the way children and adults learn—we practice *pedagogy* instead of *andragogy,* and it carries over into the way we work at motivation.

## FACTORS IN MOTIVATION

We begin our understanding of motivation by recognizing that there is a cause (usually an identifiable one) for the way people think and act. Behavior directly results from value system. Secular sociologists argue that one's value system comes from environmental influence, produced largely from factors outside of himself.

The Christian, however, knows that a biblical value system emanates from what an individual believes and has committed herself to. In a very real sense Christian leaders help people minimize the external influences that seek to condition behavior, and yield rather to internal motivations—obedience to Christ, commitment to the will of God, and a recognition of discipleship responsibility.

Paul Buchanan sets forth five principles which, though secular in the context of his book, can be adapted in Christian leadership study. He identifies these five principles "as being particularly important in exploring why people behave as they do":

1. The way a person behaves depends on *both* the person *and* his environment.
2. Each individual behaves in ways which *make sense to* him.
3. An individual's *perception* of a situation influences his behavior in that situation.

4. An individual's *view of himself* influences what he does.
5. An individual's behavior is influenced by his needs, which vary from person to person and from time to time.[1]

Buchanan's emphasis is both simple and significant. He suggests that we should not try to find only one cause of any given behavior but rather recognize the complexity of factors which produce it. If leaders can recognize what makes a person do what he does, they may be one step closer toward unleashing motivation which will help him do what he *should* do. The "should" can be defined either as "what the leader wants him to do" or "what is right according to biblical and spiritual standards." The closer motivational goals approximate biblical ideals, the more effective our ministry.

## Motivation Is Inseparably Related to Personal Goals

The name Carl A. Rogers is synonymous with the nondirective approach to counseling. In a helpful booklet entitled *A Therapist's View of Personal Goals,* he deals with the basic ontological questions of life. Based on experiences with his clients, Rogers examines the matter of personal goals and how people set out to achieve them.

Five dimensions of value in human existence are borrowed from the research of Charles Morris:

1. A preference for a responsible, moral, self-restrained participation in life.
2. Delight in vigorous action for the overcoming of obstacles.
3. The value of a self-sufficient inner life with a rich and heightened self-awareness.
4. A receptivity to persons and to nature.
5. Sensuous enjoyment and self-employment.[2]

Rogers is rather unhappy with these choices, however, and adds one of his own, using the words of Kierkegaard: "To be that self which one truly is." In effect, self-actualization (according to Rogers) is the goal of human endeavor.

Despite the freedom we find so attractive in Rogers, he doesn't quite make his way to the team goal I am emphasizing here. But he sets the psychological framework in which a group of people with various skills, abilities, and personalities can engender motivation as they work toward a group goal.

Hal Wood, of Advisory Management Services in Kansas City, distinguishes between "traditional" and "teamwork" approaches to leadership motivation (figure 10).

To this kind of a climate, Christian leaders bring the necessity of appealing to biblical motives. A Sunday school teacher, for example, is asked to teach not because it is "self-actualizing" but because service for Jesus Christ must be the normal experience of every Christian who wishes to obey the Lord. The absolute standards of Christian discipleship demand the "shoulds" and "oughts" that Rogers too willingly casts aside.

But we can agree wholeheartedly with Rogers that personal goals play a major factor in the motivation process. We realize, however, that part of our responsibility is to help people bring their personal goals into conformity with the will of God rather than establishing personal goals which pander to their own interests and desires.

## Motivation Depends upon Information

Actually, much more than information is involved here. We need to communicate a distinct philosophy of ministry in which people have a voice and to which they commit themselves. Some churches seem almost like propaganda mills in the way they promote local or denominational programs and belief systems. Others work at giving ministry back to the people, a distinctly biblical pattern. Jim Means puts it this way:

|  | TRADITIONAL | TEAMWORK |
|---|---|---|
| Structure | Formal, rigid, lines of authority | Loose, flexible, task-oriented, driven by the mission |
| Assignments and Delegation | Told what to do with little input | Team makes assignments with members often volunteering |
| Communication | From the top down, politics | Parallel, lateral, and horizontal |
| Attitude | Win/lose | Win/win |
| Motivation | For the company or the profession | For the team, for oneself, for the Lord |
| Job Satisfaction | Repetitive, routine, with few observable results | Group dynamics of collective achievement |
| Measure of Success | Individual effort | Collective results[3] |

*Figure 10*

Equipping laity inevitably involves motivation, and a church's philosophy of motivation reveals a great deal about both church and leaders. The success of any church greatly depends on effective motivation in mobilizing laity resources of time, talent, and money. Whatever else real leaders do, they motivate. Failure to motivate guarantees mediocrity, if not disintegration. Unfortunately, many churches have leaders who motivate with highly questionable tactics: coercion in a variety of forms, appeal to direct revelation, guilt, cajolery, and manipulative tactics of all sorts. An exemplary philosophy of motivation respects human dignity, gives responsibility, clarifies possibilities and choices, and encourages spiritual growth.[4]

Some say that every Christian leader is engaged in public relations. Some would claim propaganda even enters into the mix. How do these two differ? Propaganda, which tries to influence public opinion by promoting a special interest, has predetermined ends and engages in manipulation. Propaganda merely provides a means to an end. Generally, propaganda does not care whether the results obtained are detrimental to some groups or to some members of the group.

On the other hand, public relations respects truth and goes about its task with dignity and good manners, recognizing its responsibility to the various publics involved and engaging in cooperation at all points. No doubt there are propagandists in some churches, but the spiritual role of leadership motivates through the communication of accurate information to all. We make needs known, we clarify objectives, and ministry proceeds on the assumption that people respond intelligently and willingly when they feel a part of our ministry philosophy.

## Motivation Involves the Changing of Group Attitudes

Human attitude is cognitive, affective, and conative. The cognitive has to do with mental recognition of facts; the affective with one's feelings, which result from knowing the facts; and the conative deals with resultant actions. Sometimes we call these

228

three aspects intellect, emotions, and will. Leaders who motivate people must deal with all three of these aspects of attitude before we see results.

Attitudinal changes increase as ego involvement of group members decreases. In other words, as one becomes less self-centered, she becomes more motivated toward participation in group activities and, therefore, toward satisfactory achievement. Remember—*overt conforming behavior does not necessarily imply attitudinal change.* Someone has wryly remarked, "A person convinced against his will is of the same opinion still." He may withdraw his verbal attack on the leader's program, but sullen passivity does not signal cooperation.

Research in the area of attitudinal change indicates at least five principles involved in changing group attitudes:

1. *Attitudinal change increases when people spend time together.*

2. *Attitudinal change is more likely as similarity among group members decreases.* Homogeneity in a group tends to stagnate, and thought patterns conform if all members are of the same mind.

3. *Attitudinal change increases as opportunities for interaction increase.* A church member who dislikes African Americans or Caucasians might change that attitude as he allows himself more thorough personal interaction with different ethnic groups.

4. *Attitudinal change increases or decreases in response to events which take place outside of the group.* A board member may be open-minded or hostile at a board meeting, depending on the kind of conversation he had with his wife just before he left home.

5. *Attitudinal change directly relates to group crises.* If an outside force threatens the continued existence of the group, a change of attitude on the part of some members may be necessary to defend the structure of the group itself. The Epicureans and

Stoics were no friends until they united against the common foe they saw in the monotheism of the apostle Paul.

In the booklet mentioned above, Buchanan draws some final conclusions from the principles he states at the beginning of his work. Their succinctness and helpfulness justify reproducing them here:

1. Understanding one's motivation helps one to understand other people. It does so not through "doing unto others . . ." but by reducing blocks which prevent one from listening to, and thus understanding the other person.
2. Motivation, like growth, is inherent within people. Hence, the task to the leader is not so much that of "motivating others" as it is of "unleashing" and helping to harness the motivation that is already there.
3. We all respond to a situation as we see it. Thus, one way to influence another person's behavior is to help him get a more accurate view of what is reality. (This also applies to our own behavior!)[5]

## *Motivation Arises from What Leaders Give, Not from What They Take*

As Means suggests above, motivation techniques betray a leader's ministry philosophy as well as her leadership style. When we act as though people should serve us, we take from them whatever they give and use it for the good of the organization or, God forbid, the enhancement of our own personal goals. Paul says that motives are as important as actions (2 Cor. 8:12; 9:7), and the example of Jesus with the disciples repeatedly demonstrates a giving kind of leadership. Grenz offers a helpful list of responses groups should be able to make when leaders unleash biblical motivation.

- You've given us a sense of belonging.
- You've thanked us for our efforts.
- You've showered us with attention.

- You've taken interest in our personal lives.
- You've praised, recognized, and rewarded our achievements.
- You've been careful not to criticize too much.
- You've remained loyal to us in defeat as well as in victory.
- You've encouraged us.
- You've expanded our responsibilities.
- You've displayed a positive optimistic attitude.
- You've kept us informed about the church's affairs.
- You've urged us to strive for excellence in all that we do.
- You've appealed to people's emotions as well as their logic.
- You've helped us to remove obstacles and deal with problems that get in our way.
- You've supported us by providing the tools, training, and money that we need to do our jobs.[6]

## CLASSIC MOTIVATIONAL THEORISTS

### Maslow's Hierarchy of Human Needs

According to Abraham Maslow, humans are perpetually wanting organisms.[7] The wants stem from five basic human needs of relative predominance. The hierarchy concept reflects Maslow's belief that when a lower need is satisfied, it disappears and is replaced by a higher-order need. He considers gratification as important as deprivation since it releases people from dominance by a lower order and enables them to concentrate on more social or higher-order needs. Once a need has been satisfied, it is no longer considered a "need," since it exists then only in a potential fashion, although it may reemerge again at any time to dominate behavior.

Maslow's hierarchy of basic human needs, arranged in order from lower to higher, includes the following: physiological needs, safety needs, belongingness and love needs, esteem needs, and the need for self-actualization. Maslow would argue that the order is not fixed (one can always find exceptions), but that it describes the overwhelming majority of persons encountered in his research.

*Physiological needs* deal with subsistence and include

such factors as hunger, thirst, and sleep. They are relatively independent of each other and of other issues in the motivational
process, so that a person could be completely dominated by a single physiological need, such as hunger.

When the physiological needs are satisfied, *safety needs*
may emerge, particularly in emergencies such as war, disease, and
natural catastrophe. When you face an angry rattlesnake, for
example, it does not seem consequential that you might also be
hungry.

*Love, affection, and belongingness needs* emerge if the
physiological and safety needs are fairly well gratified. They
demonstrate a desire for affectionate relations with people in
general, and specifically a longing for group acceptance or group
membership.

The next step upward in the hierarchy is the *esteem-need*
level. Satisfaction of this need can be derived from self-respect or
self-esteem as a feeling of adequacy accruing from achievements
and accomplishments, prestige, status, or appreciation by others.

When all these lower needs are satisfied, then the need for
*self-actualization* emerges and becomes the significant factor in the
motivational process. It represents a longing for self-fulfillment
and a desire to become everything one is capable of becoming.

Once again, an analysis of a secular theoretician in the
light of the New Testament offers some striking insights. Surely
we understand James to be saying that talking theology to a
starving man is sheer nonsense (James 2:14–20). He only recognizes his need for inner peace and eternal salvation when physiological and safety needs have been met.

On the other hand, an organization does not motivate
people by offering them additional fulfillment of needs that have
already been met. When people have enough to eat they are not
impelled to action by the offer of more bread, or even by the
money to buy more bread.

But can Christian ministry be self-actualizing? Can a discouraged pastor or missionary ready to quit be in that position

because no one has taught him to think of his or her service as self-actualizing? Do some Christian service dropouts develop a distorted, slave-to-the-church concept of their tasks? Is it possible that some ministry roles have little self-actualizing potential?

My brother-in-law tells hilarious stories of his days as a factory worker putting screws in refrigerator doors all day long—a task hardly calculated to produce self-esteem or a feeling of belongingness and importance. How do we help people understand that Christian ministry is not the theological equivalent of putting screws in a refrigerator door on an assembly line?

## *Herzberg's Motivation Hygiene Theory*

Frederick Herzberg was professor of psychology at Western Reserve University and also served as research director of the Psychological Service of Pittsburgh for several years. Primarily through his orientation toward mental illness and health care, he developed the Motivation Hygiene Theory and detailed it in three books: *Job Attitudes: Review of Research and Opinion; The Motivation to Work;* and *Work and the Nature of Man.*[8]

Actually the three volumes represent three stages in the development of the theory. They detail the gathering of scientific inquiry and data, new research and investigation, and actual construction of the conceptual theory. The Herzberg study observes that the factors that make people satisfied with their jobs are not the same as those which make them dissatisfied, nor are these factors necessarily the opposites of one another.

Herzberg concludes that the presence of so-called "satisfiers" tends to increase an individual's satisfaction with her work, but their absence does not necessarily make that worker dissatisfied, only apathetic. Similarly, the presence of so-called "dissatisfiers" makes people unhappy or disgruntled about their work, but the absence of dissatisfiers does not necessarily keep them happy on the job. Here are the lists that came out of the research:[9]

| *Satisfiers* | *Dissatisfiers* |
|---|---|
| Achievement | Interpersonal relations (both with superiors and peers) |
| Recognition | Technical ability of the supervisor |
| Work itself | Company policy and administration |
| Responsibility | Working conditions |
| Advancement | Personal life off the job |

Notice that the satisfiers (things that keep employees content) distinctly relate to the work itself, whereas the dissatisfiers quite frequently relate to the job context or environment out of which the job emerges. Herzberg claims that the presence of satisfiers leads to higher productivity, but the dissatisfiers, on the other hand, do not necessarily lead to lower productivity. Strauss and Sayles summarize the Herzberg findings:

> The experimenters called the factors which lead to this rather sterile, non-involved attitude "hygienic factors" (since they are used to avoid trouble). We shall accordingly call management which emphasizes these factors "Hygienic Management." Such a "be good" policy may provide a pleasant environment in which to work and a considerable amount of around-the-job satisfaction, but little satisfaction through the job, and little sense of enthusiasm or creativity.[10]

Once again, we can be helped by the work of secular research. Christian organizations need to emphasize the satisfiers of achievement, responsibility, and advancement. But surely our primary deficiency does not lie here, but in our failure to recognize the presence of dissatisfiers. Too often we concentrate our attention on multiplying and enhancing the satisfiers, while the dissatisfiers may be chipping away at the morale, and consequently the motivation, of our people.

Surely a Christian employer ought to be concerned with the life of his employees off the job. Surely Christian theology teaches us to recognize that the inner factors of a leader's attitude toward personnel, self, and the leadership team will represent a crucial role in service performance.

## Zaleznik and the Individualistic View

Abraham Zaleznik is one of the few management theoreticians who seeks to place responsibility upon the worker rather than constantly harping on changing the organization. His position emphasizes an internal view of humanity and attempts to show how people, by the strength of their character and personality, can remake organizations. The effect of their personality induces a contagious desire to perform considerably stronger in directing organizations than depersonalized systems such as interlocking committee structures or shared management.

The release of this individual energy and its contagion of desire to perform may well occur within organizational structures, but the impulse and inspiration derive from individual personality. Even when people function within groups, they still perform as individuals.

Clearly then we understand the ways in which individual personality is influenced by the attributes of the groups in which people work and live, others with whom they interact, the organization within which they and their groups work, and the cultures in which they all live.[11]

Christian leaders nod vigorously when they read that Zaleznik emphasizes that individuality begins in family life. Through relationships, people influence others and are in turn influenced by them. As our world and selves broaden, we become increasingly concerned with the environment beyond our immediate, face-to-face groups.[12]

Zaleznik's theorizing appeals to me precisely because he focuses on changing people rather than organizations. Or perhaps I should say, changing organizations by first changing the people who make up those organizations. In these days of "new paradigms" for ministry and change in the church, Zaleznik's focus ought to put cautious guidelines on the massive restructuring advocated by some writers. According to Zaleznik, leaders who claim organizations can consistently be reformed to suit individuals only exert a new type of stress on the people who still must act within the framework of their own personal developmental problems.

Zaleznik also emphasizes that while behavioral scientists like Maslow and Herzberg can be enormously helpful in providing theoretical constructs, using that information ultimately falls to the leader. Of course, the information of behavioral scientists is meaningless unless leaders in Christian organizations make themselves aware of it, run it through a proper theological grid, and seek practical applications.

## McGregor: Theory X and Theory Y

This classic motivational theory again focuses on individual personality. McGregor argues, "Management has adopted generally a far more humanitarian set of values; it has successfully strived to give more equitable and more generous treatment to employees . . . *but it has done all of these things without changing its fundamental theory of management.*"

He delineates the basic assumptions of Theory X in this fashion:

1. The average human being has an inherent dislike of work and will avoid it if he can.
2. Because of this human characteristic of dislike of work, most people must be coerced, controlled, directed, threatened with punishment to get them to put forth adequate effort for the achievement of organizational objectives.
3. The average human being prefers to be directed, wishes to avoid responsibility, has relatively little ambition, and wants security above all.[13]

McGregor argues that as long as management holds such

presuppositions it can never develop a genuinely relational context for work motivation. He refers to Theory Y as "the integration of individual and organizational goals" and offers some basic assumptions in contradistinction to those held by practitioners of Theory X.

1. The expenditure of physical and mental effort in work is as natural as play or rest.
2. External control and the threat of punishment are not the only means for bringing about effort toward organizational objectives. Man will exercise self-direction and self-control in the service of objectives to which he is committed.
3. Commitment to objectives is a function of the rewards associated with their achievement.
4. The average human being learns, under proper conditions, not only to accept but to seek responsibility.
5. The capacity to increase a relatively high degree of imagination, ingenuity, and creativity in the solution of organizational problems is widely, not narrowly, distributed in the population.
6. Under the conditions of modern industrial life, the intellectual potentialities of the average human being are only partly utilized.[14]

Once again it seems that the alert reader can recognize some basic biblical undertones in McGregor's work. He suggests, for example, a high view of humanity rather than the low view so often obvious in old "carrot-and-stick" approaches to leadership. He also takes a high view of the nature of work, a position consistent with biblical rubrics as early as Exodus 20, and perhaps as early as God's activity in creation recorded in the first two chapters of the Old Testament. He also recognizes the difficulties in achieving genuinely humane management in the complex society in which we all must function today.

Since the publication of McGregor's work more than thirty years ago, we have seen a plethora of variations (e.g., Theory Z). Though tempted to explore some of those here, I must acknowledge my limited goal to review the classic theorists.

## MAKING THE MOTIVATION PROCESS WORK

In the *Master Plan of Evangelism*, Robert Coleman lists eight aspects of motivation used by Christ with His disciples: selection, association, consecration, giving, demonstration, delegation, supervision, and reproduction.[15] Note the personal emphasis in all of these. Christ's pattern was to build His life into small groups of people rather than spend the majority of His time speaking impersonally to large numbers (Matt. 10).

So perhaps first in the matter of translating theory into action comes *a commitment to the discipleship approach in our relationship to the team.* That will obviously be easier to attain in some leadership situations than in others, but that does not make it any less important.

Another factor is *a significant program of training for all responsible leaders.* A pastor should constantly be exposing lay leaders to materials in the behavioral sciences and management research as well as to a theological analysis of those fields. Obviously we are talking here about a long-term process rather than a change event.

The third ingredient of implementation is the matter of *managing the motivation.* Two aspects of unleashing motivation seem to outshine all others in importance. First, communication must provide thorough information. Second, mutual agreement upon goals and standards should pervade all organizational processes. We must *know* together and *agree* together what we are going to *do* together.

Consider also the *participation of as many people as possible in ministry functions.* We know that change occurs faster and is more lasting when accompanied by a high degree of interaction among the staff. This obviously forces us to emphasize people rather than programs. It helps us zero in on the matter of God's design through spiritual gifts, calls, and empowerings. Objectives and needs precede forms.

Participation in a realistic vision affords a significant motivational source. I'll be talking about vision at various points later in the book, but it certainly fits here. As we sink deeper into the knowledge volcano perched precipitously upon the technological landscape, the need for hands-on, personal leadership becomes evermore basic to motivation. If motivation comes from the inside (and it does), then visionary leadership is not the dream of an isolated executive overly preoccupied with the bottom line. In short, the effective team leader for the twenty-first century will become a leader of leaders.

## FOR FURTHER READING

Grenz, Arlo. *The Confident Leader.* Nashville: Broadman & Holman, 1994.

Kouzes, James M., and Barry Z. Posner. *The Leadership Challenge.* Rev. ed. San Francisco: Jossey-Bass, 1995.

Maslow, A. H. *Motivation and Personality.* New York: Harper & Row, 1954.

Nanus, Burt. *Visionary Leadership.* San Francisco: Jossey-Bass, 1992.

Schaller, Lyle E., and Charles A. Tidwell. *Creative Church Administration.* Nashville: Abingdon, 1975.

## NOTES

1. Paul C. Buchanan, *The Leader and Individual Motivation* (New York: Association, 1964), 15.

2. Carl A. Rogers, *A Therapist's View of Personal Goals* (Wallingford, Pa.: Pendle Hill, 1966), 5.

3. Hal Wood, "Continuous Quality Improvement," seminar notes used at a Dallas Theological Seminary faculty workshop.

4. James E. Means, *Effective Pastors for a New Century* (Grand Rapids: Baker, 1993), 115–16.

5. Buchanan, *The Leader and Individual Motivation,* 59.

6. Arlo Grenz, *The Confident Leader* (Nashville: Broadman & Holman, 1994), 207–8.

7. Abraham H. Maslow, *Motivation and Personality* (New York: Harper & Row, 1954), 80–106.

8. Frederick Herzberg et al., *Job Attitudes: Review of Research and Opinion* (Pittsburgh: Psychological Service of Pittsburgh, 1957); Frederick Herzberg, Bernard Mausner, and Barbara Snyderman, *The Motivation to Work* (New York: Wiley, 1959); Frederick Herzberg, *Work and the Nature of Man* (New York: World, 1966).

9. Herzberg, *Work and the Nature of Man*.

10. George Strauss and Leonard R. Sayles, *Personnel: The Human Problems of Management* (Englewood Cliffs, N.J.: Prentice-Hall, 1960), 137.

11. Abraham Zaleznik, *Human Dilemmas of Leadership* (New York: Harper & Row, 1966), 5–9.

12. David Moment and Abraham Zaleznik, *Casebook on Interpersonal Behavior in Organizations* (New York: Wiley, 1964), 2.

13. Douglas McGregor, "Theory X: The Traditional View of Direction and Control," in *An Introduction to School Administration*, ed. M. Chester Nolte (New York: Macmillan, 1966), 175.

14. *Ibid.*, 167–68.

15. Robert Coleman, *The Master Plan of Evangelism* (Westwood, N.J.: Advocate, 1990).

240

# –14–
# THE TEAM LEADER
## AS REPRODUCER

L eadership," write Kouzes and Posner, "is a reciprocal relationship between those who choose to lead and those who decide to follow. Any discussion of leadership must attend to the dynamics of this relationship. . . . If there is no underlying need for the relationship, then there is no need for leaders."[1]

That relationship governs not only the execution of immediate leadership tasks, but the preparation of the next round of leaders. In parental leadership, that "next round" refers to children who grow into adults and take over their own parenting tasks. In business, it might refer to a line manager training a foreman to take over the line manager's job when he moves up the organizational chart. In a church, it describes the modeling and mentoring a senior pastor gives to associate staff and to lay leaders.

Reproductive leadership is hardly a new idea. Paul urged Timothy to the task in the familiar language of his second epistle to that young pastor:

So, my son, throw yourself into this work for Christ. Pass on what you heard from me—the whole congregation saying Amen!—to reliable leaders who are competent to teach others. When the going gets rough, take it on the chin with the rest of us, the way Jesus did. (2 Timothy 2:1–3, *The Message*)

But, as we have seen repeatedly throughout the pages of this book, developing leadership requires much more than designing a training program. It incorporates the broad spectrum of team leadership that forms the philosophical scope of this book. If the individual leader is not functioning according to biblical and practical style and behavior, the development of other leaders may become a laborious and thankless task.

## ESTABLISHING A CLIMATE

This present decade and the early decades of the next century will emphasize adult education, if for no other reason than simply demographics. It says a great deal about the development of leadership in childhood and adolescence, but I leave that for authors more qualified. We focus in this chapter on adulthood, a stage of life when fellowship as well as education remain constantly necessary.

As we develop a climate for leadership, we do well to discard notions of position and title. As Kouzes and Posner put it,

> Leadership is a set of skills and practices that can be learned regardless of whether or not one is in a formal management position. Leadership is found in those in the boiler room and those in the board room. It is not conferred by title or degree. In fact, often those responsible for the smooth and successful operation of organizations, from the youth soccer league to the church fellowship, have neither.[2]

With that awareness, let's explore various components of the climate.

## Biblical Guidelines

The Bible is hardly silent on the subject of leadership. Chapters 1–4 bear review at this point as we remind ourselves of the kind of people God calls and equips for Christian leadership. The very concepts of "calling" and "gifting" remind us that not everyone is a candidate for reproductive leadership. An attitude of obedience and meekness; an awareness of the multitudinous examples that Scripture offers regarding leadership behavior; an allegiance to the key texts (e.g., 1 Tim. 3) which define qualifications for certain offices—these all make up our adherence to biblical guidelines. Armerding says it well: "The Christian leader should carefully examine himself to identify those characteristics in his life that may be interfering with an uncompromising devotion to the Lord Jesus Christ. Then he should be ready to learn from the circumstances into which the Lord might put him."[3]

## Team Spirit

We all know that leadership can focus on the personality and gifts of the individual leader, on group needs and goals, and on the situation. In developing leaders, the permeation of team spirit must dominate all three of those important perspectives. One task we face in adult leadership training is teaching people that they can learn. Potential candidates must be convinced of learning ability; they must have desire for growth inculcated in their minds and hearts; and we must provide adequate situations in which the training can take place. Remember, unless people see their particular ministries against the mural of the larger mission, they are not likely to feel significant on the team nor will they want to develop higher leadership skills.

## Decentralization

Since people learn leadership in an atmosphere of responsibility rather than busyness, it becomes important to create a climate in which decision making takes place on the battle line. In any organization, power and authority seek the surface like a Styrofoam fishing bobber. We must consciously and persistently push them down, thereby creating that climate of responsibility and goal achievement essential to the task.

## Delegation

Team leaders who decentralize responsibility will automatically be forced to delegate. Sadly, many leaders who give lip service to delegation still try to maintain autocratic control over crucial decisions. Reproductive leadership rarely survives in a climate of autocracy; participatory involvement at the highest possible level stimulates leadership behavior (see chapter 23).

## Purpose and Direction

As the mission gives way to objectives and goals, people begin to see how they fit into the overall scheme of things. Genuine and clearly defined purpose gives any ministry or organization the will to live *now*. The choice is not between living and dying, but living in the present rather than the past or even the future. To be sure, as mission turns to vision, we do look into the future, a posture essential for leadership development. But we do not want people so fondly remembering "how it used to be" or "how it might be some day" that they forget to apply their God-given responsibilities to current tasks so that the visionary future may be achieved.

Many Christian organizations err in providing leadership development by conceiving of this broad task as narrow technical specialization for some specific ministry role, such as Sunday school teaching or evangelistic outreach. Leadership training is much more comprehensive and embracing. Of course, teachers and outreach workers are leaders, but we want to extend that concept to parents, committee members, and all who serve in situations where leadership development provides serious potential.

## CONSIDERING THE ISSUES

While speaking at a church in an eastern state, I stayed overnight in a motel immediately adjacent to the church parking lot. After one of the sessions I attempted to walk across the parking lot and up the twenty- to thirty-foot incline when the senior pastor stopped me and suggested that a muddy ditch blocked the way. Then, as if to explain why he knew the terrain so well, he said, "You see, I own all the land between here and the motel." I shall never forget that one sentence which spoke so loudly about that man's leadership style. Presumably, he owned none of that ground; surely it was all in the church's name. But in a dominant frame of mind about his own importance, he expressed in one sentence his commitment to autocracy.

### Leadership Style

We have dealt with this elsewhere in this book, so I touch on it here only as a reminder that it is impossible to divorce what we are from whom we train. What Jesus said in Luke 6:40 about teachers certainly pertains to leaders as well: "A student is not above his teacher, but everyone who is fully trained will be like his teacher." Autocrats produce autocrats; free-rein leaders produce free-rein leaders; and participatory team leaders can reproduce after their kind. I recall some words I wrote in a foreword to Michael Anthony's book *The Effective Church Board*:

> Across the continent today churches struggle over congregational control and authority. In some churches (usually with a more congregational polity) imperial pastors tend to abuse lay leaders until the church splits or the congregation rises up and fires the pastor. In elder-governed churches, power struggles

245

between seminary trained pastors and lay elders often result in gridlock or some form of abuse by one side or the other. . . .

Leadership is a sacred trust in which the well being of other church leaders depends on the spirituality and competence of an effective church board. A certain amount of authority may rest with the title, but the right to lead and the influence to make decisions which affect other people's lives must be given leaders by followers.[4]

Whether we're talking about boards, pastors, mission executives, college presidents, business leaders, or parents, leaders who do not understand their own leadership style, who have not critiqued and refined it in accordance with biblical descriptions and sophisticated modern research, are hardly prepared to hand the torch to a developing generation of new leaders.

## Essential Maturity

We must understand that such "maturity" is not a completion of some educational pattern regardless of how long or arduous it might have been. Adults are not people who have learned all there is to learn or earned some graduate degree. Adults in the process of becoming leaders stand in need of continuing learning experiences throughout all of life. Educationally speaking, adults are "growing up," not "grown up." Hence the common terminology of our day which refers to "lifelong learning."

I have taught scores of pastors in doctoral programs, most of whom had been out in the field for several years or even decades. The common thread that unites them and makes them different from undergraduates or unseasoned graduate students is their keen awareness that questions and problems far exceed their answers and solutions. But the spirit of eagerness to keep growing and maturing is in itself a mark of maturity. When a leadership development program brings the interests and needs of adults into proper relationship to one another and with the ministry opportunities in any church or organization, we have created a dynamic situation.

## *Necessity of Credibility*

What do constituents look for in a leader? When Kouzes and Posner compared their 1987 research with 1993 surveys, they pointed out that honesty retains the top spot, with vision and inspiration holding on to second and third places. All three, however, have climbed in percentage of affirmation, i.e., they were considered more important in 1993 than they were in 1987. That was true for almost every item on their scale except competence and intelligence, which alone among the top ten dropped in importance as "characteristics of admired leaders."

In a most useful book entitled simply *Credibility*, the authors show that leadership credibility requires self-discovery, an appreciation of colleagues, the affirmation of shared values, sustaining hope in one's self and one's followers, and acknowledging the tension between freedom and constraint in leadership.

The whole point of credibility has to do with relationship, which marks it so clearly as an essential leadership issue. The authors recommend that leaders ask themselves four questions to examine their trustworthiness level among other team members:

1. Is my behavior predictable or erratic?
2. Do I communicate clearly or carelessly?
3. Do I treat promises seriously or lightly?
4. Am I forthright or dishonest?[5]

There is an obvious link between all the various constituent parts of this chapter as well as the entire book. We have already mentioned decentralization and will yet talk about empowerment. Surely credibility is enhanced when we distribute leadership across the organization through both decentralization as an administrative process and empowerment as a leadership commitment. The last paragraph of *Credibility* reflects the tone of the entire book:

Renewing credibility is a continuous human struggle and the ultimate leadership struggle. Strenuous effort is required to build and strengthen the foundation of working relationships. Constituents do not owe leaders allegiance. Leaders earn it. The gift of their trust and confidence is well worth the struggle.[6]

## Uniqueness of Women's Leadership

As the role of women has expanded among evangelicals in recent decades, this particular dimension has catapulted into the foreground. However, it is hardly the purpose of this book to deal with a biblical theology of women's ministry roles. Our concern lies in facing the fact that women have led in Christian organizations for centuries and we should long ago have examined whether that leadership is different in some ways from male leadership.

Judy Rosener's article in the *Harvard Business Review* a few years ago ought to be widely read by church and para-church leaders across the evangelical landscape. Perhaps I can best serve my readers by summarizing the findings of the research that produced that article and urging us all to keep a weathered eye for new studies on this crucial subject.

Rosener discovered a couple of interesting similarities— that men and women leaders earned approximately the same amount of money (contrary to most studies), and that just as many men and women experience work-family conflict. She then notes,

> But the similarities end when men and women describe their leadership performance and how they usually influence those with whom they work. The men are more likely than the women to describe themselves in ways that characterize what some management experts call "transactional" leadership. That is, they view job performance as a series of transactions with subordinates—exchanging rewards for services rendered or punishment for inadequate performance. The men are also more likely to use power that comes from their organizational position and formal authority. . . .

The women respondents, on the other hand, described themselves in ways that characterize "transformational" leadership—getting subordinates to transform their own self-interest into the interest of the group through a concern for a broader goal. Moreover, they ascribe their power to personal characteristics like charisma, interpersonal skills, hard work, or personal contacts rather than to organizational stature.[7]

This more "feminine" approach to leadership Rosener describes as "interactive" and ascribes to it such practices as encouraging participation, sharing power and information, enhancing the self-worth of others, and energizing others. Obviously, none of those is alien to sound leadership practice, and most can be verified as biblical concepts. We need to remember that the average age of Rosener's group is fifty-one, which accounts both for a high degree of maturity and a gender-difficult transition to leadership roles, and that she surveys women in business and industry, not in Christian organizations and churches. I have no reason to believe that the findings would be any different in the latter, but no research to affirm it either.

I totally agree with Rosener's conclusion that interactive or transformational leadership can as easily be found in men as in women, and it is not difficult to find women exercising transactional and even autocratic leadership. We want to avoid identifying "male leadership style" and "female leadership style." Rather, we want to expand our understanding of effective leadership to take into consideration the wider path people take to that goal today by allowing potential leaders to lead in ways that maximize their individual strengths. Says Rosener in conclusion,

> Then the newly recognized interactive leadership style can be valued and rewarded as highly as the command-and-control style has been for decades. By valuing a diversity of leadership styles, organizations will find a strength and flexibility to survive in a highly competitive, increasingly diverse economic environment.[8]

Obviously, I would take exception to the *equal* acknowl-
edgment of the two styles Rosener has uncovered in her survey.
This entire book argues that the "command-and-control" style
runs well outside the boundaries of biblical affirmation, especially New Testament didactic passages and early church models.
The interactive team leadership she describes ought to characterize every Christian leader regardless of gender, age, or office.

## EMPHASIZING THE BASICS

In a speech delivered at Dartmouth College in 1986,
William H. Spoor recalled the words of Winston Churchill.
Apparently, the British prime minister remarked while reflecting
on his own leadership during World War II, "There is a special
moment when a person is figuratively tapped on the shoulder and
offered the chance to do a very special thing, unique to him and
fitted to his talents; what a tragedy if that moment finds him
unprepared or unqualified for the work which would have been
his finest hour." The quote reminds us of the basics of leadership,
a section with which I will conclude this chapter.

### Competence

Even though it dropped on the Kouzes/Posner scale
between 1987 and 1993, competence still maintains a dominant
role in leadership development. Obviously, it makes no sense to
set out in a deliberate attempt to produce incompetence when
developing new leadership. But Ken Callahan indicates that
churches and volunteer organizations tend to accept willingness
as a substitute for competence and in so doing, drive competence
from the field.[9] He notes a keen scale between competence and
responsibility, indicating that increased competence must lead to
increased responsibility or the developing leader will get discouraged and perhaps even quit.

Conversely, too much responsibility unmatched by competence can only lead to frustration, disappointment for everyone, and again, perhaps the loss of the budding leader. Put another way, leadership development must set high standards for competence and measure out responsibilities in increasing doses as the competence level grows.

## Creativity

Here again, Callahan is particularly helpful. He notes that creativity grows in direct proportion to rewards for creative failure. Rather than locking the developing leader into the traditional system of the organization, free him or her to explore new avenues, to attempt new processes which may utterly fail. That very failure demonstrates what will not work. And the very attempt demonstrates courage and initiative, qualities we want to enhance in any leadership prospect. Too often we have allowed the hackneyed cliché "success breeds success" to influence our own leadership and our development of new leadership. In reality, failure breeds success, for creative failure forces the kind of exploration that ultimately leads to new and better ways of carrying out leadership tasks.

## Vision

Burt Nanus begins the first chapter of his splendid book *Visionary Leadership,* saying, "There is no more powerful engine driving an organization toward excellence and long-range success than an attractive, worthwhile, and achievable vision of the future, widely shared." He goes on to define vision as "a realistic, credible, attractive future for your organization."[10]

Too often Christian leaders confuse vision and mission. They are not the same; the former flows out of the latter. Mission describes why your ministry or organization was founded, what it is supposed to do. Vision describes where it will go in the future, what its various publics can expect to see and hear in the years ahead. Wise leaders use strategic themes to give direction and then allow considerable flexibility for other team members to elaborate and develop the central ideas. The main point, of course, is to multiply the number of visionary leaders at all levels. Here's Nanus again:

> With the proliferation of visionary leadership at all levels, a leader at the top becomes what my colleague James O'Toole calls "a leader of leaders." Not for him the image of a leader as shepherd and followers as sheep, dutifully following instructions. Instead, in a pattern now common in innovative companies, the "followers" are themselves leaders and are as qualified professionally as the leaders to whom they report. For those top executives who lead the leaders, vision is the *sine qua non*, without which there could be no common framework and hence no collaboration, no mutual trust, and no hope of organizational progress. Like the Indian scout guiding the cavalry captains, you can lead only by getting out front and showing the way, keeping one eye firmly on the distant horizon and the other looking ahead to avoid traps along the path.[11]

I can almost hear voices of dissent arising. Clearly, pastors are shepherds and congregations are sheep! In the collective sense that's true. But the modern church tends to elevate individuals to singular shepherding roles. In the ultimate understanding of this New Testament metaphor, Jesus is the Shepherd and we are all the sheep. Biblical leadership squarely depends upon our solid commitment to the doctrine of universal priesthood. God speaks to His people, not just to His pastors, principals, and presidents. No concept of vision could be more biblically correct than this emphasis on teamwork which leads us to reproduce ourselves in the lives and ministries of other people.

### Empowerment

I resist using the word "power" in describing Christian leadership in any other sense than the *dunamis* of the Holy Spirit and the gospel. Christian leaders have influence, and they have authority, but power seems a negative theme. The word itself suggests that leaders hold this quantity and parcel it out to others as they choose. But we know from solid research that power flows in an organization to numerous and varied types of people, not just chief executives. For example, people who control certain essential resources (money, time, knowledge) have power. Power also flows to the more visible, a strong argument for the appearance of numerous lay leaders on the platform Sunday after Sunday. What Christian leaders do in developing new leaders is to unleash and liberate the power and skills people already have. We expand opportunities for ministry and leadership with meaningful purpose.

To be sure, leaders can share their influence and authority with others, thereby empowering them in their own leadership roles. But in effective leadership teams, the behavior of individual team members tends to be very much like that of the leader. Self-led teams outperform tightly managed teams, both in business and in ministry.

So much more could be said on the subject of reproductive leadership, and a recent book I coauthored with Dennis Williams goes into detail on issues of retention and attrition.[12] There is no need to reproduce that information here. So I end merely with the words of our Lord which must have dented the fragile ears of His disciples when they heard them first spoken in the last week of His life on earth: "I tell you the truth, anyone who has faith in me will do what I have been doing. He will do even greater things than these, because I am going to the Father" (John 14:12).

Sometimes we get so caught up in the mansions at the beginning of that chapter that we miss the leadership impact of that single verse. Commentators speculate on what Jesus meant; I take the passage in strict literality. Measured by almost any standard of leadership, the disciples exceeded the ministry of our Lord. They served for longer duration; they covered much more ground; they shared the gospel with thousands more people; they developed the church of the New Testament, which was only a concept of theology at the time of the Cross.

True Christian leaders not only identify with the disciples in this passage; they see themselves saying to subordinates, "You will do more significant things than I have done." Parents say it to their children as they reach adulthood. Bosses say it to promising employees. Teachers say it endlessly to classrooms full of students. And we say it because it is true. Only such an attitude toward those we mentor and build can reproduce leaders who reproduce.

## FOR FURTHER READING

Armerding, Hudson T. *The Heart of Godly Leadership*. Wheaton, Ill.: Crossway, 1992.

Callahan, Kennon L. *Effective Church Leadership*. San Francisco: Harper & Row, 1990.

Kouzes, James M., and Barry Z. Posner. *Credibility*. San Francisco: Jossey-Bass, 1993.

_____. *The Leadership Challenge*. Rev. ed. San Francisco: Jossey-Bass, 1995.

Nanus, Burt. *Visionary Leadership*. San Francisco: Jossey-Bass, 1992.

Williams, Dennis E., and Kenneth O. Gangel. *Volunteers for Today's Church*. Grand Rapids: Baker, 1993.

## NOTES

1, James M. Kouzes and Barry Z. Posner, *Credibility* (San Francisco: Jossey-Bass, 1993), 1.

2. James M. Kouzes and Barry Z. Posner, *The Leadership Challenge* (San Francisco: Jossey-Bass, 1987), 156.

3. Hudson T. Armerding, *The Heart of Godly Leadership* (Wheaton, Ill.: Crossway, 1992), 193.

4. Michael J. Anthony, *The Effective Church Board* (Grand Rapids: Baker, 1993), 9–10.

5. Kouzes and Posner, *Credibility*, 14.

6. Ibid., 273.

7. Judy Rosener, "Ways Women Lead," *Harvard Business Review* (November/ December 1990): 125.

8. Ibid.

9. Kennon L. Callahan, *Effective Church Leadership* (San Francisco: Harper & Row, 1990), 165–66.

10. Burt Nanus, *Visionary Leadership* (San Francisco: Jossey-Bass, 1992), 3.

11. Ibid., 167.

12. Dennis E. Williams and Kenneth O. Gangel, *Volunteers for Today's Church* (Grand Rapids: Baker, 1993). See especially the final chapter, "Keeping That Team of Volunteers Vital."

# –15–
# THE TEAM LEADER
# AS MENTOR

W e have Homer to thank for the word. In the
*Odyssey*, Mentor is a friend of Odysseus who undertakes the education of his son Telemachus. When Telemachus
separates from his father, Mentor helps the young man find him.
In fact, however, Mentor has been possessed by Athene, the
Greek goddess of war, patron of the arts and crafts, and paragon
of wisdom. In this guise, Athene leads Telemachus past ambushes
and other hazards to ultimately accomplish his quest. From all
this fanciful mythology, we now have the common word *mentor*.

Today the word depicts a wise and helpful friend, a
teacher and leader who uses his or her experience to show others
how best to walk life's path, to accomplish goals and meet life's
challenges.

Mentoring has been primarily a family activity, carried
out by fathers and mothers or sometimes uncles, aunts, or grand-
parents. As the concept moved into society, apprentices learned
their trades under craftsmen who had gone through the same

process themselves. For centuries, that form of mentoring was the only way one could break into certain skill professions.

Already we have a hint as to the difference between mentoring and teaching. Teaching, to a great extent, deals with knowledge and information, offering a heavy emphasis on books and paper. Mentoring implies a hands-on conative approach to learning. Though we might not see it often among carpenters and cobblers today, the medical profession still practices mentoring as the major step toward becoming a doctor. Hospital internship in some specialty is crucial before one can earn the proper credentials to practice that particular form of medicine with the approval of accrediting and credentialing organizations.

Within the more defined context of leadership, mentoring means everything we have already discussed, but includes a more highly focused goal as well. According to Bobby Clinton,

> *Mentoring* refers to the process where a person with a serving, giving, encouraging attitude, the mentor, sees leadership potential in a still-to-be developed person, the protégé, and is able to promote or otherwise significantly influence the protégé along in the realization of potential. A *mentoring* process item refers to the process and results of a mentor helping a potential leader. The mentor is a special kind of divine contact, one who may offer prolonged help or guidance.[1]

Clinton goes on to call our attention to one of the great New Testament examples of mentoring: the work of Barnabas with John Mark that began after the missionary team split at the end of Acts 15. The work of Paul with Timothy, Titus, Epaphras, and others also offers us ample biblical evidence of this crucial activity.

## GENERAL QUALIFICATIONS OF A MENTOR

Can we learn anything from observing the characteristics of people who seem to have successful ministries? Obviously we can, and when we do we discover that their qualifications are not profound personality traits found only in very special types of people. We find, rather, common behaviors, which almost any experienced leader can offer with the help of God's Holy Spirit.

Certainly some leaders have greater aptitude toward mentoring than others. Those who have worked closely with their own children at home, for example, will display greater patience and willingness to work with followers on the job. Leaders who have a background in teaching or have been trained in leadership and management skills may function better in this role than those who have not.

Mentoring is not just the activity of a nice person who wants to help. In leadership, the helper must know quite precisely what it is she has done, is doing, and should do in the future, thereby guiding the follower along that general path. One is reminded of George Bernard Shaw's play *Getting Married,* in which a character says: "I am not a teacher, only a fellow traveler of whom you asked the way. I pointed ahead—ahead of myself, as well as you."[2]

Teachers who have functioned in that role for decades can point to students, perhaps all over the world, who have been influenced by their instruction and personality. Teaching is a ministry of multiplication, and its reflective recipients can very easily run in the hundreds. But only a handful of those hundreds may be the result of mentoring. Teachers stand before large groups in classrooms, but never see many of those students outside of class. Pastors preach to large groups on Sunday morning, but only a small minority of the congregation, perhaps only one or two members of the pastoral staff, could actually be called—if I may neologize—"mentees," or those who learn hands-on ministry under the direct supervision of a mentor. Furthermore, this is not necessarily something everyone can do, as Clinton points out.

> Not everyone is suited to be a mentor. Mentors are people who can readily see potential in a person. They can tolerate mis-

takes, brashness, abrasiveness, etc., in order to see potential developed. They are flexible and patient, recognizing that it takes time and experience for a person to develop. They have vision and ability to see down the road and suggest next steps that a protégé needs for development. And they usually have a gift-mix that includes one or more of the encouragement spiritual gifts: mercy, giving, exhortation, faith, word of wisdom.[3]

Mentoring holds a strategic role in the future of evangelical organizations. "Who will be the leaders in 2015?" asks Lyle Schaller before he goes on to talk about the "widely neglected issue of leadership development." Says Schaller, "Everyone is convinced of the perpetual shortage of competent, willing, and dedicated volunteer leaders and workers. On a long-term basis, however, another facet of this issue is identifying, enlisting, educating, socializing, nurturing, and training those persons who will be the leaders of the churches in the year 2015."[4]

Let me go out on a limb here and note that Schaller's book, now more than ten years old, comes out of a day when formal leadership development programs for defined groups worked rather well in the church. To some extent, churches and Christian organizations must still find some formula to conduct such "training classes," which take potential leaders beyond the basics.

But it may be fair to say, as we approach a century change, that the real development of a leader works better today through individual mentoring in which the functioning leader prepares future leader(s) to serve effectively in the same kind of ministry. Many churches today, especially those with large staffs and elaborate facilities, believe that seminaries have focused too much on the cognitive domain to the point at which their graduates know a great deal but can do very little. The reaction of these church staffs is to develop leadership in-house—a system that looks very much like informal mentoring.

## Mentors Must Control Their Own Emotions

How often Paul warns about self-control in his pastoral

epistles. Particularly in 1 Timothy 3 and Titus 2 we see repeated references to this issue. Leaders who cannot discipline their own lives and emotions cannot serve effectively as leaders and certainly do not qualify as mentors for developing leaders. If God uses us to help others develop in ministry, it will only be because His Spirit has enabled us to control the peculiarities and deviations of our own personalities.

Jay Conger and his colleagues talk about the negative side of charismatic leadership, those regressive forces that can give rise to irrational, even pathological behavior. I need to state here that I do not agree with many of the things in their book and even hesitate to use the terminology "charismatic leadership" (not because of any theological issues but because of the implications on leadership style); nevertheless, they have a strong point on the specific issue of emotions.

> It is important for both leaders and followers to be cognizant of the existence of the destructive side-effects of charisma, for this realization is the first step toward corrective action. Clinical research has revealed that if individuals are made aware of their transference reactions, these valuable insights into behavior can be stepping stones to productive change. When we notice frequent mood shifts, sudden irritability, feelings of envy, a sense of being watched, an excessive concern about what others think, or the continuous need for an audience, we may be on the track to possible transference distortions.[5]

Clearly, not every leader is a candidate for mentoring.

## Mentors Must Be Good Listeners

Listening enables a mentor to identify and understand the mentee as a person. It lays the groundwork for any help that will result from the mentoring process. As we have noted, mentoring is more than telling; it depends on thorough and adequate feedback and mutual cooperation.

## Mentors Must Be Friendly

When thinking of the history of mentoring, one can certainly imagine a snarling blacksmith grudgingly teaching his trade to a village boy while neither cared very much to be around the other. Nevertheless, it was the way of village life and it had to be done. That type of thing will not work today, especially within the boundaries of the church or Christian organization. Experienced Christian leaders and developing Christian leaders both understand the relational dimensions of biblical life and ministry. It is highly unlikely that effective mentoring could result without a significant friendship between leader and follower.

Contrast leadership mentoring with professional psychiatry. Even though the psychiatrist may be warm and friendly, one should not engage in the delusion that she is anything more than a professional doctor whose interest in the patient is less than personal. A mentor, on the other hand, counsels because she has demonstrated herself to be a trusting confidante of the person to whom she ministers. Obviously this involves keeping confidences and the warm receptivity that encourages people to seek out the mentor for help with their problems.

Remember, mentors must hold on to friendship regardless of the mentee's decisions. In the mentoring process, mentees may often yield to the voice of Satan and the influence of the sin nature within, choosing paths obviously opposed to the will of God. The mentor faces the temptation of discouragement. He wants to turn away from one who has so clearly rejected the will of God for his life. But to turn away from the learner at this time only guarantees that he will develop destructive self-doubt. Many such disappointing moments occur in the ministry of mentoring, but we must live with them, and through them try to help another day as God gives the opportunity.

## Mentors Must Learn to Ask Catalytic Questions

The questioning process so crucial to effective mentoring is, in effect, part of good listening. There is no need for mentors to appear overly inquisitive or even just plain "snoopy." Questioning seeks to uncover the real issues involved in the mentoring process and to direct the thoughts and behavior of the mentee.

Kouzes and Posner talk about "moments of truth." They argue (along with Tom Peters) that the most powerful mechanisms for modeling (mentoring) are found in the way a leader goes about his daily routines, observed, of course, by the follower.

> The message about what really counts in the organization is delivered, demonstrated, pointed out, and emphasized by the leader's moments of truth and how well these moments are orchestrated. Leaders, and would-be leaders, must consciously structure moments of truth to communicate and reinforce their intangible values. The most typical moments of truth center around:
> • how leaders spend their time.
> • questions leaders ask.
> • leaders' reactions to critical incidents.
> • what leaders reward.[6]

When dealing with the actual questions, Kouzes and Posner emphasize that *routine,* not *formal,* questions highlight issues. This holds true primarily because the questions demonstrate the leader's values and therefore convey on a regular basis to the mentee what priority system that particular ministry holds high. They argue, "Questions provide feedback about which values should be attended to and how much energy should be devoted to them. . . . When we examine how leaders make people aware of key concerns or shifts in organizational focus, it is readily apparent that the leaders' questioning style has a pervasive effect on the issues that organizational members worry about."[7]

## Mentors Must See Things in Total Perspective

Thought fragmentation characterizes immature people. They fixate on one event or idea and do not seem to be able to bring it into proper relationship with other matters. In short, they do not see the whole picture. This makes it difficult for some would-be mentors to identify their own leadership properly, though their failures may be quite obvious to friends and family. The particular problem at hand may have a history deeply rooted in the relationships and interrelationships of a very complex society.

Part of this perspective requires us to recognize the vocational aspect of ministry. As Christian leaders and teachers draw heavily from secular research and integrate those findings with Christian theism, vast progress can be made in our understanding of leadership development. But one uniquely biblical dimension is the idea that God calls and gifts people for leadership positions. In dealing with the subject of the leader's example, Hudson Armerding talks about "long-term accountability" and says,

> For me, the prospect of divine assessment is a stimulus to excellence and an antidote for indolence. In addition, our experience of God's love powerfully motivates us to "climb the steep ascent of Heaven through peril, toil and pain." The challenge to the Christian leader . . . is this: "Who follows in our train?" . . . I believe our example of accountability can summon others to this kind of life. They will need to see specific, tangible instances, however, to assure them that what we propose is practicable.[8]

## Mentors Must Resist the Temptation to Be Only Tellers

I have mentioned this at least once already, but the temptation is complicated by the fact that many followers want precisely this kind of relationship. At times it may seem logical simply to tell a mentee what he ought to be doing. Such telling, however, takes the burden of thinking through the problem off the shoulders of the learner and makes him even more dependent upon his newfound "adviser." Should the solution be effective, the mentee will return again and again for solutions to other problems of ever-increasing complexity. If the advice proves inadequate, however, he can always pass along the blame for any negative results directly to the mentor by simply saying, "I was only doing what he told me to do."

## THE PROCESS OF CHRISTIAN MENTORING

Mentoring is most effective when the contact is initiated by the mentee. Therefore, the leader who wishes to function effectively in this role should recognize some of the basic principles involved in the process.

Narramore in *The Psychology of Counseling* answered the question, "To whom do they turn?" when speaking of functioning in the counseling role within a Christian context. He suggests seven "drawing characteristics" of successful counselors, which relate to mentoring as well:

People usually turn to someone they know.
People take their problems to someone they like.
People take their problems to someone they respect.
People are most likely to seek help from Christian leaders who indicate their interest in counseling.
People turn for counseling to someone whom they feel is competent.
People take their problems to someone who observes professional ethics.
People turn to the counselor who knows God.[9]

## *Be Available*

A mentor must be accessible to his protégé. This involves

more than geographical location; it represents an entire attitude toward other people. The "available" mentor somehow escapes from the workload on his own desk. Depending on the mentoring situation, the mentee may or may not need vast blocks of the leader's time. As maturity and experience develop, we can delegate individual tasks, which is very much a part of the mentoring process. Our "apprentices" are not necessarily rookies, just people who need to take the next step or two in the leadership process. Nevertheless, there are times when the mentee needs you, and he or she needs to be able to find you and obtain the necessary guidance so essential for that critical moment in progress.

Availability also implies an allowance of sufficient time for each learner so that her problem can be satisfactorily handled. Obviously, this puts a limitation on the number of mentees a mentor can handle at one time. My own experience indicates that, in addition to my staff with whom a mentoring relationship is always ongoing, I can probably deal with one or two developing leaders in a mentoring relationship over the course of a year. Sometimes the relationship will extend longer than a year; sometimes shorter, depending upon circumstances.

### *Be Credible*

Let the mentee see your insides, understand how you make the decisions you do and why you hold the values and priorities that characterize your leadership style. Leadership is primarily relational, and in the mentoring process there is a greater connection between the leader and learner as persons than there is between *leadership-followership roles.* In their most recent book, *Credibility,* Kouzes and Posner emphasize that credibility requires self-discovery, appreciation of colleagues, the affirmation of shared values, developing capacity, serving a purpose, sustaining hope, and acknowledging the contention between freedom and constraint in leadership.[10]

The leader who has operated his leadership role within a team framework, who has involved people and related to them satisfactorily from day to day, will be the leader who stands in a satisfactory position to mentor them. Other leaders, students, and people in the organization already feel an attitude of confidence toward the ability and commitment of the properly functioning leader. Nevertheless, in the actual mentoring process, we must allow our mentees to relate to us in an informal way. A relaxed, natural, open, and vulnerable posture avoids stiffness in attitude and jargon and attempts to speak in the learner's language at all times.

## Be Ethical

We all know that parents talk about their children, teachers talk about their students, and leaders talk about their followers. Within the boundaries of discretion, this is not necessarily harmful behavior. But the mentor/mentee relationship carries with it boundaries of confidentiality that are not unlike the counseling situation. Ethical behavior in mentoring requires that the mentor at times must invoke a lawyer-client or doctor-patient relationship unless prohibited by some institutional or civic legal structure. Part of the vulnerability, of course, is letting mentees see that we struggle with the same problems they find so enormous in their own lives.

The wise mentor will never minimize a problem that the mentee describes, and he will never show shock at anything the mentee tells him. Throughout the process he is constantly alert for underlying struggles which hinder leadership progress: physical exhaustion, emotional disturbances, financial difficulties, and evidence of sin.

In a fascinating approach to this subject, Peter Koestenbaum turns our words around. Instead of suggesting that mentoring means ethics, he suggests, "Ethics in leadership means mentoring. Rather than developing people for the sake of jobs, it is wiser to develop jobs for the sake of people. This statement may seem excessive, for companies must make a profit; but profit comes when people find meaning in their work."[11]

In higher education I have long lived by a hiring philosophy rather reminiscent of the professional sports enterprise— "take the best player in the draft." Sometimes one must fill a certain vacant position and can only use an employee with certain skills. Other times, there comes along a highly gifted, highly motivated, deeply spiritual person who doesn't seem to fit any particular niche at the moment but whose maturity and leadership potential have been thrust in our paths by a sovereign God who almost shouts, "What will you do with this one?"

### Be Instructive

Having belabored some of the distinctions between teaching and mentoring, it may be useful to dwell for a moment on the similarities. Obviously, all three learning dimensions are at stake in both teaching and mentoring—the cognitive (knowledge), affective (attitudes), and conative (behavior). Since conative deals with doing, mentoring often focuses on that dimension. How does one conduct a meeting? How does one make public announcements? How does one go about the process of hiring or firing? These are all conative issues, but they carry enormous baggage from the cognitive and affective domains. There is basic knowledge involved in the structuring of that meeting. There are extremely important attitudes in the hiring and firing process. So the mentor is always a teacher and more, as we define the process in this chapter. Let's return to Koestenbaum:

> A leader's obligation is to develop the people for whom he or she is responsible—to help them become more marketable, more qualified professionals, to further their careers, to help them feel better about themselves, to equip them to confront the toughest vicissitudes of life. Mentors are like loving parents who feel fully responsible for developing the independence of

their children. This kind of teaching is based on a high degree of loyalty and commitment to the individual employee and on the recognition that human beings are not expendable. Employees can also be expected to adopt a similar attitude of dedication to the organizations for which they work.[12]

## Be Committed

In the mentoring process there will be times when protégés feel let down by their mentors and other times when mentors feel let down by their protégés. What bridges these difficult gaps? What keeps us together in these moments of tension? The answer is commitment. When mentor and mentee link up, one of the first things they discuss is their long-term commitment, perhaps even defining the time boundaries involved.

Commitment means that mentors empower mentees with portions of their own influence and authority. Commitment means that mentees go out of their way to please and satisfy the suggested requirements of the mentoring situation. They don't cut corners; they don't offer excuses; they don't fall into sloppy, shoddy work.

Within the realm of Christian ministry, this attitude becomes even more binding by our mutual allegiance to the Savior. Precisely the same glue which binds Christian husband and wife closer together than those outside the faith, namely, that they are "one in Christ," applies in a lesser impact to Christian mentoring. Hudson Armerding puts it this way:

> The yielding of the self to Christ, making death with Him the working principle that informs the whole life of the redeemed individual, was Paul's desire when he said, "For to me, to live is Christ . . ." (Philippians 1:21). Such a life effectively and succinctly answers those who ask, "Why didn't God call more brilliant and powerful people?" Simply put, He desires followers fully committed to Him. Part of the impact of our example, shown by the level of our consecration, will be manifested in such commitment. Then those who follow us will not place

their trust in our brilliance or eloquence but rather in Christ and His cross and in the sovereign power of our Almighty God.[13]

Effectiveness in mentoring is determined by a number of things: the degree of rapport we establish, the effectiveness of the process, and the willingness of the mentee to grow. In Christian mentoring, as Armerding has noted, there resides a supernatural ingredient, both in the life of the leader and the learner, which introduces a dimension that can never play a role in secular mentoring. Christian leaders capitalize upon this factor as we apply the power of the Word of God, the supernatural dynamic of prayer, and the vitality of the Holy Spirit in every mentoring situation.

### FOR FURTHER READING

Finzel, Hans. *The Top Ten Mistakes Leaders Make*. Wheaton, Ill: Victor, 1994.

Koestenbaum, Peter. *Leadership—The Inner Side of Greatness*. San Francisco: Jossey-Bass, 1991.

Kouzes, James M., and Barry Z. Posner. *Credibility*. San Francisco: Jossey-Bass, 1993.

Longenecker, Harold L. *Growing Leaders by Design*. Grand Rapids: Kregel Resources, 1995.

Miller, Calvin. *The Empowered Leader*. Nashville: Broadman & Holman, 1995.

### NOTES

1. J. Robert Clinton, *The Making of a Leader* (Colorado Springs: NavPress, 1988), 130.

2. Quoted in "Acting as a Mentor," *Royal Bank Letter* 76, no. 4 (July/August 1995): 2.

3. Clinton, *Making of a Leader*, 131.

4. Lyle Schaller, *Getting Things Done* (Nashville: Abingdon, 1986), 259.

5. Jay A. Conger et al., *Charismatic Leadership* (San Francisco: Jossey-Bass, 1988), 250.

6. James M. Kouzes and Barry Z. Posner, *The Leadership Challenge* (San Francisco: Jossey-Bass, 1987), 201, 203.

7. Ibid., 203.

8. Hudson T. Armerding, *The Heart of Godly Leadership* (Wheaton, Ill.: Crossway, 1992), 47.

9. Clyde M. Narramore, *The Psychology of Counseling* (Grand Rapids: Zondervan, 1960), 14–17.

10. James M. Kouzes and Barry Z. Posner, *Credibility* (San Francisco: Jossey-Bass, 1993), 52–55.

11. Peter Koestenbaum, *Leadership* (San Francisco: Jossey-Bass, 1991), 160.

12. Ibid., 161.

13. Armerding, *Heart of Godly Leadership*, 64.

# PART THREE

---

# FUNCTIONS OF
# TEAM LEADERSHIP

# –16–
# SETTING AND
# ACHIEVING GOALS

Helpful, practical, and reasonably thorough, the third volume in the series *Leadership Handbooks of Practical Theology* hit the market in 1994. Its 524 pages focus on "Leadership & Administration," but the words "goal" and "objective" appear neither in the extensive table of contents nor in the index.

That astonishing omission in a very fine volume reflects the failure of so much modern evangelical leadership when it comes to setting, nurturing, and achieving goals. Somehow we have been unable to translate MBO from "Management by Objectives" to "Ministry by Objectives." Of course, there is nothing negative about the former, but many Christian leaders feel a sense of squeamishness in picking up such secular terminology.

So this chapter deals with ministry by objectives. We need to begin with a focus on mission and move on to note how that focus leads to an effective conclusion.

Let's begin with three basic assumptions. Leaders in any

church or Christian organization may operate on the following premises:

1. *The organization has goals.* They may be unwritten, they may be fuzzy, they may be forgotten by most, but the existence of the organization implies some kind of goal orientation.

2. *The organization has some structure to facilitate goal realization.* In a small church that structure might mean the pastor attempting to do everything as the church's only paid staff member. Or it might mean a large and complicated bureaucracy in which goal achievement is actually impeded by the multiple layers of supervisors and assistants.

3. *The organization requires effective leadership if goals are to be reached.* The achieving of goals does not just happen. There are specific procedures through which we move in order to look back on what God has allowed us to achieve in the service of the Savior.

## DEFINING THE MISSION

The word "mission" (identical with purpose) simply describes what the ministry organization was designed to do. Goals, objectives, action steps, structure, and administrative process all flow from the mission statement. A confused mission statement, or a group of people who are confused about their mission statement, should raise an immediate red flag in any organization. The mission is usually very brief and not always vastly different from similar organizations. For example, the mission of one congregation in Eden Prairie, Minnesota, can be summarized in a single sentence: "The purpose of Wooddale Church is to honor God by bringing lives into harmony with him and one another through fellowship, discipleship, and evangelism."[1]

Obviously, the broad concept of mission narrows as we move into setting goals, objectives, and action steps. The most important singular word in this process is "specification." The broad understanding of why God has created a ministry gives way to the breakdown of how we are to carry it out.

That leads us again to the distinction between mission and vision, the difference often being confused in our day. To repeat, *mission describes why an organization exists; vision describes what that organization will do about its mission in the future.* Aubrey Malphurs says: "I define an institutional vision as a clear and challenging picture of the future of the ministry as its leadership believes it can and must be."[2] We'll get into this more in the next chapter since vision has more to do with planning than with developing and achieving goals (though in practice the two are virtually inseparable).

Dr. Donald Bubna of the Christian and Missionary Alliance states:

> Where church workers are saying the same thing and often with the same words, I know they have leadership that is keeping the mission before them. They know what they are doing.
>
> The process of arriving at a good mission statement is important. The leadership needs to work on it collectively. The congregation deserves input. Such involvement brings good ideas and thereby people take ownership.[3]

Bubna suggests five questions that every congregation ought to ask with respect to its mission, and they all relate as well to other types of Christian organizations.

1. What is it that God wants us to do?
2. Whom are we trying to reach?
3. How are we going to accomplish this?
4. Where is our geographic target?
5. What are the results we anticipate?[4]

One further thought before we leave the concept of mission. The reality of purpose is just as important to individual leaders as to their organizations. It may seem a bit driven to talk about "a lifetime mission," but a life purpose statement is a realistic and practical way to facilitate planning and decision making throughout your ministry. Many years ago I wrote a ten-page document describing what I thought God wanted me to accomplish during my adult life. I was just over thirty-five years of age at the time, so I had some handle on where I had been as well as a fair grasp of my gifts, abilities, and professional preparation. David once observed, "You have made known to me the path of life" (Ps. 16:11). Sybil Stanton addresses this process in *The 25-Hour Woman*:

> You can't pull a purpose out of a hat. You can't force or fake it. You must find it deep within you, and that may require some hard soul-searching.
>
> Your purpose may not seem unusual to others, but it will be unique to you. It has nothing to do with grandiose goals, lofty achievements or universal fame. It is the quiet confidence that, even if you never leave your neighborhood, you will have lived fully.[5]

Stanton suggests preparing your life purpose by dividing a piece of paper into three sections labeled "Past, Future, and Present." The past deals with influences, an understanding of God's call, and a review of some of the dreams you once held, or perhaps still hold.

The future requires that you identify yourself in ten years or even thirty years. It suggests several potential scenarios and asks for a response and a perspective on the total package.

The present deals precisely with the material in this chapter. What are the goals and objectives that can make possible the kind of future you have described?

I would suggest also that you divide your life purpose preparation into various sections so that you can identify goals, objectives, and action steps for key areas of life such as the spiritual, professional, social, domestic, physical, and so on.

## MINISTRY BY OBJECTIVES

Leaders who practice this kind of MBO identify purpose, objectives, and goals, and then establish a program for achieving those results and evaluating their achievement. They understand what the old cliché really means—if you aim at nothing, you are likely to hit it.

### Process of Ministry by Objectives

For as long as I have been teaching this material, students have been confused about the difference between goals and objectives. (Part of the problem may very well be my inadequate explanation!) But we all face the fact that different writers in the field of leadership and management use the terms in different ways. Sometimes, for example, goals will be broader than objectives, and sometimes the reverse will be true. In *Feeding and Leading* I identified purpose-objectives-goals-realization procedures.

Let me revise the process a bit here and talk about mission-goals-objectives-action steps. The process remains the same; only the terms change. Ministry that moves forward by objectives that are based on goals derived from its mission must take several specific steps along the way. What will you do in this crucial process?

1. *Assess your environment.* What is the current surrounding? What type of financial, theological, sociological climate surrounds you? What is your "parish"? Wesley's wonderful motto, "The world is my parish," has a beautiful missiological ring, but of course it was not true. Likewise, a small Christian college facing the twenty-first century may have to acknowledge that it is distinctly a regional school with little appeal to forty-five of the fifty states or perhaps no more than one or two provinces.

2. *Identify strengths and weaknesses.* Every organization

does some things well and other things at a lower level of quality. In order to develop the vision based on a solid mission, we have to know which things fall into each category. Not only that, but we have to know whether the things we do well are the things we ought to be doing. If that is not the case, some major overhaul may be required.

Like a mission statement, the identification of strengths and weaknesses serves individual progress as well as corporate aims. You have certain leadership strengths and certain leadership weaknesses. Again an old maxim rings true: "Lead to your strength; staff to your weakness." Do those things you do well, and hire people to fill in your gaps with their strengths.

*3. Assume reasonable trends.* Trend analysis is no longer sanctified guesswork for Christian organizations. The science of demographics has made it possible to get hold of data that enable us to project foundational statistics as they relate to the future of our organizations. Sometimes this has to do with the ethnic changing of a neighborhood or even a city. Often it projects age-group shiftings such as the current trend toward older adults throughout North America.

To be specific, churches and schools should not have been surprised by the huge number of kindergarten children enrolling in the fall of 1995. We had known for five or six years about the so-called "echo boom" which formed the largest entering class in elementary school since 1960, the height of the baby boom era. In the same pattern, we still have a shortage of teenagers and can anticipate that reality for another eight or ten years.

*4. Write specific and measurable goals and objectives.* Goals and objectives hold value insofar as we can identify whether they have been achieved or not. A goal which cannot be evaluated is not a goal at all. A Christian teacher who says regarding a given day, "I want to be a blessing to my class," may articulate a sincere prayer but does not speak in the language of objectives and goals.

My own suggestion here is to use the prepositions "to,"

"through," and "by" to distinguish between goals, objectives, and action steps. For example, "Our congregation aims *to grow* to attendance of three hundred *through engaging* in active community evangelism by *conducting* an outreach program to every home in our community by the end of 1998." Of course, that is something of a rough generalization, but it gives a hint of the specification these prepositions can afford as we nail down what we want to do.

*5. Strategize action steps.* As important as the mission is, the action steps form the key to achieving goals. Unless we can create statements to which we can answer yes or no, we do not have specific action steps. In the illustration above, action steps might read something like this:

1. By forming an evangelism committee by November 1 of 1997.
2. By segmenting the community into quadrants and developing a strategy to reach each quadrant during one quarter of 1998.
3. By designing, preparing, and distributing an attractive brochure that will both present the gospel and explain the ministries of our church.

Regarding each of these statements we can ask, "Did we do it or didn't we?"

*6. Provide for evaluation, reinforcement, and reward.* Goal achievement moves forward step by step, and its progress must be monitored. For example, time frames are critical. Notice above the references to months and years in which things will be finished. People involved in the process must not only see the progress but should participate in reinforcement and reward as we move toward fulfilling goals and objectives we have set. Evaluation deals with both process and product. Product describes the outcome, the actual goal-achievement dimension. Progress, however, describes how we went about it and refers to our ethics, the satisfaction of the people involved, and the general reputation we have developed in the community by the way we handle our evangelism project.

Van Auken states it well:

> When managed effectively, goal-setting can be a strong motivating force within the Christian organization. This is because goals give people a sense of united purpose, channeling their energy in productive directions. Goals serve as performance standards, providing ministry team members with a rudder to guide daily job activities. Goals also let people know which ends and means will be endorsed and sanctioned by the organization.
>
> In the absence of strategic goals, ministries must pay the price of slackened motivation, wasted energy, and inferior productivity. To say the least, goals are one of the most important items in any manager's tool kit.[6]

## Principles of Ministry by Objectives

By what guidelines do good leaders handle goal setting and achievement? Let's look at eight that seem to keep reappearing in the work of both secular and Christian organizations.

1. *All staff know and understand the objectives of the ministry.* In a church, one could hardly expect every member or attender to articulate clearly the congregation's goals and objectives. However, if there are four pastors on the staff, they should speak with one voice on what the church is attempting to accomplish in its community.

2. *Members of the leadership team mutually exchange goals on a regular basis.* I don't mean they give them to one another, but rather they communicate them openly and frequently, so that all members of the management team know what the other members are doing. This helps prevent overlap of effort and, even worse, a bifurcation of goals that finds members of the leadership team going off in different directions.

3. *Each leader's goals flow from the mission statement.* If you have a leader on your team whose activities can't be justified

by the mission statement, you have cause to wonder if he or she should continue in that position. Too often Christian organizations allow individuals to follow their own agendas, thinking it will keep peace and avoid conflict, but the more common result is chaos and stagnation.

4. *Keep the main thing the main thing.* People and organizations have a tendency to stray from priorities. But if we have not prioritized our goals and objectives, we are in danger of achieving the wrong things. We may be efficient (doing things right) without being effective (doing the right things). A college is an educational enterprise in which public relations, fund-raising, bookstores, and radio stations are secondary enterprises. A church should not own and operate any kind of business, profit or non-profit, which does not directly relate to its mission.

5. *People claim goals.* We can't talk about visions and dreams in a vague sense, and we certainly can't place them on the shoulders of a singular leader. Objectives must be capable of conversion into specific targets and assignments that key people in the organization take on as their responsibility and really make happen.

6. *Sound goals and objectives make possible concentration of resources and efforts.* In a time of tight budgeting, something has to go in order for something else to stay. Those decisions are not made on the basis of who squawks the loudest, nor is it best to achieve budgetary balance by cutting across the board, thereby assuming everything we do has equal importance. Good leaders face the difficult but essential choices of determining where resources will be allocated, and they do that by understanding the mission, goals, and objectives of the ministry.

7. *Both goals and objectives are multiple, never singular.* The mission statement is singular and very general as we have said. But each goal gives way to multiple objectives, and each objective gives way to multiple action steps. The diagram might look something like this:

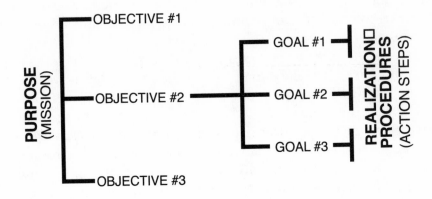

*Figure 11*

8. *Goals and objectives relate to all areas of the ministry.*
We cannot afford to neglect an area just because it does not have
a spokesperson on the board. We cannot afford to pay less attention to areas in which we have less interest. A group of elders, for
example, may have intense concern for evangelism and worship
and prepare very specific goal patterns in those areas. Less interested in church finance, however, they fail to set clear-cut goals,
objectives, and action steps with respect to budgetary matters
and soon discover that worship and evangelism strategies suffer
because there is no money to make them work.

Kouzes and Posner write passionately about "developing
cooperative goals." They state, "In the more than 500 cases that
we studied, we did not encounter a single example of extraordinary achievement that was accomplished without the active
effort and support of many people."[7] That sentence describes
their analysis of the Amdahl Corporation from which they devel-

oped several general principles, chief among which is that management alone cannot make goals happen.

> Teamwork is essential for a productive organization. Collaboration is needed to develop the commitment and skills of employees, solve problems, and respond to environmental pressures. Fostering collaboration is not just a nice idea. It is the key that leaders use to unlock the energies and talents available in their organizations.[8]

## THE POWER OF PURPOSE

Clearly defined mission, goals, objectives, and action steps can do amazing things for ministry organizations. Groups of any size, floundering in a morass of confusion and lacking direction, can immediately begin to move down the field if they understand how to get there. What can you expect if you make this process work for you?

### Present and Future Awareness

Have you ever noticed how many people in some churches live in the past? They can quickly tell you about the effectiveness of former pastors or how large and worshipful the choir was ten years ago. Others live only in the future, talking about vision and dreams of how things might be someday. To be sure, we prefer the latter to the former, but people in our organizations need to live now. Goals and objectives provide the wherewithal, the stepping-stones by which we move from where we are *now* to where we would like to be in the future. Without them, we have only dreams.

### Enthusiasm

If the goals are achievable and not ridiculously exaggerated, people can get excited about where their church or mission is headed. But again, the map is more crucial than the destination. We can say, "Our church will have an attendance of 1,000 by the year 2000," and make catchy mottoes about that sort of thing. But if our current attendance is 500, how do we propose to double that attendance in less than five years? *Remember, there are few things more demoralizing in any organization than a history of unfulfilled goals.*

## Basis for Evaluation

I have repeatedly said that goals must be measurable, because if they are not we have no way to assess our progress. This is best exemplified in the classroom in which a teacher has taught a unit of study with general and fuzzy goals and then discovers that making the test is extremely difficult because she had no target in the first place. We talk about things like "knowing the material," a poor substitute for carefully designed lesson plans that identify for students in advance what they will be expected to know or do at the end of that unit of study.

## Forced Planning

We can't jump ahead to the next chapter yet, but these two chapters are consecutive for a reason—a goal needs a plan to make it work. Even if we don't talk about long-range planning, once we get serious about setting goals and objectives, we are virtually in the planning process.

## Emphasis on Productivity

Effective leaders focus on output rather than motion. Busy people do not necessarily affirm the significance of any ministry organization. Goal-achieving people do. Activity becomes a poor substitute for productivity.

## Reduction in Conflict

This is the cooperation that Kouzes and Posner talk about. When people move in concert toward the same goals and objectives, there is less threat of conflict than when everyone marches to his or her own drum.

> Shared visions and values bind employees together in collaborative pursuits. Group tasks, complementary roles, and shared rewards also play a role. Tasks that require people to exchange ideas and resources reinforce the notion that participants have cooperative goals. As individuals jointly work together, seeing that they need information from each other in order to be successful, they become convinced that everyone should contribute and that by cooperating they can all accomplish the task successfully.[9]

In his article "Go for the Goal," Robert Witty wonders, "Does the football coach have a message for the pastor and the church?" In response, he asks us to consider the following conversation:

> Reporter: Coach, what is your goal for the big game?
>
> Coach: To win the game.
>
> Reporter: How will you attain your goal?
>
> Coach: By making one touchdown after another. We'll make touchdowns by making yardage. And we'll make yardage by line drives, end runs, and completed passes. If one play doesn't work, we will try another until we find the right combination. We won't change our goal—just our methods.

> Even so the church has an ultimate mission: to do the will of God. To fulfill that mission, the church must adopt varied and adequate goals.[10]

FOR FURTHER READING

Anderson, Leith, et al. *Mastering Church Management*. Portland, Oreg.: Multnomah, 1990.

Gangel, Kenneth O. *Feeding and Leading*. Wheaton, Ill.: Victor, 1989.

Kouzes, James M., and Barry Z. Posner. *The Leadership Challenge*. Rev. ed. San Francisco: Jossey-Bass, 1995.

Van Auken, Philip M. *The Well-Managed Ministry*. Wheaton, Ill.: Victor, 1989.

NOTES

1. Leith Anderson et al., *Mastering Church Management* (Portland, Oreg.: Multnomah, 1990), 43.

2. Aubrey Malphurs, *Vision for Ministry in the 21st Century* (Grand Rapids: Baker, 1992), 31.

3. Donald L. Bubna, "The Draft Mission Statement—What Are We Trying to Do?" *Briefing* (September 1995): 2.

4. Ibid., 1.

5. Sybil Stanton, "How to Write a Life Purpose Statement," *Worldwide Challenge* (January/February 1989): 25.

6. Philip Van Auken, *The Well-Managed Ministry* (Wheaton, Ill.: Victor, 1989), 39–40.

7. James M. Kouzes and Barry Z. Posner, *The Leadership Challenge* (San Francisco: Jossey-Bass, 1987), 133.

8. Ibid., 135.

9. Ibid.

10. Robert Witty, "Go for the Goal," *Church Administration* (May 1992): 13.

# – 17 –

# PLANNING

# FOR THE FUTURE

S andy is not a great deal different from other home-makers—she has a house in the suburbs, three children, a minivan, and is very involved in her church and community—but she seems to be the envy of her peers because she always gets things done. While other mothers barely keep up with school events, Sandy seems to be a step ahead, anticipating what will be happening in the next month and thinking through options and scenarios that affect her and her family. Though hardly chief executive officer of a major corporation, Sandy functions in an organized planning mode, partly the result of her own well-organized childhood, plus a course or two in leadership and administration in college.

Planning, simply described, means nothing more or less than predetermining a course of action. Like Sandy, every leader must understand what has to be done and figure out a way to do it—in light of what we know about the future. Remember, a goal needs a plan to make it work. Everyone in a leadership position is thrust into the planning process, whether we understand how to do it or not.

## PRINCIPLES OF PLANNING

As I have suggested often in these chapters, axioms and mottoes regarding the leadership process abound in leadership literature. Likewise with planning. I have selected six as a foundation for understanding how the planning process works.

### Planning Invests Time; It Does Not Spend It

Walking to the candy store to buy a quarter pound of fudge offers a pleasant experience both before, during, and after the purchase. But eventually the fudge will be gone along with the money. Buying fudge is an expense. Waiting in the drive-through lane at the bank irritates us, especially when traffic is already building for the drive home at the end of a workday. But handing over that check as it beams through the bowels of the air lock system on its way into the bank building should elevate our emotions. Putting money in the bank is an investment.

We understand this clearly with respect to money, but somehow lose the idea in regard to time. Some people don't take fifteen minutes to read a map before starting on a trip through unfamiliar territory, so they end up losing forty-five minutes when they get lost. A housewife (not Sandy, of course) starts out with a list of chores to do in town but does not prioritize them geographically, so she ends up driving helter-skelter from one shopping center to the other when a simple numbering system could have cut the driving time in half and even gotten her to the bank before it closed. Effective planners know the time they take to plan will ultimately pay dividends.

## *Planning Requires Careful Attention to Immediate Choices*

Neophyte planners look too far ahead. They get too wrapped up in the concept of vision and can only see what the church or mission might become ten years from now without understanding that one reaches the tenth year in incremental steps. The point, of course, is that immediate choices determine future options. The college that decides to invest $200,000 in a residence building better know that resident students will be a part of its population in the future; once that $200,000 is invested in a campus building, it cannot be spent any other way.

Actually the process works both ways. We make immediate choices in light of long-range planning, and the effectiveness of long-range planning depends on immediate choices.

## *Planning Is Cyclically Based on Evaluation*

Poor evaluation leads to poor planning, but sloppy objectives lead to poor evaluation. The better your database, the better your options for planning.

This explains why planning is so difficult in a new organization. Church planters must plan ahead, but much of their planning is speculation since they have no history on which to base it. Even more complex is the church or organization that has not kept satisfactory records for the last ten or twenty years. The current leaders find themselves attempting to carry out future planning for an organization that has a history but no decent record of it. They work in a vacuum trying to re-create word-of-mouth testimony as to what has happened in the past. Incidentally, should you be in that situation, help the leader who will follow you—keep careful records right from the first day: minutes, reports, statistics, trends, and any other kind of information that will help in the planning process.

## *Planning Requires Acting Objectively Toward Goal Realization*

Planning is impossible without goals because we have no target at which to aim. A student who wants to enter medical school after completing his baccalaureate degree must select those chemistry, biology, and science courses required for that next step. He cannot decide on commencement day that it would be nice to enter medical school, having treated the undergraduate curriculum like a buffet. A 3.8 average with courses in advanced criminology and statistical marketing is useless because the target lies in a different direction.

## *Planning Should Allow for Maximal Participation*

We'll get back to this in a moment, but here I simply want to emphasize the principle that planning is not the vision of a single person. Moses' handing down the Ten Commandments was a unique and never-repeated event. As participation of the stakeholder group increases, cooperation in the planning process increases and resistance decreases. Not representation; not majority vote; not unanimity; just participation. But more on that later.

## *Planning Increases in Specificity as the Event Draws Nearer*

Remember our chart of mission—goals, objectives, action steps? The same principle works here. If we need a one-year plan for a missions conference next February, the details may be sketchy and quite general this February; but the road narrows throughout the year so that by Christmas we have a very clear focus on program, personnel, venue, and other important matters. There are two extremes to avoid here—staying too general too long, and becoming too specific too soon.

## BASIC PLANNING MODELS

Sophisticated models such as PERT (Program Evaluation and Review Technique) are readily available to help you in the planning process. Even if you do not choose a complicated model, you should understand that paradigms are important in planning, as they are in decision making, and a sound approach to getting where you need to go requires some type of model. Since I dealt with PERT in *Feeding and Leading,* I will not repeat that information here, but readers are encouraged to review that chapter as a corollary to this one.

### Planning Step Model

A long-range plan develops out of the mission statement. Once we understand why we exist, we can develop *information sources,* both external and internal. External information has to

## STEPS IN PLANNING

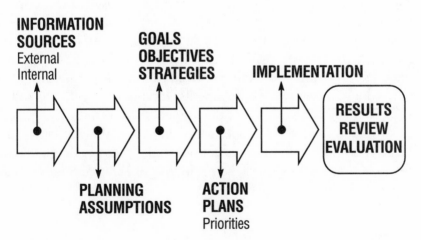

INFORMATION SOURCES
External
Internal

GOALS
OBJECTIVES
STRATEGIES

IMPLEMENTATION

RESULTS
REVIEW
EVALUATION

PLANNING ASSUMPTIONS

ACTION PLANS
Priorities

*Figure 12*

293

do with demographics and changes in our ministry's surrounding environment. Internal information provides statistics on attendance, age-group involvement, giving, spending, and so on.

The next step, *planning assumptions,* does not mean guesses. These relate directly to the information sources and essentially force us to say, "Because we know *this* about our ministry, we should assume *that* will occur over the next five years." Assumptions should be made about every area of the organization, from the recruiting of personnel to the availability of finances to the quality and repair of facilities.

We have talked in the previous chapter about *objectives and goals,* and this step really shows how they fit into the planning process.

*Action plans* (action steps) are the same as strategies. Once we have identified the steps of the first three arrows, what exactly do we plan to do, and when, and who will take responsibility for it?

*Implementation* is the process of putting the plan into action. Perhaps I should stop here and say that, though I use "plan" as a noun, in reality, planning is an ongoing, present tense verb. That will become more clear in the next model.

Finally, we look at the target to see how we've done. If you've ever done any pistol or rifle target-shooting at a well-equipped range, you know that you pull the rope to bring the target back to you so you can see where your shots have landed. Having done that, and having noticed that the firearm pulls a little to the left, you make adjustments, fix a new target, and roll it back to its place at the end of the range. Of course, the new target looks exactly like the old one; what changes is the way we try to hit it. Without evaluation we cannot make those midcourse corrections that take us from the beginning of the planning process to the achievement of goals.

## *Progressive Three-Year Model*

In what he calls a church's "blueprint for mission," Ken

*The processive approach is more developmental and dynamic and has a more flexible spirit. We could diagram this approach as follows:*

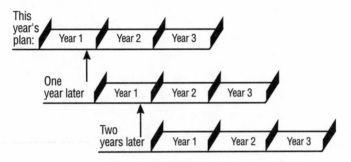

Kennon L. Callahan, Effective Chruch Leadership *(New York: Harper & Row, 1990), 240.*

*Figure 13*

Callahan suggests the following pattern, "the processive approach" as opposed to a block approach.

I think Callahan is right when he says, "The process of approach is more developmental and dynamic and has a more flexible spirit." He continues:

> The art of long-range planning is to keep as many options open as possible. The purpose of long-range planning is to keep the future open, not to close it down. The mistakes some make is to develop a unilateral long-range plan that they are going to follow "come Hades or high water." They will be disappointed.[1]

According to this model, planning leaders take two steps at the end of the first year: they advance, improve, modify, or delete objectives for years two and three; and they add a new third year. Furthermore, they practice this ongoing process annually—testimony that planning is a systematic aggressive operation.

## Annual Planning Model

Though Callahan argues vigorously that churches should not plan just one year at a time, many Christian organizations that do no planning at all would enhance their ministries by planning at least annually. As my aging memory attempts to plod back through the years to one of my pastoral opportunities, I recall raising the question of long-range planning to a group of elders. They offered no opposition whatsoever, thought it a splendid idea, and suggested that I go ahead and do the whole thing.

This hardly reflects what we want in terms of cooperative participation, but that situation offered no other choice. The usual planning models rarely work where planning has never before been done. So I designed an annual sheet that would help us decide what we wanted to do during the next calendar year. The process began by identifying ten areas of ministry in which we were involved in that church. (The number is hardly consequential; some churches can identify twenty, perhaps others only five.)

On the next page you will find one of the ten sheets developed that first year. The model is self-explanatory, built as it is upon the patterns of the last chapter. Note the specificity of the action steps. Remember, this is only one of ten areas of ministry. Others included such things as evangelism, finance, Christian education, and so on.

Before we leave this section, let me add a word about the difference between long-range and short-range planning. Sometimes short-range planning is viewed as anything up to a year and long-range planning anything beyond a year. But one can get more precise. For example, Drucker argues that short-range planning is the organization's way to carry out "systematic abandonment of things that don't fit."[2] We begin with a lofty vision and then submit it to the reality of feasibility studies until it becomes something we can actually do. Consequently, there is a distinct difference between vision and planning. Some writers have talked about planning as a "history of the future."

ANNUAL PLANNING OUTLINE

MINISTRY:_____

OBJECTIVE A

   I. To _____

       _____

     GOALS

        A. Through _____

        B. Through _____

        C. Through _____

     ACTION STEPS

     ("We will") 1. By _____

          2. By _____

          3. By _____

OBJECTIVE B

   II. To _____

       _____

     GOALS

        A. Through _____

        B. Through _____

        C. Through _____

     ACTION STEPS

     ("We will") 1. By _____

          2. By _____

          3. By _____

*Figure 14(a)*

ANNUAL PLANNING OUTLINE

MINISTRY: Worship

OBJECTIVE A

I. To increase the congregation's understanding of biblical worship.

GOALS

A. **Through** preaching on worship passages.

B. **Through** explaining worship behavior.

C. **Through** singing worship songs.

ACTION STEPS

("We will") 1. By selecting at least 2 worship hymns in each service.

2. By providing explanation of each hymn's docrine.

3. By reviewing the story behind the hymn.

OBJECTIVE B

II. To increase the the congregation's participation in worship.

GOALS

A. **Through** designing various small group experiences.

B. **Through** inviting ideas and comments on our worship.

C. **Through** asking more people to share in leading worship.

ACTION STEPS

("We will") 1. By reading Scripture.

2. By giving personal testimony.

3. By sharing music ministry.

(1 each Sunday for 1, 2, 3.)

*Figure 14(b)*

For example, they may be asked, "Imagine it's one year from now, and you are talking with a colleague. You are delighted by how the organization has progressed over the past year, beginning with a strategic planning retreat. Imagine what has been accomplished that leads you to feel so positive. Describe the steps and the new initiatives. How are they linked with existing services and operations?"[3]

## ORGANIZING YOUR PLANNING GROUP

Sandy has no planning group except for total family projects such as a vacation or the renovation of some part of the house. Most of her work she does on her own because homemaking represents essentially a one-leader small business. But you and I don't operate that way. We are responsible for (and to) dozens or perhaps thousands of people in an organization, and their involvement in the planning process is important. But who makes up that planning team, and how can we spot them?

In some cases, such as my earlier illustration about the elder board, one has little choice. However, in many organizations, even in some churches, it is possible to put together a carefully constructed planning team whose members are unrelated to other positions or titles they may hold in the organization. What kind of people do we want?

1. People who know the organization, its history, and its goals.
2. People who are spiritually mature and can work comfortably with one another.
3. People who are flexible and not rigid regarding the future.
4. People able to disassociate their ideas from their persons and thereby willing to have those ideas effectively critiqued by other members of the team.
5. People who will stay with the project over the long haul —a planning team is not a task force.
6. People who are positive and optimistic in their outlook.

Gilmore reminds us:

Paradoxically, a good sign of effective strategic planning work
can be a somewhat depressive tone, which indicates that group
members recognize the difficulties of linking their ideas to a
changing reality. By contrast, a manic feeling can suggest that
the group has fled from the difficult implementation issues and
has remained stuck, playing with ideas but not linking them to
existing constraints.[4]

Interestingly, there are tests we can use to see whether
people will fit well on a planning team. Indeed, you can determine whether or not you yourself are an appropriate planning
team leader. In my opinion, no biblical or sociological mandate
requires that a senior pastor or a CEO be a member of a long-
range planning team. In Appendix C, I have reproduced a simple
but effective test to ascertain whether you or someone else in
your organization is a good candidate for a planning team. It is
adapted from a very fine work called the *Local Church Planning
Manual,* which I strongly recommend.[5]

## PLANNING AND THE BUDGET

Starstruck visions of the future often hit the ground with a
thud when we look at the bottom line of the budget. The budget
is simply a plan for handling money. It comes in two parts—
income and expense. The general operations of any organization
include a financial plan for each ministry segment unless, of
course, the organization operates on a unified budget. Simple
budgets rarely segment income items unless ministry units have
their own budgets treated separately. Current fund budgets
almost always run for a calendar or fiscal year. Special project
budgets are kept separate and may run for indefinite terms, but
they really do not affect long-range planning.

While not trying to make this chapter a monotonous

rehash of budgeting procedures, we must at least look at some basic guidelines.

## Budgets Should Generate from
## the Bottom Up as Much as Possible

1. *Sunday school classes should have a voice in the things they need and equipment that will enhance their ministry for the next year.* That budget item then moves up through departmental superintendents, general superintendent, and perhaps pastor of Christian education before it lands on the board's desk. In educational institutions we say *academic planning must always precede budget planning.*

2. *Ultimate budget balancing decisions should be made by a finance committee, not by one person.* If a senior pastor or a chief executive officer has ultimate control of the budget's bottom line, the organization will reflect only his attitudes toward its priorities and ministries. Whether we call them trustees, a finance committee, or a budget control group, there ought to be financial wisdom in multiple counselors.

3. *A budget is useless without controlled buying such as purchase orders and appropriate signatures.* When those Sunday school teachers have identified certain equipment and the equipment appears in the budget, somebody (probably the pastor of Christian education) has authorization to approve a purchase order. In many organizations every purchase order must be signed by the head of the department requesting the item and cosigned by another administrator.

4. *Avoid inter-fund borrowing.* Inter-fund borrowing simply means that at a given crisis point during the budget year you borrow money "from yourself," probably from a building program account or some other block of funds specifically designed for a future project. The intent is never to keep the money out of that account, of course, but to repay it when gift income improves or when student tuition moneys become available.

Many institutions do this regularly, and when done with extreme caution, it will not lead to financial collapse. But it does open the door to shady practices, and when inter-fund borrowing is not paid back within the fiscal year, difficulties will arise.

5. *Designated gifts are sacred.* If Grandma Johnson wants to give the church five hundred dollars for a new pulpit, we can accept it only if we spend the money on a new pulpit. If a Christian organization does not want or will not do what a potential donor wants done with designated funds, those funds must be refused. Obviously, we can ask Grandma if she will allow us to use the five hundred dollars toward new hymnbooks if we need them, but she must decide.

### Donor Records Must Be Maintained Accurately

This is not just a nice in-house financial practice, but an absolute legal requirement. Churches and Christian ministries are nonprofit organizations and therefore must abide precisely by the rules the Internal Revenue Service has laid down. We are required to produce an exact record at the end of the fiscal year (or the calendar year) of what people have given to the organization.

### Financial Reports and Disclosures Must Be Thorough and Frequent

This means an annual audit as well as some form of public financial statement that we can give to potential donors or to anyone who asks about the institution. A Christian ministry that keeps its finances strictly secret invites unwanted, unpleasant, and probably unnecessary investigation by informal or formal means.

### Keep Your Total Debt Within 2 1/2 Times the Total Annual Current Fund Receipts

If your church has an annual income of $60,000, then

debt should not rise above $150,000. Immediately you see how this affects long-range planning. A church with an annual income of $60,000 has no business planning a $750,000 building to be completed within three years. Yes, I know it's done all the time. But that does not make it right, nor does it make it wise for leaders to engage in what can only be called foolishness, not faith.

Perhaps we can end this chapter by briefly highlighting some common pitfalls in planning.

1. *Failure to make the tough decisions.* The planning process requires decisions which demand vision and breadth of thinking. Sometimes these decisions carry with them painful budgetary cuts. Failure to make tough decisions will bog down the planning process.

2. *Sloppy data collection and analysis.* This takes us back to early steps in the first model. The cliché "garbage in/garbage out" certainly applies to the planning process. If we have distorted information regarding the organization's past, we will probably distort its future.

3. *Bureaucratic centralization.* No single person or group of powerful persons should dominate the planning process. God speaks to His people, not just to pastors, principals, or presidents. Wide, cooperative involvement in the planning process is recommended by every management book worth reading.

4. *Failure to keep constituents informed.* Not everybody will be on the planning team, and not everybody will take the opportunity to speak to a planning team member. But we can post announcements, send out periodic letters, and print paragraphs in the weekly bulletin describing the planning team's progress.

5. *Timidity—lack of vision.* With the wrong members on the planning team, we can easily end up in narrow, restricted thinking lines. When it comes to protecting orthodox doctrine, that kind of conservatism is laudable. In long-range planning, however, it's a trap. Richard Love puts it this way:

The leader who would be effective must thus make the organizational vision the top priority. He must recognize its importance and commit himself to the development of the vision in collaboration with the other team members that will become the life blood, the heartbeat of organizational purpose. For the Christian leader, this vision must follow God's heartbeat as spelled out in Scripture and illuminated in space and time to the seeking believer. But getting to this point is not enough. The vision must then go through the specification of the short-range or goal-setting operation in order to develop a common road map to the organization's destination, a destination to be reached by everyone . . . together.[6]

## FOR FURTHER READING

Callahan, Kennon L. *Effective Church Leadership*. New York: Harper & Row, 1990.

Gangel, Kenneth O. *Feeding and Leading*. Wheaton, Ill.: Victor, 1989.

Gilmore, Thomas N. *Making a Leadership Change*. San Francisco: Jossey-Bass, 1988.

Hesselbein, Francis, Marshall Goldsmith, and Richard Beckhard, eds. *The Leader of the Future*. San Francisco: Jossey-Bass, 1996.

Mason, David E. *Voluntary Non-Profit Enterprise Management*. New York: Plenum, 1984.

Rusbuldt, Richard E., Richard K. Gladden, and Norman M. Green, Jr. *Local Church Planning Manual*. Valley Forge, Pa.: Judson, 1977.

Schaller, Lyle E. *Effective Church Planning*. Nashville: Abingdon, 1979.

## NOTES

1. Kennon L. Callahan, *Effective Church Leadership* (New York: Harper & Row, 1990), 240.

2. Peter Drucker, *Innovation and Entrepreneurship* (New York: Harper & Row, 1985), 154.

3. Thomas N. Gilmore, *Making a Leadership Change* (San Francisco: Jossey-Bass, 1988), 181.

4. Ibid., 183, 184.

5. Richard E. Rusbuldt, Richard K. Gladden, and Norman M. Green, Jr., *Local Church Planning Manual* (Valley Forge, Pa.: Judson, 1977).

6. J. Richard Love, *Liberating Leaders from the Superman Syndrome* (New York: Univ. Press of America, 1994), 134.

# —18—
## DEVELOPING
## MINISTRY TEAMS

W e can surely understand how pastors and teachers dealing with Old Testament passages emphasize singularity of leadership. Yes, there are multiple passages like Exodus 18 that emphasize a participatory philosophy, but people like Abraham, Moses, Samuel, and David dominate the horizon of pre-monarchical and monarchical times.

Yet, as I have repeatedly emphasized throughout the pages of this book, when one turns to the New Testament, everything changes. The only earthly kings are the bad guys like Herod and Caesar, and ministry, biblically defined, almost always takes place in groups, especially when we focus on the developing of new covenant churches throughout the book of Acts.

Van Auken concludes his helpful booklet emphasizing that "Christian ministry is teamwork with a difference, teamwork that makes a difference. This is because Christians are different in the goals they pursue and in the way they pursue them.

God intends for His family members to work together in unified cooperation, the very essence of teamwork."

He then goes on to identify specific ways in which Christian ministry teams are different.

> Christian ministry is teamwork with a difference because of the pervasive sense of family.

> Christian ministry is teamwork with a difference because personal sacrifice is elevated above rugged individualism and self-serving competitiveness.

> Christian ministry is teamwork with a difference because followers are just as important as leaders.

> Above all, Christian ministry is teamwork with a difference because God is in the driver's seat. He charts the ultimate course.[1]

Some will immediately suggest that Van Auken's list represents an ideal situation, the church or ministry which does not exist. I disagree. Not only do ministries like this exist, but they represent precisely the kind of organizations which God blesses in a biblical way (not necessarily in numerical or financial statistics). They are places where people really enjoy serving God and are grateful that He has called them to minister in such a setting.

Aubrey Malphurs talks about "ministry matching," in which individuals discover how God has called, gifted, and led them into specific kinds of ministry situations and to serve in ministry teams.

> Ministry matching starts with the various positions in the ministry organization and matches them to the personal ministry design of the individual. For example, a local church may be adding a small-group program to its ministry menu and needs people to lead and shepherd those groups. First, it focuses on the ministry position of a small-group leader, drawing up a reasonably detailed ministry description (similar to a job descrip-

tion) that consists of the necessary spiritual gifts, passion, temperament, and so on needed for this ministry. Then it will seek someone with a design that most closely matches the small-group leader's ministry description.[2]

## PRINCIPLES OF AN EFFECTIVE TEAM

This entire book has discussed principles of an effective team in chapter after chapter. But let's get specific; let's try to identify several characteristics of an elder board, a missions committee, the academic affairs committee of a Christian college, or a Christian camp staff. What does a leadership team look like when it operates according to biblical standards?

### Effective Teams Understand Team Goals

Remember our Getzells/Guba model of transactional tension? That will always exist. Individuals bring their own needs and personal agendas to any ministry position. The key to serving on a team is to sublimate those concerns for the good of the corporate ministry group. At the same time, however, the leader of the ministry team makes every effort to see that personal needs of group members are served, neither ignored nor abused. It simply makes sense to recognize that when members of a ministry team do not understand their corporate goals they cannot successfully move toward them.

### Effective Teams Utilize Group Decision Making

Again, it has been popular for decades to describe leadership as singular activity ("groups discuss; individuals make decisions"). This archaic notion, however, has been maligned in recent years by both secular and Christian writers. Em Griffin's book *Getting Together* not only explains the values of group decision making but actually teaches us how to do it, as we explored in chapter 8. Scripture tells us, "Plans fail for lack of counsel, but with many advisers they succeed" (Prov. 15:22). But somehow we have failed to transfer the acknowledged truth of that verse to the way we do business in churches and Christian organizations. There are times, usually in emergency situations, or perhaps where absolute confidentiality is essential, that the individual leader must make a decision alone. My experience demonstrates that when the group shares in 80 percent of the decisions that govern the future of the organization, they are more than happy to let the leader make the other 20 percent when necessary and will trust him or her to do so.

## Effective Teams Share Leadership Responsibility

Larry Osborne talks about building leadership unity through shepherding meetings, times when leadership teams (like boards) meet together to pray; interact with general, devotional, or theological materials (not business); and recognize their corporate rather than competitive function.

> This team building has had a significant impact on our business meetings. They have lost their confrontational edge. I can't remember the last time we had an honest-to-goodness argument. Not that we don't disagree, sometimes strongly, but we found truth in the old saying, "Friends discuss; strangers argue."[3]

But sharing leadership responsibility is more than just agreeing or even agreeing to disagree. Members of a serious leadership team understand that they corporately manage the progress of the church or Christian organization and take collective responsibility for the outcome. They don't blame the pastor; they don't blame the circumstances; they don't blame each other; they don't blame the congregation or the employees; they function as one, anticipating what God will do to honor their commitment, their work, and their prayer.

## Effective Teams Maintain Good Communication

The importance of communication during meetings seems too obvious even to mention. Good team members communicate between meetings as well. If something isn't clear in the minutes, they call each other to make sure they are moving in the same direction. If one is working on a project and another can provide information or connections that might be helpful, they network to make that possible.

Obviously, length of time together is a factor here. Steve Young can communicate with Jerry Rice or John Taylor with a nod of the head or a movement of a shoulder, but a rookie receiver may take years to learn what his quarterback is thinking if he changes the play at the line of scrimmage. Like everything else on an effective team, communication is something all team members work at all the time.

## Effective Teams Evaluate Process as Well as Product

I can't belabor this point again here; it has been so much a part of what we've talked about throughout these chapters. *Product* describes outcome—the final decision, the achievement of the missions conference, or completion of the building project. *Process* describes what went on in the lives of the leadership team as they moved from beginning to the end or from any point to any future point in their relationship. Usually, positive process begins with flexibility in selecting procedures by which the group will operate and includes a good balance between productivity and individual needs. An effective group is cohesive, attractive, and utilizes the abilities of its members.

### STEPS IN TEAM BUILDING

We need not look far for a model of team building. That is precisely what the first four books of the New Testament describe. Of course, they do detail for us the birth, life, death, and resurrection of the Son of God, but along the way they let us watch Jesus finding, grinding, and binding twelve men into a team. Harold Longenecker talks about the selection.

> Servant leaders are not just there, waiting to be picked. They require a suitable climate in which to grow and mature, and it is the task of Christian leaders to help create that climate. A church or group that creates a climate in which God's people can become all that His grace can make them will inevitably grow leaders. . . . Read the Gospels carefully, and the story leaps right out at you. The planting of His church in the world required the training of this little group for leadership in that church.[4]

## Teach Effective Leadership

One more time: *leaders are not born, they are made.* Let's stay with our biblical illustration. Most of us would not have selected the group that Jesus handpicked to change the world. They were not well educated; their experience did not particularly prepare them for ministry; they showed little potential for becoming a unified group; they had a frightening propensity toward intramural quarreling; and they seemed relatively unable to function on their own, stumbling through their assigned duties unless Jesus was right there to watch them every minute.

By the time we find them in the book of Acts, however, they have become a well-functioning, unified group of leaders (with the exception of Judas) whose influence and example marked the early church. Acts offers us a real-life enactment of what these men understood the teaching of Jesus to mean. They learned leadership.

## Build Team Unity

Nothing is more crucial for churches and Christian organizations. How foolish for a congregation to enter an elaborate and perhaps even expensive community evangelism project when at the core of everything they do is a squabbling, backbiting deacon board. As Osborne discovered in his shepherding groups, "It would be nice if unity in Christ guaranteed unity on the board. But human nature being what it is, most groups also need to spend significant time together in order to gel."[5]

## Make Use of Team Abilities

Of course you can't do this until you first discover what those abilities might be. Spiritual gifts, natural talents, experience, skill—all these come in the package of a leadership team. And until we discover how God has gifted and led team members, bringing them to precisely this point in His kingdom purposes, the blend of abilities is hampered by our ignorance. Remember, *lead to your strength; staff to your weakness.* That staffing means building a leadership team with people whose gifts, interests, and abilities complement your own.

## Practice Mutual Submission

Ephesians 5:21 may lead into a passage on husband-wife relations, but the principle of mutual submission applies to all believers. This lies at the core of servant leadership biblically practiced. I cannot say it better than Paul Cedar put it in his wonderful book *Strength in Servant Leadership:*

> In my opinion, every Christian minister, Christian parent, Christian coach—indeed, every Christian involved in any vocation or responsibility of leadership—has one common need: to be a "servant leader!" A leader who serves as Jesus served; a leader who leads as Jesus led! I believe that God is calling all of us to become servant leaders![6]

313

## Teach People to Follow Creatively

Once again, the disciples provide an excellent model of how one learns followership before he or she learns leadership. Indeed, it would probably not be an overstatement to say that one who has not learned followership can never accurately and completely learn leadership.

Picture a Christian college in which the newly appointed academic dean has been brought from another institution after one or two years of service as an instructor. The appointment was made through board influence, or perhaps nepotism, and now senior faculty of twenty and thirty years' experience are expected to follow a neophyte who, though intellectually brilliant, has no idea how to function as an administrative leader.

In a book which deserves more spotlight than it has received, Thomas Gilmore talks about "managing the boss." He offers six explicit points, the last of which fits precisely here:

1. Negotiate shared expectations of the strategic challenges.
2. Think explicitly about the style differences between your old boss and the new one.
3. Build up a picture of the boss's world and assess the relative stakes that are located in your area of responsibility.
4. Assess the boss's strengths and weaknesses and how they fit with your own.
5. Periodically ask your boss for feedback on how you can better support him or her.
6. Work explicitly on followership.

In expanding the sixth point above, Gilmore suggests,

New leaders sometimes tend to over-concentrate on the challenge of leading and underattend to that of following, especially if they have been upwardly-oriented, watching their prior bosses to learn how to lead, reading about leadership, and fantasizing about what they would do when they took charge. In that frame of mind, it can be difficult to confront honestly those aspects of one's role in which the challenge is to be a good follower, aspects that may not have been visible in role models.[7]

## EXAMPLES OF TEAM LEADERSHIP

Perhaps we could have begun the chapter with this section, but I like to let principles precede examples so readers can find the principles illustrated in those examples. I referred earlier to the consistency of team leadership in the book of Acts. Let's look now at four specific segments that give us a life-size, historical, and accurate picture of how Christians work together in ministry teams.

### Selection of Servants—Acts 6:1–7

How easy the apostles would have found it to call all the shots in this situation. A dispute had arisen in the early church regarding cultural discrimination—Greek-speaking widows were being neglected in the congregational care program. Instead, they transferred the entire project immediately back into the hands of those who faced the problems on the front lines. Greek-speaking (Hellenistic) Christians, elected by the Greek-speaking portion of the congregation, formed a ministry team to solve the problem.

Notice the careful wording of the text in verse 3: "We will turn this responsibility over to them." The apostles themselves were a ministry team, and now a second ministry team had been created to take care of other functions. With great emphasis this passage seems to say that the ministry of the Word was not more *important* than the ministry of taking care of widows, just *different*.

### The Antioch Church—Acts 11:19-30

This portion of Acts is one of my favorite passages of Scripture. A church founded by laymen on the run, and led by a lay leader (Barnabas), clearly becomes its own cooperative congregational group when the people themselves decide to send an offering for famine relief in Judea. No special program; no signs, posters, placards, logos, or thermometer charts on the wall! They had been studying the Scriptures for more than a year and understood that believers take care of other believers in need. The entire congregation had become a ministry team after watching Barnabas and Saul work together as their leaders. Talk about modeling! All this seems to come alive after only a year or so of spiritual growth. It can be done!

### Sending of the First Missionaries—Acts 13:1-4

If you miss the plural pronoun throughout the early verses of this chapter, you miss again the function of the Antioch congregation as one large ministry team. In this case they give birth to a smaller ministry team. They pick the candidates; they discuss the attributes; they trust God for the selection; and they send them on their way, a clear indication that the missionaries will report back to the sending congregation. Dennis Williams and I conclude our joint effort, *Volunteers for Today's Church,* with this paragraph:

> When people in any congregation exercise ministry for which God has gifted them through the power of the Holy Spirit, they can, under a caring, nurturing leadership, make exciting things happen. So put words like *duty* and *drudgery* behind you. Stop focusing on maintenance and accept the exciting challenges of the future. Help people find the places God wants them to serve and turn them loose to function effectively in those volunteer ministries.[8]

## The Council at Jerusalem—Acts 15

A cursory reading of this passage might yield some credence to the idea of singular, even autocratic leadership, since James obviously chaired the session. But a more careful study will notice how cautious he was to allow every voice to be heard, to make sure the traditional, as well as the nontraditional, viewpoints were given proper airing and respect, and then to formulate policy for the Gentile churches. Most New Testament scholars believe that James merely verbalized what the entire group had decided and did not originate the regulations for the Gentile churches. Group decision making, clarity of team goals (particularly the Paul/Barnabas mission to the Gentiles), the sharing of leadership responsibility, good communication, and a concern for process as well as product all surface in this passage.

All of this is neither fiction nor foolishness. If we really believe the Bible to be the accurate and absolute Word of the living God, then Christian leaders cannot ignore the overwhelming evidence for participatory leadership style and the development of ministry teams. We find it on page after page of the New Testament. Van Auken calls it "the spirituality principle: teams engaged in Christian ministry are supernaturally empowered, generating a rare kind of fruitfulness nurtured by team member unity, vision and sacrifice. God lovingly shepherds His teams, helping them succeed despite human fallibility and frailty."[9]

FOR FURTHER READING

Cedar, Paul A. *Strength in Servant Leadership*. Waco, Tex.: Word, 1987.

Gilmore, Thomas N. *Making a Leadership Change*. San Francisco: Jossey-Bass, 1988.

Henricksen, Walter A. *Disciples Are Made Not Born*. Wheaton, Ill.: Victor, 1988.

Johnson, Douglas W. *Empowering Lay Volunteers*. Creative Leadership Series, ed. Lyle Schaller. Nashville: Abingdon, 1991.

Longenecker, Harold L. *Growing Leaders by Design*. Grand Rapids: Kregel Resources, 1995.

Malphurs, Aubrey. *Maximizing Your Effectiveness*. Grand Rapids: Baker, 1995.

Senter, Mark. *Recruiting Volunteers in the Church: Resolve Your Recruiting Hassles*. Wheaton, Ill.: Victor, 1990.

Tillapaugh, Frank R. *Unleashing the Church*. Ventura, Calif.: Regal, 1982.

Van Auken, Philip M. *The Well-Managed Ministry*. Wheaton, Ill.: Victor, 1989.

Williams, Dennis E., and Kenneth O. Gangel. *Volunteers for Today's Church*. Grand Rapids: Baker, 1993.

## NOTES

1. Philip Van Auken, *The Well-Managed Ministry* (Wheaton, Ill.: Victor, 1989), 237.

2. Aubrey Malphurs, *Maximizing Your Effectiveness* (Grand Rapids: Baker, 1995), 126.

3. Larry W. Osborne, *The Unity Factor* (Waco, Tex.: Word, 1989), 91.

4. Harold L. Longenecker, *Growing Leaders by Design* (Grand Rapids: Kregel Resources, 1995), 28–29.

5. Osborne, *The Unity Factor*, 91.

6. Paul A. Cedar, *Strength in Servant Leadership* (Waco, Tex.: Word, 1987), 27.

7. Thomas N. Gilmore, *Making a Leadership Change* (San Francisco: Jossey-Bass, 1988), 220.

8. Dennis E. Williams and Kenneth O. Gangel, *Volunteers for Today's Church* (Grand Rapids: Baker, 1993), 154.

9. Van Auken, *Well-Managed Ministry*, 238.

# −19−
## RECRUITING AND
## RETAINING LEADERS

Tim had always wanted to serve his church in some significant way, and now the opportunity had arrived. The pastor put out an all-points-bulletin appeal for someone to serve as a youth sponsor, and Tim, a thirty-five-year-old computer programmer with a working wife and two elementary school children, signed up.

From day one the mix looked and felt wrong. Tim was too far away from his own teenage years to remember what they had been like. Actually, clear memory wouldn't have helped since the cultural and sociological issues facing teenagers had changed dramatically in two decades. Furthermore, his own children were still too young for him to have any taste of what kids deal with in today's world.

Susan did not favor this extra family responsibility from the beginning. The church apparently had no program of leadership development or training for the task, so Tim muddled through as best he could. Amazingly, he continued to serve as a

319

youth sponsor at that church for nearly ten years. He didn't quit. He didn't make any parents angry at him (at least not very often), and he didn't turn off any kids to the gospel and involvement in the church. At first glance, Tim seemed an unlikely but documentable success.

But no one noticed that Tim emerged from the ten years' experience no closer to significant leadership ability than the day he began. Yet he had served faithfully, willingly, and sometimes sacrificially. Because his gifts and abilities lay in something other than sponsoring junior high youth ministries, they disallowed leadership development. Take a look at the diagram below.

The message of the model is simple: *leadership development only takes place when one's strengths overlap a given ministry situation.* Probably in Tim's case we could identify some overlap, so he did make a modicum of progress toward leadership, but, as in all diagrams of this kind, the more the circles overlap,

*Leadership potential is activated whenever a person's strengths overlap with the needs of a given situation.*

Figure 15

the greater the level of leadership development. The situation alone has no flaws in itself, nor does the strength of the potential leader on the right side. The point is that growth in leadership skills only occurs when these two important facets *overlap*. A simple understanding of this diagram can explain a great deal of the leadership vacuum we see in so many churches and Christian organizations.

Someone has suggested that we face three basic problems in helping people serve Christ: misuse, disuse, and abuse. The first refers to employing unqualified teachers and workers; the second, to the many uninvolved Christians who throng our church pews; and the last, to the problem of overburdened workers.

## WHY IS THERE A LEADERSHIP VACUUM TODAY?

Actually, most of the answers here are either spiritual or organizational. The spiritual problems direct attention to the individual Christian's relationship to Jesus Christ; the organizational problems focus on programs and processes that hinder rather than promote leadership development.

### Some Christians Seem Indifferent to Their Responsibility

Some choruses used in music ministry with children and youth give the impression that the purpose and end of salvation is service. Not according to Scripture. The New Testament indicates that believers have been brought to God through Christ in order that our lives might be a witness to Christ's glory and grace. Nevertheless, service forms a distinct part of Christian living. The dynamic passage in Matthew 9:35–38 indicates that the necessity of harvest laborers that originated in the days of Christ continues on to the present. A Christian unwilling to share responsibilities for service demonstrates a deficient spiritual life. He has not come to grips with the New Testament demands upon his time, talent, and entire being.

## Some Lack Confidence in Their Ability to Lead

This problem could be either organismic or organizational. If it results from an unwillingness to trust Christ and the Holy Spirit for effectiveness in service, then the cause points once again to a spiritual inadequacy. If, on the other hand, people lack confidence because of confusion and chaos in the structure of our ministries or because we have not adequately trained them, the problem becomes organizational.

## Some Lack Consecration to Christ

"I don't have time" is a common excuse offered when the nominating committee begins contacting potential leaders. But everyone has the same amount of time—twenty-four hours in a day and seven days in a week. The difference comes in the priority use of that time!

Sometimes Christians should bypass an offer to serve Christ in the church because they must work additional hours to support a family or spend more time with the family in biblical parenting. Often, however, time withheld from ministry ends up in some materialistic enterprise. Income produced may be wanted but not needed. The attention and time of such people may have been directed to a life of self-centeredness and pleasure rather than Christ-centeredness and service.

## Some Misunderstand the Task We Ask Them to Perform

To the question, "Will you serve on the board?" a potential leader ought to direct a number of counter-questions. How long? How often? What do I have to do? What other duties or standards do you expect of me?

The necessity of role analysis (job descriptions) for all ministry tasks seems obvious; no leader can satisfactorily function in a given role unless she understands exactly what that role entails. She should have this information before she is expected to decide whether she will undertake the task. Some workers turn out to be misfits because they have not been placed in positions that correspond to their qualifications and interests.

Remember Tim and his youth group? He was a classic demonstration of an old Peter Drucker cliché: "There are no bad people, only people in the wrong place." Of course Drucker knows there are bad people, but he wants to emphasize that we leaders err repeatedly by confusing willingness with competence and putting good people in places where they can't really function, or at least in places where their leadership strengths cannot develop.

Here again we face an old nemesis—the conflict between organizational roles and individual goals. Christian organizations must realize that people have personal and spiritual needs of their own which must be met and, although they might not be able to specify them accurately, goals which must be satisfied. *When the goals of the individual can correspond directly with the goals of the organization, we are on our way to developing an effective leader.*

## Some Are Ill-Prepared for Ministry Leadership

Secular business organizations spend millions of dollars recruiting new talent. They assume that the organization's progress and continued existence depend upon its ability to enlist, train, and retain people who can competently perform the tasks that form organizational goals. Many churches and ministry organizations, on the other hand, expect workers to walk through the door and ask to be used. We often give little concern to their capabilities since it would be foolish to turn down any volunteer (or so it seems).

This business of willingness and competence has not had sufficient attention in nonprofit organizations, especially in churches. Listen to Ken Callahan:

People learn leadership best in an environment of competency, not willingness. When the team of persons with which one is working is competent, then one can most fully develop one's leadership abilities. It is not necessary that all of the team be extraordinarily and outstandingly competent. Such teams rarely occur. Rather, most effective mission teams have a reasonable range of complementary competencies present.

One mistake pastors make is to look for someone who is willing, not someone who will do it well. **The art is to look for someone who will do it well, not someone who is willing.** Sometimes pastors convince themselves that there is a shortage of leaders in their church, which then becomes their *excuse* for recruiting someone who is willing to do some leadership post rather than someone who would do it well. That simply makes it more difficult to recruit competent leaders.[1]

If Christian organizations want adequate staff, we must employ adequate methods to secure good people. This does not undermine for one minute the essential call of God and the importance of prayer in bringing people into ministry. Indeed, sensitizing people to the call of God and praying clearly for them form a large part of biblical, spiritual recruitment.

### *Some Have Never Been Asked*

Their number may be small, but they are out there. I remember one time being called in by a local church to assist in leadership recruitment. One of the tasks to be filled was the leadership coordination of a nursery program. The pastor told me the committee had looked carefully over the church lists and asked three or four people, all of whom had declined. There was simply no one left.

But in looking over the list one more time, we found a name not previously discussed. When I asked about this woman, they told me that she surely would not be interested and so had not been considered. Talking to the woman herself, however, produced a completely different story. She was not only interested but delighted to serve in this way. With a brief period of orientation and training, she understood the task and performed at a high level of competence.

A single best way to recruit leaders? Probably not. People best learn Christian leadership in principles adapted to a number of different situations. These principles culminate in specific techniques applied to varying situations to achieve satisfactory results. The following eight-step pattern is no magic formula, but I have seen it increase leadership development in a number of churches and ministry organizations who put it into operation in one form or another.

## Conduct a Need-Task Survey

Dennis Williams and I have dealt with recruitment and training in *Volunteers for Today's Church,* and the procedures I want to review here are explained in more detail in that book.[2] Here it will only be necessary to review them briefly. In that book we talk a great deal about the "Need and Task Survey" and the "Talent and Ability Survey." These are considerably more important in a volunteer organization (especially a church) than in an organization that pays its staff.

Usually the human resources (personnel) department of an organization of any size picks up a lot of this information. We would not have hired people in their present positions unless we understood the needs. In the church, however, it is easy to fall into that "willing worker syndrome" so eloquently described by Callahan.

The first time these data are procured they may take the form of a complete listing of every ministry in the church. However, it is actually a *continuing survey.* Departmental superintendents, sponsors, and leaders regularly report through their supervisors to the board of Christian education concerning projected needs, long-range goals, and patterns of growth in their particular ministries.

Every organization should keep a long-range projection on need analysis at all times. Then the leaders can look forward to the kind of people it will carry on and the kind of leaders it will need in one, two, and even five years. On occasion it may happen that a ministry post becomes vacant without warning. This should be the rare exception. If it happens with any amount of frequency, it denotes a deficiency in recruitment policies and long-range planning.

A survey of talent and ability establishes a personal file on every church member. Information in the file could include service interests, experience, abilities, and other pertinent data that will be helpful in placing a given worker in a given position. Team leaders act as a "personnel office" in properly matching people and ministries.

## Relate Every Position to the Mission

The early chapters of this book are not just for pastors and missionaries. Every Christian must become familiar with basic ecclesiology. He must understand his relationship to the collective body and to the ministries of that body in conformity to Ephesians 4. She must grow up unto Christ through engaging in the process of mutual edification with other saints.

We have no room in Christian organizations for self-focused entrepreneurs; a Christian leader dare not view a particular ministry as his own piece of work. *Stewardship is not ownership, and discipleship is not lordship.* Students in a Sunday school class belong to Christ and not the teacher. Money in an evangelism crusade budget is God's, not the treasurer's.

Yet you should not be discouraged or disheartened because your ministry seems small. First Corinthians 12 teaches that the less attractive parts of the body are just as important (and sometimes more important) for bodily functions as those parts more pleasant to look at. Just as the human body must have all the parts working together to function satisfactorily, so it is with all parts of the spiritual body.

No need to bring up the issue of mission again here. Chapter 16 covered that. But we do not develop a mission and then forget it. Every ministry post links its goals and objectives to the central mission of our overall ministry.

## Continually Review Goals and Objectives

Promoting and instructing a congregation in the church's total ministry is not something we do once in a general meeting. We use all the media open to us: sermons from the pulpit, bulletin boards, church bulletins, mailings, church newspaper, personal interviews, Sunday school classes, and even casual conversation. The same holds true in a mission board or college. Reviewing our goals intentionally tells people what our ministry really is and shows them the urgency of total unity and commitment to those ministry outcomes.

## Enlist People to a Common Vision

The field of leadership studies has always had its buzz-words, vocabulary that comes and goes with the popular ideas of a given era. Today you should use *vision* frequently if you want people to sit up and take notice. We have already spelled out the absolutely essential difference between vision and mission if we are to order our ministries correctly. It is also easy to remember the old King James rendering of Proverbs 29:18: "Where there is no vision, the people perish." Calvin Miller argues that "vision plus communication is the winning profile of leadership. Those who can articulate their vision become for God a fulcrum with which He moves the world." But how to keep the fire burning? He continues:

Perhaps it needs to be said that your visions will serve you best, not when you keep them, but when they keep *you*. I want to suggest two ingredients for the recipe of vision keeping. Number one is an adequate quiet time. When you are quiet before the altar of your own trust in God, vision will hold a strong place in your life. Visions grow in quietness, never in the hurry and noise of life. A second ingredient of vision keeping is rehearsal. You must constantly rehearse your dreams. It is never enough to claim that you rehearsed them in the past and that you have memorized their form. Visions require a central altar in our continuing lives. They must be a part of each new day, or soon they will not keep faith with *any* day.[3]

Miller's treatment of vision as a singularity, that is, the possession of a central dominant leader, does not fit the ministry philosophy of this book. Nevertheless, what he says about maintaining corporate and collective vision rings true in a team ministry situation.

### Keep the Team Spirit Fresh

I regret that I came so late in my writings to a strong focus on team leadership. It certainly appears in *Feeding and Leading,* and in numerous journal and magazine articles I have written over the past ten years. But in both earlier editions of this volume I failed to place sufficient emphasis on the corporate and cooperative role of ministry teams.

In the book I coauthored with Dennis Williams, we talk about how "team ministry requires effective nurturing."

Nurturing is not a difficult word to understand, especially for gardeners and parents. Plants and children need a special climate, careful watering and feeding, and sometimes pruning. . . . That's the function every team leader carries out if he wants to be effective in that role. We have already emphasized showing appreciation, finding the right place of ministry for each person, helping people get along together, providing adequate resources, and defining peer fellowship groups. All these are basic.[4]

## Make the Approach Person-Centered

Conveying crisis in a ministry indicates that the organizational structure and its recruiting policies have not functioned properly. Rather than a general call from the pulpit ("Anyone interested in being a youth sponsor please see the pastor after church"), the appropriate board should send its representative to *ask specific people for specific jobs for a specific length of time.* We assume the board will consider the person's gifts and interests.

One progressive St. Louis church has a member on the Board of Christian Education whose only responsibility is to seek out and contact potential church leaders. He makes the initial contact which marks that person for training and service in some appropriate church ministry. He takes people to lunch, visits in their homes, and talks with them about what it means to serve Jesus Christ in the church. The results of such a ministry are rewarding.

## Offer Each Potential Leader a Carefully Prepared Job Analysis

Job analysis (sometimes called "job description" or "role definition") outlines what we ask a leader to do when she accepts a given position. If, for example, the church wishes its Sunday school teachers to attend prayer meeting, make a minimal number of calls each week, spend a certain amount of time in lesson preparation, and arrive at church at a given time on Sunday morning, all this should be specified in the job description or some similar document.

Included in the job description should be some indication of what new leaders may expect from the church, as well as what the church expects from them. Consider the following items adapted from a local church vacation Bible school personnel letter:

(What We Expect from You)
 1. Willingness to serve
 2. Spiritual readiness to serve

3. Preparation for service
4. Faithfulness in service

(What You May Expect from Us)
   1. Competent administration
   2. Training sessions
   3. Early and thorough planning
   4. Guidance at all points

## Do Not Hurry the Candidate's Decision

If we really present an opportunity, a responsibility, and a need rather than a predicament, there should be no need to hurry the decision. The potential leader should be allowed to study the job description carefully, consider the matter in prayer before the Lord, and finally make a decision. If divine sovereignty works within the framework of our ministries (and it does), then we must view a leader's response to the request after prayerful and intelligent consideration by the church leadership as God's will.

This procedure is not particularly profound. On the contrary, its very simplicity can succeed in almost any organization, regardless of how limited the administrative structure. If properly followed, it will provide more leaders who will approach their tasks with a greater sense of responsibility, a more positive attitude in service, and a willingness to accept and utilize the training we provide.

## HOW DOES PHILOSOPHY OF MINISTRY RELATE TO RECRUITMENT?

Philosophy of ministry simply describes why we do what we do instead of something else. The church that decides to go to two services instead of opening a branch church in a nearby town acts upon a philosophy of ministry. A church that conducts a highly concentrated and publicized annual missionary conference exhibits philosophy of ministry.

These various emphases and strategies come from numerous sources. Sometimes tradition plays a major role; the leadership of the pastoral staff and what they have found effective in previous ministry posts hold high profile in ministry philosophy; the competence and assertiveness of elders and deacons as they see the history and mission of that particular congregation; the interpretation of the mission statement that leads a college, for example, to refuse to organize a graduate degree program (or to design one) stems from philosophy of ministry.

Throughout this book I have emphasized the elevation and dignifying of volunteers. Satisfactory recruitment standards actually provide leaders with these necessary elements:

## 1. Incentive

God's people should *want* to serve Him. That desire, however, does not spring up automatically in the heart of the Christian—particularly the Christian whose level of maturity is somewhat slow in developing. It becomes our responsibility as team leaders to try to build incentive into the recruiting program. When the potential leader looks at ministry, she tries to determine whether or not she wants to be identified with it. If the standards are high and the requirements significant but reasonable, she will respond more positively than if it appears that she may be joining a shoddy enterprise.

## 2. Improved Efficiency

In any given leadership situation, some current problems cause difficulty to the ministry. Perhaps nothing can be done about them now without upsetting the whole program. What ought to concern us, therefore, is that these problems do not breed more problems. Mediocrity can only reproduce itself or its

331

retarded offspring, inferiority. Effectiveness in ministry ought to be always improving, but this can't happen if people do not grasp our ministry philosophy.

## 3. Evaluation Guides

If we evaluate our ministry, we will have to use some acceptable norm or standard as a comparative measure. To ask anyone to assume a task and then evaluate that task on vague and emotive measures yields a distorted situation. Leaders must know what we require of them and expect that they will be judged on how they have measured up to that requirement. Evaluation always relates to objectives, and objectives ought to demonstrate clear indication of standards.

At times it will seem that high standards in a ministry philosophy impede recruitment, but in the final analysis they will lead to better leaders and a higher opinion of ministry among the congregation or constituency. Churches and Christian organizations ought to have clear-cut expectations of their leaders, having provided them with the wherewithal to do the task well.

A periodic check of staff accomplishments, needs, and problems will benefit them and us. Self-evaluation is important as well, and can be carried on through workers' conferences, questionnaire sheets, and group discussions.

### HOW IMPORTANT IS RECOGNITION?

Elevating and dignifying Christian leadership includes a genuine demonstration of appreciation for those who have served. There are some very obvious benefits in a thorough appreciation program:

1. *People feel noticed.* They can see that leaders do not take them for granted but rather thank God for the work they do.

2. *Potential leaders can see that we really consider ministry important—important enough to recognize publicly.*

3. *The total organization is made aware of the importance and centrality of volunteers.* Every member may not be invited to some special event, but the announcing and carrying out of such gatherings will serve as a reminder that ministry happens by design and not by accident.

A number of methods can demonstrate appreciation for volunteers; the following is only a partial list:

- an annual appreciation banquet
- a dedication service at the beginning of each year
- personal letters from the pastor and/or other church officers or organizational leaders
- periodic notes of appreciation in the church bulletin or other literature produced by the church or organization
- special elections such as "teacher of the year" or "deacon of the month"
- a public wall chart that shows who takes responsibility for what particular ministry in the church and perhaps even a listing of what training courses each has completed
- free transportation and expenses to special seminars or professional training conferences
- an annual appreciation picnic
- giving of gifts (such as a book or magazine subscription) at Christmas
- a regular and sincere personal "thank you" regularly given by the senior pastor, principal, district superintendent, and other leaders or officers

The recruitment and enlistment of workers and teachers in ministry organizations depend upon the alleviation of spiritual and organizational problems. When we raise spiritual standards and immaturity gives way to maturity in Christian living, the innate conviction of dedicated lives will solve any spiritual problems we face in recruitment.

But the central role of climate or environment looms large

in the recruitment process. Leadership must be broadly understood to affirm and practice the universal priesthood of believers
in Christian organizations. This breadth of understanding now
permeates solid secular leadership work as well.

> We frequently fall into the habit of associating leaders and
> leadership characteristics only with the top of the organization:
> senior business executives, political figures, military top brass,
> sports team captains, and coaches. It is a natural tendency,
> since they are the most visible and highest-profile leaders.
> However, in the past, the present, and certainly in the future,
> true leadership is needed across and throughout all types of
> organizations. The character and qualities that are found in
> true leaders are essential at all levels of responsibility.[5]

So what does all of this have to do with Tim and his
junior high youth group? Two keys dominate this chapter:

1. *Leadership only develops when a person's strengths fit
the ministry situation in which he or she is placed.*

2. *In recruiting and retaining leaders, willingness will ultimately drive out competence if we focus only on the former and
ignore the latter.*

We find good people and hold on to them because of the
general leadership climate into which we invite them to serve.
Tim liked what he saw and enjoyed his ten years with the kids in
the youth group. The fact that he made little progress in leadership was not his fault but ours. Recruitment done correctly is not
necessarily easy, but it is certainly possible. And we enhance
recruitment dramatically by a serious and professional commitment to the retaining of leaders whom we have begun to develop
and in whose lives God is clearly working.

### FOR FURTHER READING

Callahan, Kennon L. *Effective Church Leadership*. San Francisco:
Harper & Row, 1990.

Gangel, Kenneth O. *Feeding and Leading*. Wheaton, Ill.: Victor, 1989.

Johnson, Douglas W. *The Care and Feeding of Volunteers.* Creative Leadership Series, ed. Lyle E. Schaller. Nashville: Abingdon, 1978.

Ratcliffe, Donald, and Blake J. Neff. *The Complete Guide to Religious Education Volunteers.* Birmingham, Ala.: Religious Education, 1992.

Stevens, R. Paul. *Liberating the Laity: Equipping All the Saints for Ministry.* Downers Grove, Ill.: InterVarsity, 1985.

Tillapaugh, Frank R. *Unleashing the Church.* Ventura, Calif.: Regal, 1982.

Westing, Harold J. *Multiple Church Staff Handbook.* Grand Rapids: Kregel, 1985.

Williams, Dennis E., and Kenneth O. Gangel. *Volunteers for Today's Church.* Grand Rapids: Baker, 1993.

Wortley, Judy. *The Recruiting Remedy: Taking the Headache Out of Finding Volunteers.* Elgin, Ill.: David C. Cook, 1990.

## NOTES

1. Kennon L. Callahan, *Effective Church Leadership* (San Francisco: Harper & Row, 1990), 165.

2. Dennis E. Williams and Kenneth O. Gangel, *Volunteers for Today's Church* (Grand Rapids: Baker, 1993).

3. Calvin Miller, *The Empowered Leader* (Nashville: Broadman & Holman, 1995), 67.

4. Williams and Gangel, *Volunteers for Today's Church,* 145.

5. C. William Pollard, "The Leader Who Serves," in *The Leader of the Future,* ed. Hesselbein et al., (San Francisco: Jossey-Bass, 1996), 256.

# —20—
# TRAINING AND
# PLACING VOLUNTEERS

W ayne Jacobsen illuminates the theme of this chapter in a paragraph that appeared a few years ago in *Leadership* magazine:

> If I had a choice between getting all the people in my city to an evangelistic crusade or having a lay person with an infectious love for Jesus work beside each of them at their jobs for one week, I'd certainly choose the latter. The same goes for our church's gatherings: Rather than have a few professionals participate while most watch, I'd choose to see every member actively involved.[1]

The church's strategic task can only be accomplished through the use of an army of volunteers serving effectively under the direction of a few professional leaders. And effective service requires more than willingness; it requires training.

To become a teacher in even the youngest grades, one must study content and methods for several years after high school. In contrast to this requirement, willing people in churches and ministry organizations assume responsibility without even knowing what is expected of them, much less having been trained for the job. Long ago Wyckoff reminded us,

> Leadership is a function of the church. Leadership training is basically a matter of making the nature and mission of the church clear, establishing the functions of leadership in light of the nature and mission of the church, and selecting and educating persons to know those functions well and to perform them skillfully.[2]

Leaders should be given basic training in the content of Scripture and the process of ministry. In the progressive organization, however, the trained leader will also understand the entire ministry mission and see his place in it. Many individual problems that face the leader will be dealt with in the training sessions. Also, a certain fellowship develops as leaders learn side by side in a training program. Jacobsen continues:

> The challenge to use every person in ministry presents us with the same alternatives. If a tidy church is our objective, we'd better make sure every important task is put in the hands of full-time professionals.
> But if our eyes are on the harvest, we'd better involve everyone, and cleaning up messes occasionally is just part of the price. As a young father said recently, "It took me a lot longer to make breakfast this morning; my kids helped me."
> That won't always be so as believers mature. And in the meantime, as we risk the problems in equipping the laity, they'll reap a harvest no team of professionals can match.[3]

## INFLUENCES ON LEADERSHIP BEHAVIOR

Team leadership development means more than offering a certain program, studying key books, or viewing a set of videos. It produces future leaders by any process available, providing the process lines up with biblical principles.

Ability to lead depends to some extent upon previous leadership experience, because the leader transfers learning from what he has done before to the new task. The traditional principle of *apperception,* developed and described by Herbart, plays a significant role in the process of leadership development. As we watch developing leaders move through various age levels, attempting different and increasingly more difficult and responsible tasks, we recognize that all of life prepares us for leadership.

The transfer of learning that takes place can be either positive or negative:

1. *Positive transfer of learning facilitates team leadership performance.* The more a new leadership situation approximates previous ones, the more behavior patterns may be transferred. A person who plays the trombone, for example, would not find that skill particularly helpful in learning to play the organ. On the other hand, a person who plays the piano for several years could make a transfer to the organ with minimal difficulty.

One church with which I worked designed an attractive and effective elder-in-training program. We searched for young men in the congregation who loved the Lord but had little background in leadership behavior. The basic qualification was an admission that they did not presently meet the biblical qualifications for elders but would be willing to work toward that end.

We designed a three-year program, taking them through those kinds of ministry experiences—from person to public, from private to platform—which accentuated transfer of learning. We couldn't guarantee that at the end of the three years the congregation would elect them elders just because they'd finished the program, but our purpose (and theirs) was to get them ready.

2. *Negative transfer of learning is detrimental to performance.* Negative learning transference can happen when a leader carries old behavior patterns into a new situation. Consider, for example, a rural pastor whose homespun, folksy style helped his rural congregation feel right at home. Moving into the city and assuming the pastorate of a larger and more sophisticated church,

he applies the same jargon, uses farming illustrations, and acts as though he had not changed positions. The negative carryover of behavior in this situation hinders effective leadership.

A similar situation occurs when a high school student enters college. In high school a fixed schedule required her presence in a given room at a given hour all through the day. Assignments were specified, and she found little need for independent thinking and decision making. Now in college she not only chooses her courses but must do individual research and be responsible for her own learning. If she expects the same kind of enforcement that characterized high school days, she may soon be listed among college dropouts.

We say that all of life prepares us for leadership; certainly most kinds of experiences and situations during various age levels either help or hinder team leadership development.

## Childhood Influences in Leadership Training

The earlier one's effectiveness as a leader, the greater the present success in leadership. Leadership training does not begin in senior high; it begins during preschool years. Children are influenced in many ways. Some influences are negative, others positive. Parents, churches, and schools need to revitalize various opportunities for leadership influence during childhood years.

1. *The family.* How we teach a child to act and react within the context of his own home is the most crucial factor in leadership development for the first five years, and maybe for the first fifteen. There must be a climate of acceptance, love, and faith bounded by a clear-cut fence of obedience. Discipline is extremely crucial during these years and is not to be confused with punishment. It is the setting of boundaries—the narrowing of the line so that the child walks in the path which his parents have set up for him. Punishment becomes necessary only when discipline fails.[4]

A child properly loved in her own home—who learns to live within the proper biblical bounds of obedience and discipline; who learns to accept herself, her parents, and her social status with ease and understanding; who learns consideration for others as well as proper care for her own things; and who develops a perception of God's will and Word in her own life—has begun the path to satisfactory Christian leadership.

2. *The local church.* A church that is serious about training leadership will set up its entire educational program so that, from the earliest years in the nursery, children will learn to grow to maturity in Christ and accept a proper responsibility for serving Him. Such a church will construct a curriculum that helps the child early develop an appreciation for the Word of God. She learns how to apply it in her everyday life and understands how to relate to other children.

Proper and competent organization of training experiences all through childhood years contributes to the establishing of a team leadership climate. Children should also establish and maintain a proper concept of the church so that, as soon as possible, they can comprehend their roles and responsibilities in the body of Christ.

3. *The individual classroom.* Perhaps we should say here "training experience" rather than refer specifically to a "classroom." Increasingly churches and Christian organizations are moving away from formal classroom training programs to mentoring, internships, and on-the-job preparation. But certainly in the childhood years the classroom is important.

Teaching procedures and the atmosphere in which children learn at church are significant factors in their growth into leadership. Simple participation, such as reciting Scripture verses, giving reports, involvement in groups, and various kinds of responsibility, lays a foundation for accepting more significant leadership in later years.

4. *The Christian school.* Public schools focus on the development of civic leadership and social responsibility. Christian schools develop Christian leadership. Many believe that ministry leadership develops more thoroughly in a Christian school than

in a public school. In recent decades many churches have begun Christian elementary and secondary schools as part of their educational programs.

An increase in size and quality of church educational programs, a result of the church education movement of the last forty years, now makes it possible for some congregations to provide satisfactory educational activities for the entire week instead of just on Sunday. In a parochial organization the church controls the educational program and the selection of teachers. It can therefore provide an instructional setting that lends itself to the preparation of leadership. Some students will become effective lay people. Others will go on to further Christian education and become professional leaders heading up ministry teams in a variety of Christian organizations.

## Adolescent Influences in Leadership Training

As children mature into adolescence, the leadership pattern changes from coercive to persuasive, from overt enforced discipline to less dependent, problem-solving procedures. As independence increases, leadership potential becomes more apparent and leadership opportunities more frequent.

In training adolescents in leadership, the greatest single factor, both negative and positive, is the team. Teenagers are profoundly influenced by the thought and behavior patterns of their peers; we cannot deny that. But strong Christian parents still hold great influence. In either case, effective group work and team cooperation create essential experiences.

The team provides several essential ingredients of teen life:

1. *Social relationships with members of his or her own sex and members of the opposite sex.*

2. *Competition within the crowd and between the particular crowd and other crowds.*

3. *The sharing of peer problems.* These problems may

never be solved, but the opportunity to share them without adult interference is one of the attractions of the group.

4. *Opportunities to exercise leadership in various capacities.* This can range from being the toughest kid on the block to being a duly elected student-body president in high school.

5. *A source of strength against adult authority.* Any Christian leader developing leaders at the youth level must face and handle the matter of peer pressure in the teen years. Many social proficiencies, essential to leadership, must be learned during this time of life:

- Christian social ethics and relationships
- Christian etiquette
- proper grooming
- group activity, both as a follower and as a leader
- public oral communication

Other skills, such as athletic development, may not be essential to present and future leadership but can be very beneficial. A pastor who played basketball in high school can use that skill later in working with the teenagers in his church. A missionary who sang in various high school music groups will almost surely use that experience on the field.

The influences of peers are not necessarily bad. The wise Christian leader will use them to positive advantage in training teenagers for present and future leadership.

## *Adult Influence in Leadership Training*

At this point many churches, and to a lesser extent, other kinds of Christian organizations, have not kept up. They fail to move from pedagogy (the process of teaching children) to andragogy (the process of teaching adults). We cannot prepare adults for leadership by spoon-feeding them increasing doses of information. Of course they need to know the Scriptures, basic Christian doctrine, and other content essential to effective ministry. But teaching adults is different, which we know from vast amounts of research that have been carried out in the past twenty years.[5]

1. *Different needs.* Adults approach learning with a different set of development tasks than do children and young people. Educationally, a need is not a need until the adult learner realizes it. So forcing adults through training programs they don't think they need is a useless and frustrating experience. Always begin with need analysis through group interviews, observation, self-evaluation, and other kinds of testing.

2. *Different experiences.* Adults bring an enormous background to any leadership training situation. In many cases, that background includes work habits, good and bad, that were learned in previous positions. In addition, throw in their educational years, family and domestic lifestyle, and we begin to see immediately that the issue of leadership training becomes very different at the adult level.

3. *Different attitudes.* We have conditioned children to learn because it is their duty. They go to school because they must; they study algebra because geometry is coming next year; they work through science and civics with the ever-present promise, "Trust me—you'll need this some day."

All of that no longer influences adults where the key word is "immediacy." In any kind of leadership training program, the adult says to the training director and the organization, "Show me something I can use now and I may take time to listen."

4. *Different groupings.* The age grading so crucial to us throughout childhood and teen years tends to fade into insignificance in adult years. To be sure, people twenty-five years of age probably have more in common with each other than they do with fifty-five-year-olds. But a young couple of thirty-five with a ten-year-old child have more in common with a couple forty-five who also have a ten-year-old than they would with another couple of thirty-five who have no children at all. See the connection?

Needs and experiences have become the dominant issues of life; age has faded into the background.

5. *Different methods.* Teachers in classes across the world still teach adults as though they were children. The teachers plan the objectives, do all the study, talk for forty-five minutes, and wonder why nobody seems interested. This is not a book about teaching, but we do precisely the same thing in many leadership training programs.

One error that many churches and other ministries make in providing training situations for adults is to conceive of this training only as technical specialization for a particular task. Adult leadership training should be a much more comprehensive and embracive program. Certainly we want more effective teachers in our Sunday school classrooms, but we also want more effective parents in the homes of our congregation. Leadership is just as important at family devotions as it is in the worship services at church.

## COMPONENTS OF A TRAINING/PLACING PROGRAM

Often when we talk about standards in leadership training, we refer to standards we want to inculcate in potential leaders. That's proper and necessary; but we must also place high-quality standards on the training program itself. It doesn't matter whether you work with Young Life, Campus Crusade, a college or seminary, or a local church—any effective leadership development program that trains and places people in positions of ministry carries certain basic qualities.

### Clear Objectives

You knew this was coming, didn't you? Unless we understand what we're trying to do in training, we'll end up with frustrated people and frustrated training directors. As indicated earlier, the program may at times be general since not everyone knows exactly what ministry God has called him or her to perform. But when that crucial piece of information becomes available, then we train toward specific leadership goals. Training an elder, for example, is vastly different from training a preschool director. The end results of what they know, feel, and can do aim toward two totally different, but equally important, types of ministry.

## Quality Personnel

Here we have a two-sided coin. Obviously we want quality personnel to head the training program. That does not necessarily mean the pastor or regional director. We need someone who understands team leadership development even if he or she is not the highest titled person in the organization.

But of course we're also looking for quality personnel to participate in the program. I thought through this a great deal as a pastor and concluded I am looking for at least four basic qualities in volunteers who enter training programs:

1. *Spiritual maturity.* Perhaps I should say spiritual "maturing" since we are all on a journey which leads to the ultimate goal of perfection in heaven, not on earth. But any leadership development program takes a giant step forward when you can begin with people who demonstrate a reasonable level of spiritual maturity.

2. *Leadership skills.* We do not just look for the potential to eventually develop some leadership skills, but some present evidence. Obviously I'm talking about adults or perhaps late teens who have had some opportunity to gain these skills. Leadership is learned behavior, but I'd like to at least start with some skill level.

3. *Learning potential.* Here we must consider intelligence, willingness, and, if possible, even eagerness to move forward in the challenges of Christian ministry. Every Christian leader knows it is nearly impossible to break through the shell of an adult who

has convinced himself that he cannot learn, or who believes she does not need what you have to offer.

4. *Cooperative attitude.* Leadership is relational. People who cannot get along with each other in a basic training program have little chance of getting along on a leadership team.

## Growing Responsibility

If a program with clear objectives trains quality people, we can expect a growing responsibility level—even among those often-criticized boomers. Remember the elder training program mentioned above? We wanted to be sure we started out with foundational things that wouldn't frighten candidates away from the program. We learned that leadership candidates felt most comfortable starting with *physical* kinds of ministry tasks (setting up chairs, taking roll, handling something about the overall plant and property of the church); then they began to feel increasingly comfortable with *program* responsibilities (reading the Scripture on Sunday morning, hosting a Bible study class in their homes); and finally they worked to the highest level of leading other *people*. If we reversed that and threw our trainees immediately into some leadership responsibility where they encountered lack of interest, unfaithfulness, absenteeism, and many other things that leaders deal with all the time, they would quickly become discouraged and begin to talk about dropping out of the program.

## Persistent Communication

People involved in a training program need to stay in touch with each other and with their training leaders. We can't be too busy to stay in touch, answer questions over the phone, and offer a Barnabas-like relationship all the way along the line. We keep their needs in mind and tailor the program to their rate of growth. We deny and denounce a closed leadership style that keeps them shut out from the very people who should be mentoring them. And as they grow, we welcome them into the circle of leaders. Paul Hiebert warns of the mixed blessings and dangers in such openness:

> Training leaders is a more difficult task for we must train them to think and to make decisions on their own. But this is threatening, for it means that they can and must challenge our own beliefs and plans. Key to the process is to teach them to critique what we ourselves have taught. There is no ego trip involved in this. Rather, we expect in the end to be set aside as new leaders take over, teach new ideas and set new courses of action.[6]

Are you ready for that?

### Niche Selection

Training and placing are not the same, but they are inseparably related. People who have worked through a training program of any rigor expect to be involved in useful ministry just as college graduates expect to find a job after they receive a diploma. Van Auken talks about "the niche principle" in which "people who occupy a special place on the team feel special and perform in a special way. Team niches humanize team work."[7]

### STRUCTURING EFFECTIVE TRAINING

We cannot divorce a discussion of leadership training from the issue of ministry philosophy discussed earlier. All ministry groups must have a clear understanding of how their particular service contributes to the total church mission and its strategy to achieve the goals that derive from the mission. When we keep this clear, each group or individual plans training experiences in cooperation, not in competition, with other ministries. Then we have a synchronized schedule of training processes, a cooperative balance in the recruitment of possible workers, and a sincere appreciation for ministries other than our own.

No specific training courses can be effectively designed until preparatory work has provided a satisfactory organizational climate for leadership. That climate (to hammer it home yet one more time) includes involvement in a ministry team with clear-cut goals and harmonious working relationships.

The church or organization that is able to employ a full-time director of training (or perhaps minister of education) will certainly benefit from his leadership in this area. A properly trained missions director will supervise training as well as teach several of the courses. A Christian school board must give wholehearted support to training new faculty. Enthusiasm and cooperation must accompany every approach to developing new leaders in Christian organizations.

## _Various Methods of Training_

There is probably no single best method of leadership training in any ministry. A church, for example, that actively produces leaders usually utilizes various approaches to training. Perhaps no organization will utilize all the following methods, but a flexible approach with several opportunities to prove one's leadership skills is preferred over a single course program.

1. _The coaching plan._ This personal approach to leadership training focuses on the pastor's or team leader's working with one or a few developing leaders through personal mentoring.

2. _Utilization of a training consultant._ Sometimes it is helpful to hire a specialist to direct a training program that may include evaluation and recommendations for change.

3. _Apprenticeship._ In this system new leaders are trained by watching and helping experienced leaders. After serving in this capacity for three or perhaps even six months, the rookie may be ready to assume responsibility for her own ministry. Apprenticeship should probably be accompanied by a more formal leadership training approach.

4. _Support leaders._ Every organization should have a

corps of people who serve periodically under the supervision of a veteran. This is different, for example, from a cadet teacher program in that a person may serve as a substitute for a number of years, teaching quite sporadically until he or she finally takes a class of his or her own.

5. *Visits to other ministries.* New leaders learn by watching a better trained leader in action, not with the goal of importing methods from another place but in order to involve themselves in observation.

6. *Workshops.* Bible conferences and campuses periodically conduct laboratories or clinics in Christian leadership, and emerging leaders should be involved in such programs.

7. *Conventions.* Regional, state, and national conventions sponsored by professional organizations (like the Professional Association of Christian Educators) or denominations provide much help for local church leaders.

8. *Cooperative training schools.* Leadership training can be conducted on a one-night-a-week basis for a period of three months or so. If a single church can't provide this kind of training program, perhaps a cooperative venture with several other churches would work.

9. *Regularly scheduled training classes.* Classes can be held annually in any Christian organization serious about leadership training.

10. *Staff meetings.* We should view staff meetings as a leadership training time. Although informal in style, the exchange of information and agreement on goals during these weekly or monthly sessions are crucial to teach unity and effectiveness.

11. *Library.* College and seminary libraries make books available on all phases of Christian leadership. Active use is necessary here. Having the books on the shelves will not help us.

12. *In-service training.* This general term involves many of the above methods. Its main distinguishing feature emphasizes the training of people already involved in the program rather

than potential leaders. Leaders should never be allowed to feel they have "arrived" because they have earned a diploma or certificate. New methods, new ideas, and resolution of continuing problems are brought into focus in a proper in-service training program.

13. *Correspondence courses.* Your organization actually has less control over this kind of program, and it is more difficult to build motivation. Nevertheless, satisfactory courses are available from Moody Bible Institute (Chicago), Taylor University (Fort Wayne), the Institute of Theological Studies (Grand Rapids), as well as other sources.

All these and many more approaches to training can be very effective. But as we point out in *Volunteers for Today's Church,*

> The most effective training for the people in your church is that which you design and carry out locally. Usually the broader the outside training experience, the less likely it will meet the specific needs of your workers. A program designed in your church can address your particular needs and will be much more effective.[8]

## *Enlisting Trainees*

Christian ministries have a task even more difficult than providing training—getting our people to use it. In a church, need and task surveys are essential and the Christian education committee has access to this information, so we can approach specific people for specific jobs for a specific length of time. We use the same approach for leadership training—personal and precise invitation.

The other part of training, however, aims to train all adults of the congregation so that they will be ready for specific leadership opportunities as they become available. The following seven steps may be helpful:

1. *Use personal appeal.* It's fine to advertise a leadership

training class and attempt to inform everybody through various media. In the final analysis, however, we must speak to specific people about becoming involved in the program. Just as some volunteer for service and others need to be asked, so some will volunteer for training, but others will need to be asked, even coaxed.

2. *Use all available public promotion and publicity.* This will include bulletins, periodic mailings, announcement boards, posters, and verbal announcements. No one should be able to say that she did not know leadership training was available.

3. *Impress present leaders with their responsibility to produce leadership.* They should see themselves not only as holding office in a given agency or organization but also as sharing in the developing process of other leaders for that agency. Every leader becomes a potential recruiter of other leaders (see chapter 14).

4. *Recognize leadership achievement.* One church has an entire section of the vestibule devoted to the names and pictures of congregational leaders, specifying what ministries they perform in the church. Under each name and picture hangs a long ribbon upon which everyone can see the diplomas or achievement awards earned through leadership training programs. It reminds me of a medical doctor displaying his credentials on his office wall. Such a high respect for leadership development tends to dignify training and draw others to it.

5. *Set high standards for all ministries.* The use of certificates or diplomas is helpful in this regard, as well as genuine appreciation of the leader's desire to better herself. As we have noted earlier, a dedication service at the beginning of the educational year and an appreciation banquet at the end help build incentive for training and service.

6. *Put people to work.* Even more than college students, adults want to see the practical value of what they learn. To always sit in adult education classes or training programs and never utilize the information is a stagnating experience. That is

why in-service programs more highly motivate trainees than programs that are designed for potential leaders only.

7. *Require reports of all leaders.* The reports should record what professional growth has taken place during the year and how the leader has sought to improve himself in his leadership role.

We will continue to hear the standard objections: "no time," "not interested," and "we've never had a training program here before." We must not be discouraged when these problems arise, however, but we must work even harder to pinpoint the fallacy of such reasoning and the absolute necessity of training leadership in ministries.

What Christian organizations attempt to do in securing and training leadership is not dissimilar to what industry does to obtain employee commitment. Milton Valentine and Robert Graham, writing in *Northwest Business Management* magazine, apply the so-called "stages of identity development" to this problem. They demonstrate the process of bringing a worker from mistrust to trust, from self-doubt to initiative, from inferiority to industry, and from despair to integrity. In their conclusion they say:

> What all of this seems to suggest is that the pattern of identity development also fits the pattern of work development. . . . Specifically, what is suggested is a planned induction of each employee through each level and stage of development. Begin by providing a firm, clear structure, modify this to allow the employee greater individual involvement and commitment as time goes on; and be consistent with general recognition. Begin, too, by developing trust. Look for signs of trouble and provide possible answers: poor quality performance, for example, perhaps suggests feelings of inferiority and non-involvement. . . . Management is, after all, an individual and clinical business, an art based on several sciences, but it is always and necessarily a spontaneous and ever-changing art. It involves the activity of maintaining and advancing the human condition by human beings and through perception.[9]

The same basic principles operate in a church or mission. True, we want new leaders to commit not to the organization but rather to its Head, Jesus Christ. Nevertheless, the New Testament demonstrates that a greater commitment to Christ will bring a greater commitment to the work of His kingdom. The kind of training suggested in this chapter is a vast undertaking for any local organization. Yet the benefits outweigh the trouble and expense involved. Too long has the church floated down the ministry stream using broken oars to propel a leaky boat. The time has come to patch up the holes, mount the motor, and head for specific ports of new vision.

This last decade of the twentieth century must be a time of adult education. Christian organizations that want to get serious about growth will evaluate and enrich their adult team leadership development.

*Developing a climate in which effective leadership training can take place is more important than constructing specific training experiences.* People of all ages must feel that we want to help them become better disciples and more effective leaders for Christ. When we deliver, we can design and develop leadership teams that advance our ministries and the global cause of the gospel.

### FOR FURTHER READING

Gangel, Kenneth O. *Feeding and Leading.* Wheaton, Ill.: Victor, 1989.

Gangel, Kenneth O., and James C. Wilhoit. *The Christian Educator's Handbook on Adult Education.* Wheaton, Ill.: Victor, 1993.

McKillip, Jack. *Need Analysis: Tools for the Human Services and Education.* Newbury Park, Calif.: Sage, 1987.

Van Auken, Philip M. *The Well-Managed Ministry.* Wheaton, Ill.: Victor, 1989.

Ver Straten, Charles A. *How to Start Lay-Shepherding Ministries.* Grand Rapids: Baker, 1983.

Williams, Dennis E., and Kenneth O. Gangel. *Volunteers for Today's Church.* Grand Rapids: Baker, 1993.

## NOTES

1. Wayne Jacobsen, "Five Reasons Not to Equip Lay People," *Leadership* (Summer 1988): 44.

2. D. Campbell Wyckoff, *The Gospel and Christian Education* (Philadelphia: Westminster, 1959), 165.

3. Jacobsen, "Five Reasons Not to Equip Lay People," 49.

4. Kenn Gangel and Betty Gangel, *Your Family* (Gresham, Oreg.: Vision House, 1995), 145–55.

5. Kenneth O. Gangel and James C. Wilhoit, *The Christian Educator's Handbook on Adult Education* (Wheaton, Ill.: Victor, 1993).

6. Paul G. Hiebert, "Training Leaders, Training Followers," *Theology, News and Notes* 36, no. 2 (June 1989): 23.

7. Philip Van Auken, *The Well-Managed Ministry* (Wheaton, Ill.: Victor, 1989), 238.

8. Dennis E. Williams and Kenneth O. Gangel, *Volunteers for Today's Church* (Grand Rapids: Baker, 1993), 111.

9. Milton Valentine and Robert Graham, "A Method for Obtaining Employee Commitment," *Northwest Business Management* (Spring 1967).

# —21—
# Supervising
# Staff

In Christian ministry we must maintain a dynamic tension between the concepts of *gift* and *call*. We know from the New Testament that the Holy Spirit sovereignly gives to each believer a spiritual gift which He intends that person to use in the service of Christ through the church. Often Christian leaders evidence multiple gifts; some Bible scholars believe God calls these people into positions of "professional" leadership in the church, both in local congregations and in education, literature, and world mission. Remember, we can only properly understand our roles in Christian leadership when we understand our spiritual gifts and develop their capacity.

But the other dimension, the concept of call, is rather like the rudder that steers the ship. None of the spiritual gifts delineated in the New Testament carries any geographical or age-group connotation. No one, for example, has the gift of "missionary work in Africa" or "ministry to inner-city youth." The gift describes the *what* of ministry; the call designates the *where*. We should not be upset when a missionary who has been serving, let us say, in Germany, decides at one point that God has called her to switch to a ministry among German-speaking people in Argentina.

Supervisory leaders must recognize both of these crucial ingredients as biblical components. Both Sunday school superintendents and college deans must consider the gift of teaching in their faculties, and also impress upon them the issue of being called to that specific ministry rather than to club work, parachurch ministry, or youth leadership. Both Peter and Paul used multiple gifts for Christian ministry, certainly including the gift of proclamation (prophecy). But God distinctly called Paul to utilize his gift as an itinerant missionary-evangelist establishing new churches among the Gentiles, whereas Peter served primarily among Jewish Christians.

The concepts of *gift* and *call,* if taken seriously, have profound implications for the way we recruit workers, the way we supervise their activities, and the way we evaluate their performance. This chapter will explore some of those implications.

## DEVELOPING A CHRISTIAN
## CONCEPT OF WORK AND MINISTRY

Already in this book I have referred to Abraham Zaleznik's *Human Dilemmas of Leadership.* Zaleznik concerns himself with the relation of an individual to the organization, and he writes out of a secular, industrial-management context.

Perhaps the key concept of his book has to do with the acceptance of human tension and conflict as a condition of existence and an opportunity for change and progress in the interrelationships between the people and organizations. His psychoanalytical framework, with emphasis on Freud and Piaget, drifts far from a biblical frame of reference. Nevertheless, he explores several crucial issues: conflicts in work, authority and self-esteem, subordination, equality, rivalry, status, group formations, and other common problems.

We have often failed to recognize that these problems do not exist only in the management-labor relations of the UAW or AT&T. They also present cardinal points of interpersonal difficulty in a Christian publishing house, an evangelical college or seminary, and a local church.

## *Understanding Human Nature*

Interestingly enough, Zaleznik attacks what he calls "the Utopian View" of human nature, denying inherent good and rejecting the idea that the natural course of human life moves toward personal growth or self-actualization. He substitutes his own position, which he dubs "the Individualistic View," emphasizing human capability and the necessity for assuming responsibility in work relationships. According to Zaleznik, the historic model of work unfolds in three parts: tension represents a need; activity results from the tension; and a discharge results from the gratification of the action. Both rivalry and equality afford developmental crises for the individual.

No organization can solve this problem, but it can "foster ideas which make developmental gains worth pursuing." Perhaps the most significant sentence in the book is Zaleznik's perceptive analysis of the key problem in personnel relations: "The unsolved problem in understanding man in organization centers around the inability of existing theory to grasp the essential dynamics of the individual, and from this understanding to formulate a true psychosocial theory of organization and leadership."[1]

What does all this have to do with a Christian view of work and ministry? Simply this: Zaleznik identified the crucial problem as a failure of all existing secular theories to correctly analyze the nature of people, their understanding of themselves, and their relationship with each other. Unfortunately, his neutral view of human nature also misunderstands the issue, and, as in all rejections of revelational truth, ends up with a perverted concept of reality. The Bible teaches that people are neither good nor neutral, but essentially evil in nature (Isa. 53; Rom. 1–3).

The Christian view of humanity, so often characterized as low, is really a very high view. The Bible teaches that we were created in the image of God and that Christians are bona fide members of His family. Even Christian administrators involved with personnel in a secular organization must understand that the people they lead are potential restored images and therefore deserving of genuinely Christian treatment (Col. 4:1).

## Understanding the Reality of Vocation

Consider another important factor in a Christian view of work and ministry. For Christians there are no menial jobs. Many contemporary psychologists have shown us (even though their views may not be based on a biblical philosophy) that the foundation for a sense of well-being and meaning in life depends not so much on external circumstances as it does on a deep-down belief that we are worthy human beings. In other words, rather than some menial job thrusting its impersonal clutches of despair upon us, we recognize the dynamics of gift and call, responding in a totally renewed way to whatever ministry God gives us (Col. 3:22–25). Call it a Christian work ethic if you will, but do not identify it with Puritanical capitalism, for a biblical view of work transcends time and culture.

But there is more at stake than just a leader's attitude toward others. That attitude influences administrative style and supervision. The Survey Research Center at the University of Michigan once conducted a national analysis of more than fifteen hundred workers. I find some of the results most interesting. For example, construction workers and the self-employed landed at the top of the contentment scale, with only about one in twenty registering job dissatisfaction. In technical, professional, and managerial occupations, the dissatisfaction rate was about 10 percent, but it climbed to 25 percent for workers in service occupations and in the wholesale-retail industry. Among workers with low incomes, college experience emerged as a handicap to attaining job satisfaction.

Generally in the survey, women were more dissatisfied with their jobs than men, and age did not seem to be a significant factor in that dissatisfaction. Marriage, however, figured big since unmarried young people were twice as likely to be dissatisfied with their lives as their married counterparts.

Perhaps the most significant finding, for those of us concerned with team leadership and ministry, was the seeming lack of emphasis on salary. Of the five work features rated "most important," only one had to do with tangible or economic benefits. Indeed, people ranked "interesting work," "enough help and equipment to get the job done," and "enough authority to get the job done" higher than salary levels. Church leaders who constantly work with volunteer personnel should pay attention to the message of those statistics, which remind us of the findings of Maslow and Herzberg.

The twelfth chapter of 1 Corinthians reinforces the concept that there are no menial jobs in Christian service. Given the human value system and the cultural priorities of our society, certain ministries, like certain jobs, appear to be more important and prestigious than others. But in God's value system, all parts of the body are equally important, and all must function at acceptable levels if unity and collective health are to be maintained.

In their classic volume *Counseling in an Organization,* Roethlisberger and Dickson identify what they call "five basic concerns" of employees:[2]

> 1. Keeping a job
> 2. Friendship and belonging
> 3. Felt injustices
> 4. Authority
> 5. Job and individual development

These concerns, the authors tell us, stem from three sources: organizational requirements, group values and norms, and individual needs. If we can "Christianize" their research by recognizing spiritual needs and sin as a part of that third concern, we may have a workable model by which to analyze our understanding of a Christian view of work and ministry. Such a model can help us identify the kind of attitudes and administrative styles Christian leaders bring to their important tasks.

## SECURING AND SERVING VOLUNTEER LEADERS

Notice the double emphasis in this heading. We know responsible team leaders have the task of recruiting other leaders. But, as I have repeatedly tried to show, a New Testament style of leadership requires that we see ourselves as their *servants* rather than their *lords* once they become members of the ministry team. Surely the difference between paid employees and volunteer workers has no bearing here. It seems to me that with both we adopt a distinctive kind of managerial technique that protects both productive outcomes and biblical norms.

Perhaps the following four guidelines represent a mixture of competent administration and biblical leadership.

### *Evaluate Your Recruitment Process*

How do you go about securing workers? Does your leadership largely depend upon initiating structure? Or do you emphasize the other end of the continuum, consideration? According to research in administration, *the most effective leaders score high in both dimensions of leadership behavior.*

We must avoid such intensity upon getting a job done that we forget we work with human beings, not cogs in a machine. At the same time, we want to steer away from a leadership style that may ooze the milk of human kindness but contributes little to effective performance or goal achievement.

The conflict of roles and goals will always be with us. Organizations and ministries structure specific roles with job descriptions and expected outcomes. People understand their own gifts and their own personal goals and ponder whether they comfortably approximate what the job asks of them. In volunteer ministry it becomes essential for us to bring these two dimensions together like overlapping circles. The greater the overlap between what the ministry role asks of a person and that person's perception of gift and call, the greater the potential for effective ministry and leadership development.

## *Emphasize Strengths in Followers*

In Peter Drucker's book *The Effective Executive,* one of the most significant chapters is entitled "Making Strength Productive." The initial paragraph warrants reproduction here:

> The effective executive makes strengths productive. He knows that one cannot build on weakness. To achieve results one has to use all the available strengths—the strengths of associates, the strengths of the superior, and one's own strengths. These strengths are the true opportunities. To make strength productive is the unique purpose of organization. It cannot, of course, overcome the weaknesses with which each of us is abundantly endowed. But it can make them irrelevant. Its task is to use the strength of each man as a building block for joint performance.[3]

Drucker goes on to suggest, "Effective executives know that they have to start with what a man can do rather than with what a job requires."[4] That implies getting the right person for the right role in staffing any organization, including a Sunday school, mission board, or college faculty.

The creative team leader in a world of challenge can never be content with the desires of Sancho Panza in *Don Quixote,* who wished to be lord of an island if it were offered to him "with little trouble and less danger." Nor, of course, does she wish to follow the frenetic neuroticism of Sancho's lord and spend years of service tilting at windmills. Somewhere between lies that happy, median ground of sane and scriptural ministry as divine power operates through a human instrument.

### Appraise Potential Leaders

Good leadership always breeds leadership—that is the thrust of what we have come to call the "Paul-Timothy approach." The effective Christian leader assesses and records how well each person performs in her present position, and what kind of ability she demonstrates for other tasks. Which of the teachers in the primary department has the potential to become a superintendent? Which of the missionaries would make a good field director? Who are the potential deacons or elders who could give leadership to the congregation?

Effective appraisal of potential leadership is only possible when we do three basic things well:

1. Help people gain a clear-cut knowledge of their roles in the organization.
2. Establish objectives and goals (including reasonable time lines).
3. Design regular opportunities for personal interaction to discuss mutual problems and progress.

### Develop Adequate Personnel Policies

The term *personnel policies* is simply a handy label to describe the guidelines affecting the dealings that leaders have with followers. Positive personnel policies center on a biblical view of people, a biblical understanding of the importance of individuals in the institutional framework, and a biblical commitment to the strategic position of the "gift-call" analysis of ministry. Such policies should be clearly defined and understood by potential leaders, so that they will not suffer from that organizational disease sometimes called "normlessness"—the idea that your ministry will overlook questionable means in order to achieve important goals.

In volunteer organizations, we do not deal primarily with pay raises, promotions, and attractive retirement benefits. We do, however, face problems of isolation, self-estrangement, and the inability of an individual to achieve his own goals while helping the organization achieve its mission. Positive team leaders emphasize meaningful relations, competent administration, participation in the decision-making process, and a high level of flexibility in roles and expectations.

## FUNCTIONING IN THE ROLE OF SUPERVISOR

Supervision means directing other people toward the accomplishment of ministry goals. As a leadership function, it links with staffing and delegation. These distinct people processes account for success or failure in leadership and administration.

At the heart of supervision lies a concern for improvement and the continuous development of new leaders. In a large business or industry, we could probably separate executives from administrators, administrators from supervisors, and so on. But in small ministry organizations we all hold responsibility for these crucial functions. We attempt to build people into the leadership team—which is the central focus of this book from cover to cover.

In reality, we don't supervise programs, we supervise people. Kenneth Pohly picks it up beautifully in the title of a helpful book—*Transforming the Rough Places: The Ministry of Supervision.* In the introduction he writes:

> My purpose in writing this book is to show that supervision offers a historic and effective means for equipping persons for ministry. I recognize that in doing so I invite resistance, because

supervision is a term that is loaded with baggage. It carries an image of "bossism," of someone in authority looking over one's shoulder and controlling every move, rewarding or punishing at will. It suggests a hierarchy of superiority/inferiority and dredges up threatening associations with the past. For this reason some people suggest abandoning the term and substituting something more palatable, but that is a false solution because it fails to deal with the condition that produces the resistance.[5]

Pohly develops some interesting concepts throughout the book, including an analysis of Jesus as supervisor and His relationships with the disciples. He talks about the transformational nature of supervision and its capacity for facilitating the empowerment of persons in their journey of development. In short, he sees supervision as a means by which leaders produce other leaders and build the leadership team.

Supervision accompanies persons and communities through significant times of their development, times that are filled with both obstacles and opportunities. Those times lead into ways that are filled with rough places. The supervisory task is not to prepare the way but to point the way to what God is already doing to transform the rough places into a highway that can be traveled in the fulfillment of ministry. This is a theological task; to do supervision is to do theology in the midst of daily experience. This is a salvatory process, because it provides a framework for confession and forgiveness; it establishes the conditions in which covenant, relationship, incarnation, judgment, and grace can occur.[6]

## PRACTICING ADEQUATE
## ADMINISTRATIVE PROCESS

Let me say here that implementing efficient administrative guidelines in a Christian organization does not necessarily lead to the abuse of executive power so common among what Jesus called "the kings of the Gentiles" (Luke 22:25). When practiced in love and concern for developing leaders, this kind of supervision can produce a blend of spiritual fervor and ministry competence, which is precisely what we pray for in team leadership situations.

## *Placement*

The supervisor usually has a voice in the initial appointment of leaders to their tasks. In the properly functioning Sunday school, for example, the authority for the appointment probably comes from the board of Christian education. But the Sunday school superintendent makes the personal contact and asks the person to accept the task. Therefore she becomes involved in a supervisory capacity from the very first.

## *Observation*

Effective seminary faculty members can focus clearly on the importance of their roles only when their deans or department chairs make a specific point to observe them in the classroom with regularity. Certainly one does not want to be legalistic about that in colleges, churches, or any other kind of Christian organization, but the reality of observation and its importance cannot be overstated in our focus on supervision. Good supervisors know how developing leaders are doing because they have watched them do it.

## *Evaluation*

Evaluation is an objective, written measurement of the developing leader's performance. The supervisor's evaluation should be supplemented by self-evaluation and other assessments (see chapter 22).

## *Resource*

In addition to guiding new leaders regarding strong and

weak points, the supervisor also serves as a resource person for improvements. She should be ready with ideas and helpful books and be prepared to encourage all efforts growing leaders make toward improvement.

## Team Needs

Supervisors, especially those who want to be team leaders, focus on meeting team needs. Keep in mind three elements we have talked about before—team, task, and individual. Let's reverse those for better understanding.

1. *Individual needs.* Members of the developing leadership team we supervise need our acceptance; they need to know we value them; they need to know their contributions are important and that they are doing what we expect of them. Obviously, frequent and clear communication makes this possible.

2. *Task.* Members of the team need clear goals, reasonable standards, adequate resources, and complementary roles. A good weekly staff meeting will make sure people work together, do not overlap work, and help each other toward their collective team goals.

3. *Team building.* As people work together under your supervision, they should develop a common sense of purpose in a supportive climate and recognize their collective achievement to be something far greater than any of them could do alone.

David Cormack offers a model entitled "Adair's Interlocking Needs of a Team"[7] which graphically picks up all of these items. As in all diagrams of this kind, the more the circles are pushed together (overlapped), the greater the central common area and the more team needs are being met.

## FOLLOWING SOUND PRINCIPLES OF SUPERVISION

Supervision must relate to specific tasks and specific personnel. Nevertheless, certain principles of effective supervision,

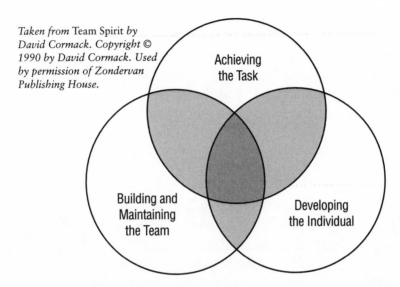

Taken from Team Spirit by David Cormack. Copyright © 1990 by David Cormack. Used by permission of Zondervan Publishing House.

Achieving the Task

Building and Maintaining the Team

Developing the Individual

ADAIR'S INTERLOCKING NEEDS OF A TEAM
*Figure 16*

when followed, may not guarantee success but will most likely lead the supervisor to perform tasks more satisfactorily.

## Be Open with Your Team

Openness especially counts when you are in your supervisory role. Don't prowl around in the dark looking for things to complain about. Explain to the entire staff how you view supervision and seek their cooperation and prayer in attempting to do it.

But what if someone reacts negatively, either in a public meeting or in private conversation with you? That situation requires more time, more prayer, and more personal counseling with that person. It may be necessary for a time to leave that person and others like him out of an observation and evaluation system. Eventually, however, one should achieve the goal of complete supervision which includes all people in the group.

### Predetermine What to Look for in a Leader

It does little good to go into a classroom and sit in the back of the room unless we have an organized format for observation and evaluation. It may be necessary for us to take some training in proper evaluation procedures before beginning the suggested program.

### Be Positive in Personal Interviews

We never want to be dishonest with people by telling them they are satisfactorily doing the job when we know they are not. Surely though, we can offer some note of praise, and the interview should emphasize commendation as much as possible. Weaknesses can be described as "areas that need improvement" rather than "faults" or "things you are doing wrong." Keep the interview on a spiritual plane and share some prayer time with the worker.

### Emphasize the Collective Nature of the Task

Each person has an important role on the team. We communicate to everyone our genuine desire to see them improve. We assure everyone that we do not want negative control but only to serve and assist them to become the best they can possibly be.

### Cut Down on Resignations

This is obviously the next level of responsibility in the matter of dealing with grievances. "I quit" are words heard too frequently in Christian service, and particularly in the church. Yet the words of Jeremiah the prophet haunt us in our contemporary situation: "His word was in my bones like a roaring fire, I was tired of trying to hold back, and I simply could not quit" (Jer. 20:9, author's paraphrase).

The rate at which employees resign or are dismissed from jobs in some companies is more than 100 percent a year. Perhaps an even more pressing problem is the people who do not leave but continue at their jobs disgruntled, unhappy, and making themselves and everyone around them constantly miserable.

In a way, this entire book attempts to confront the problem of resignations. To be specific, the key to retaining good leaders may be summed up in three words: *challenge, recognition, and reward*. We must recognize that they need opportunity to pursue individual goal achievement as well as assist in institutional goal achievement. They need to participate in decision making and receive recognition for their importance in the organization. To put it another way, team members must understand that their gifts and call are very much a part of the functioning body, and that they fulfill strategic roles.

All we learn from administrative science needs to be filtered through a theological sieve before we apply it in the life and ministry of Christian leadership. Perhaps the key concept of a genuinely biblical attitude toward service is found in the words of the apostle Paul in Ephesians 6:6–7: "Don't work hard only when your master is watching and then shirk when he isn't looking; work hard and with gladness all the time, as though working for Christ, doing the will of God with all your hearts" (TLB).

### FOR FURTHER READING

Callahan, Kennon L. *Effective Church Leadership*. San Francisco: Harper & Row, 1990.

Hesselbein, Francis, Marshall Goldsmith, and Richard Beckhard, eds. *The Leader of the Future*. San Francisco: Jossey-Bass, 1996.

Pohly, Kenneth. *Transforming the Rough Places: The Ministry of Supervision*. Dayton, Ohio: Whaleprints, 1993.

Schmuck, Richard A., and Philip J. Runkel. *The Handbook of Organization Development in Schools and Colleges*. Prospect Heights, Ill.: Waveland, 1994.

Van Auken, Philip M. *The Well-Managed Ministry*. Wheaton, Ill.: Victor, 1989.

Williams, Dennis E., and Kenneth O. Gangel. *Volunteers for Today's Church*. Grand Rapids: Baker, 1993.

## NOTES

1. Abraham Zaleznik, *Human Dilemmas of Leadership* (New York: Harper & Row, 1966), 207.

2. F. J. Roethlisberger and William J. Dickson, *Counseling in an Organization* (Boston: Harvard, 1966).

3. Peter Drucker, *The Effective Executive* (New York: Harper & Row, 1967), 71.

4. Ibid., 73.

5. Kenneth Pohly, *Transforming the Rough Places: The Ministry of Supervision* (Dayton, Ohio: Whaleprints, 1993), 2.

6. Ibid., 129.

7. David Cormack, *Team Spirit* (Grand Rapids: Zondervan, 1989), 98.

# —22—
# EVALUATING
# MINISTRY EFFECTIVENESS

E valuation is the process of getting answers to the question, How are we doing? The cycle of leadership requires us to engage in effective evaluation. Evaluation inseparably relates to the clarity and specificity of objectives stated at the outset of the process.

The evaluation step measures the degree of success or failure in our achievement of ministry objectives. What we learn from evaluation establishes the basis for changes in the organization which may result in reidentifying needs, re-clarifying objectives, and restructuring methods and ministries.

Improvement is a biblical concept. The Scriptures continually remind Christians to put their lives to the test of God's holy standard. Note the emphasis of the following passages:

> That is why a man should examine himself carefully before eating the bread and drinking from the cup. (1 Corinthians 11:28 TLB)

Check up on yourselves. Are you really Christians? Do you pass the test? Do you feel Christ's presence and power more and more within you? Or are you just pretending to be Christians when actually you aren't at all? (2 Corinthians 13:5 TLB)

Dear brothers, if a Christian is overcome by some sin, you who are godly should gently and humbly help him back onto the right path, remembering that next time it might be one of you who is in the wrong. Share each other's troubles and problems, and so obey our Lord's command. If anyone thinks he is too great to stoop to this, he is fooling himself. He is really a nobody. Let everyone be sure that he is doing his very best, for then he will have the personal satisfaction of work well done, and won't need to compare himself with someone else. Each of us must bear some faults and burdens of his own. For none of us is perfect! (Galatians 6:1–5 TLB)

Before they are asked to be deacons they should be given other jobs in the church as a test of their character and ability, and if they do well, then they may be chosen as deacons. (1 Timothy 3:10 TLB)

Dear brothers, what's the use of saying that you have faith and are Christians if you aren't proving it by helping others? Will that kind of faith save anyone? If you have a friend who is in need of food and clothing, and you say to him, "Well, good-bye and God bless you; stay warm and eat hearty," and then don't give him clothes or food, what good does that do? So you see, it isn't enough just to have faith. You must also do good to prove that you have it. Faith that doesn't show itself by good works is no faith at all—it is dead and useless. (James 2:14–17 TLB)

At least three terms are commonly used almost interchangeably within the framework of evaluation. _Testing,_ considered the most narrow of the three, refers to information about a given person, group, or program. The data are usually obtained through objective and written means.

A second word is _measurement._ Perhaps we can say that measurement over a period of time consists of gathering a body of information through the process of testing. It still emphasizes obtaining data rather than formulating conclusions about the data.

A third term, _evaluation,_ is the broadest of the three. When we evaluate we move from the process of objective data gathering to the interpretation of that data, and we develop con- clusions that will ultimately result in change.

Much evaluation is subjective. Every honest leader admits that she subjectively evaluates most of the time. The teacher eval- uates her students continually. The director of Christian educa- tion or dean evaluates teachers and staff to a much greater extent through subjective observation than through objective testing. But when both results are brought together, they provide a data- base for decision making.

Evaluating ministry effectiveness follows much the same pattern that accredited educational institutions are now required to conduct with respect to their programs. Most accrediting insti- tutions now require the establishment of adequate procedures for both planning and evaluation. In the language of education, the steps in the process look like this:

1. The establishment of a clearly defined purpose appro- priate to collegiate education.
2. The formulation of educational goals consistent with the institution's purpose.
3. The development of procedures for evaluating the extent to which these educational goals are being achieved.
4. The use of the results of these evaluations to improve institutional programs, services, and operations.

That's what this chapter is all about. Some confusion may arise here because, while many colleges look alike in their pro- grams, the kinds of ministries we are discussing in this book run the gamut and globe of diversity. So I've decided to focus throughout the chapter on local church illustrations as much as possible since we all understand that common connection. Nevertheless, as in every chapter, we want to be thinking broadly across the spectrum of ministry.

## Evaluating Organizational Structure

### Is Our Ministry Organization Genuinely Unified?

Evaluation should demonstrate singleness of purpose in the minds of staff and in the overt functioning of the ministry itself. Do all our people really feel a part of the team? Is the whole really greater than the sum of its parts? What built-in organizational structure can produce the desired unification of our ministry?

### Does Our Board Function Properly?

Here we look for proper representation of constituencies on the board, clear-cut specification of responsibilities of board membership, productive meetings, evidence of vision and long-range planning, and an awareness of the significance of the board's ministry.

### Who Is Responsible for Planning and Supervising Our Ministries?

Biehl and Engstrom list "evaluating board members" as the sixth step in "the board process chart." Ultimately, the effectiveness of the institution rests on the board. If the chief administrative officer does not achieve institutional goals or does not focus on the mission, the board may need to remove him or her. Board members don't actually do the evaluation, they simply make sure it gets done and analyze the final results. Regarding the evaluation process, Biehl and Engstrom suggest:

> A standard evaluation process provides a systematic, orderly way of helping people know where we feel they are strong and

where we feel they need to grow in order to make an even more significant contribution.

When each person understands that everyone on the board and staff is going through the same evaluation process, resistance tends to be reduced.[1]

## Is Our Organizational Chart Written and Available for All to See?

Such a chart, accurately drawn, should show proper line-staff relationships and lines of authority. Each leader should have a copy and be able to perceive the basic issues involved in organizational relationships and span of control.

## Do We Require Reports from Ministry Leaders?

Reports may be at times verbal, but more frequently they should be written. They include information such as needed additional equipment, equipment repair, and plans and programs for the coming year. These data aid the planning team in its responsibilities.

## How, by Whom, and How Often Are Leaders Appointed?

Many ministry organizations appoint workers annually for terms of one year, after which time they are evaluated and either reappointed for another year or directed toward another type of ministry in the organization. Remember—the way we appoint or elect leaders reflects our informal organization.

## Do We Have Job Descriptions for All Workers?

Job descriptions should be brief, effectively utilized in leader appointments, and demonstrative of the responsibilities of both the individual and the organization.

## Do We Use Our Officers Effectively?

A good case study here is the vice presidency of the United

States. The butt of many jokes, any sitting vice president can be either a figurehead or a major force in government.

## What Ministries Are Presently Being Carried on by Our Organization?

If the congregation has a properly written organizational chart, this question can be answered at a glance. If not, the evaluator must write down exactly what the church is doing now and compare that information with what the church should be doing now and in the future.

Perhaps it is useful one more time to differentiate between mission and vision. Mission describes what we exist to achieve; vision describes how we will go about that in the future. Objectives and goals are built on the mission but point forward toward the vision. *Vision* is such a buzzword in the nineties that we tend to apply it to anything and everything. When we talk about what ministries we are currently doing and what we might do in the future, however, we look back to the mission statement and make sure that the vision corresponds with our central purpose.

## How Do Our Various Ministries Relate to Each Other?

The issue here again is correlation. Do we have clear communication of goals, curriculum, and programming among the teacher of teenagers in the Sunday school, the captain of AWANA, and the director of the young teen youth group? Do they realize that they all affect the life of the same young people and should contribute harmoniously rather than competitively to their growth in Christ?

## Does Each Ministry Have Distinctive Objectives?

These objectives should be written and followed. A mere random verbalization on the part of the leader is inadequate.

Exactly why does a mission focused on Africa send missionaries to Brazil? If all our staff were asked separately about the objectives of their cooperative work, would their responses be identical? Would they be even similar?

## EVALUATING PERSONNEL

The key to evaluation is *improvement*—we must convince people that that is our goal. As we carry out the process, we will want to build in checkpoints between evaluation sessions that might occur only annually. Good team leaders press for constant self-analysis and emphasize solving problems along the way. Here are some guidelines for evaluating personnel.

### Examine All Key Areas

Evaluation should not deal just with the person's output (though productivity is considerably more important than activity) but with process. A church could be stifled by an elder who gets a great deal done but hurts people along the way.

In examining Sunday school teachers, for example, you would want to reconsider call, reexamine the dedication to the ministry, analyze teaching competence, discover whether they are taking advantage of training opportunities, assess their relationships with both students and other teachers, and look at what is happening to students in their classes.

### Evaluate with Various Measures

Almost all evaluation systems include some kind of questionnaire, and that's fine. But the written evaluation instrument (for example, a department chairman's evaluation of faculty in a Christian college) should be followed by personal discussion. It should also be supported by some form of observation; in addition, people being evaluated by others should have opportunity to fill out evaluation forms on themselves as well.

## Establish a Person-Centered Climate

Evaluation is at best awkward, and for some people it is downright distasteful. The wise team leader diffuses the fear and frustration connected with evaluation by making it a two-way experience. Subordinates evaluate the boss at the same time she evaluates them. In the personal interview, discuss the job before you discuss the person and always ask for self-evaluation first. What you say and how you say it may very well be determined by what the staff member has said about his own work and feelings regarding the job. Whenever possible, emphasize strengths and consider the environment in which mistakes were made.

## Provide Corrective Feedback

Having a job description guarantees nothing except that the staff member has been told what is expected of him. We need to ascertain whether he has followed proper procedures, developed proper attitudes, and is developing job control.

Remember to evaluate experienced staff as well; tenure does not guarantee quality.

## Set New Goals

Every evaluating interview, at least those which take place on a semiannual or annual basis, should end with the agreement of goals for the future. The evaluation describes the successes and failures, the strengths and weaknesses of the past year. Now we need to look ahead to see what goals we will mutually set for next year because they will become the foundation for evaluation at that time.

EVALUATING MINISTRY EFFECTIVENESS

As I noted earlier in the chapter, ministry effectiveness relates directly to such things as mission, goals, and relationships. It may take vastly different forms in different kinds of Christian organizations. Consequently, in this section we will look at a dimension of ministry with which most readers will be familiar, the educational process in a local church.

## Do Teachers Use a Variety of Methods in the Classroom?

We want effective communication. From whatever information she can obtain—written reports, suggestions from students, and counsel with supervisors and teachers themselves—the evaluator attempts to determine the degree of achievement in the actual teaching process. Variety is only one of the characteristics of good teaching; the achieving of learning goals forms the foundation.

## Do Teachers Use Media Effectively in the Classroom?

Good teaching methods assume good teaching media. Is there evidence that marker boards, videos, slides, computers, and other accessible teaching aids form part of the instructional process in the church's education program? Note that we must evaluate not only the *fact* of use but also the *effectiveness*. If available materials are not being used, evaluation asks why. The answer might lie in the area touched by the next question.

## Do We Train Teachers to Communicate Effectively in the Classroom?

We have dealt with questions about leadership training in previous chapters, but insofar as lack of training has a direct detrimental effect upon the achievement of learning goals, an analysis of the instructional process requires some inquiry into the teacher's competence for the task.

## Do Students Participate in Classroom Procedure?

The principle of involvement simply states that students will learn better if they are part of the teaching-learning process rather than just passive spectators to the teacher's performance. Evaluation discovers whether teachers involve students and, more important, whether we have trained teachers to implement this principle of valid instruction.

## Do Teachers and Students Use Bibles Effectively?

Church educational ministry deals primarily with biblical instruction. Part of that instruction directly ties in with the student's ability to utilize the Word of God for herself rather than just listen to information transmitted by a teacher or leader.

Closely akin to the proper use of the Bible in the classroom is the misuse of other curricular items. In Sunday school classes and public worship most pastors prefer regular Bible usage, and we can evaluate our effectiveness level in issues like this.

## Do Teachers Demonstrate Christian Love and Enthusiasm in the Classroom?

Someone has said "teaching is contagious enthusiasm." Students cannot develop excitement for biblical studies unless they see excitement communicated by teachers. A genuine *agape* love should be evident in the classroom as teacher and student share alike in the Spirit-controlled atmosphere of Christian nurture.

## *Do Curricular Materials Reflect Theological Accuracy, Educational Adequacy, and Adaptability to Local Needs?*

Curriculum evaluation should be conducted about every three years. Consistency in the use of curriculum depends upon proper educational programming. Confusion can result when one department uses material produced by one publisher and another department uses a different publisher's curriculum. We can allow wide flexibility in the adult department, but most churches should give greater attention to curriculum scope and sequence.

Instructional poverty can also result when a church allows budgetary considerations to negate the use of helps and aids available as a part of curriculum. Here again we must not only purchase such items but also train classroom teachers to use them properly.

## EVALUATING STRUGGLING LEADERS

Remember the central purpose of evaluation—improvement. In some cases, effective evaluation will uncover deficiencies in performance and struggles our leaders face, either with themselves or people they supervise. Experienced team leaders sense quite early in the process when they must deal with a "problem performer." Immediately they switch to a "nickel defense" designed specifically for this kind of situation. Exactly how do you evaluate a struggling leader?

### *Disarm Tensions*

Ministry tensions seem to fall into three types—equipping, administrative, and personal. *Equipping tensions* deal with such things as inadequate training and knowledge of how the work is done. Commonly this type of person has not yet gained job control, and we need to find out what she is missing and where we have failed to train or place adequately. *Administrative tensions* come from weak delegation, poor staff meetings, and a generally adversarial attitude between followers and leaders. Again, since we might be directly involved in the cause, we need to find out how to help such a person. *Personal tensions* may cover a myriad of diverse struggles that the developing leaders may or may not want to talk about. In some cases we may need to help find some solutions to health problems or perhaps even recommend a counselor for some family conflict. The trick here is to offer assistance without appearing to pry into private matters.

## Offer Encouragement

Start by recognizing what has caused discouragement—coercion in recruitment, failure to achieve objectives, personality conflicts, fuzziness of responsibilities—and then simply behave like Barnabas and be an encouraging leader. That grand apostle offers us some significant guidelines all leaders need to learn:

- Abandon personal rights (Acts 4:37).
- Take risks with people (Acts 9:26–27).
- Rejoice at God's work in and by others (Acts 11:23).
- Don't be defensive about your own leadership role (Acts 11:25–26).
- Don't abandon your people (Acts 15:38–40).

## Handle Obstinance

Once we have looked at every possible aspect of the problem which our own failures may have caused, we may have to recognize that the worker in front of us is batting his head against the organization's systems, its rules, and perhaps even its leadership. We try to understand the source and talk it through, but *modern research indicates that an increasing number of people are not signaling "recognize me" or "treat me well" but rather "use me effectively."*

## Discipline When Necessary

Be natural, be friendly, and be fair, but there are times when developing leaders, even those who showed promise in the early months of their service, must be redirected. The discipline interview is no time to philosophize about the organization. Instruct the worker where he stands and offer whatever "due process" the constitution and bylaws or the staff handbook might call for. Above all things, be prepared; this kind of leadership task is not usually pleasant.

## Negotiate and Compromise

When you cannot arrive at a mutual agreement on evaluation, work at it until some compromise can be reached. Compromise or negotiation is the antithesis of force and certainly fits a Christian organization. In negotiation you must listen more than talk. What does he want? What will she settle for? What underlying problems do these demands suggest? Remember, you must have patience here, and you are not required to say either yes or no. Once the agreement has been reached, you must figure out a way to make it stick.

Throughout the process ask God to keep you calm and unthreatened. Assuming you have gathered all necessary documentation and are acting graciously under the control of the Holy Spirit, you can comfortably leave the results in God's hands.

## EVALUATION OF PERSONNEL RECRUITMENT AND RETENTION

### Do We Follow Written Standards in the Selection and Development of New Leaders?

When the board or administration meets to decide prayerfully upon new staff, the members should have before them clear-cut objective criteria by which those people are chosen. Such criteria or standards may be a part of the constitution or may be developed in connection with other documents (handbooks) that represent the official position of the organization on various matters. Within legitimate bounds of flexibility these standards become the basic guidelines for leader procurement.

## Do We Conduct Effective Staff (Faculty) Meetings?

The properly functioning staff meeting should emphasize professional growth and development as well as goal and task coordination. Such conferences represent our minimal level of leadership training. Format will vary from leader to leader, but the importance cannot be overstated.

## Is There a Conscious Program of Leadership Retention?

Every college admissions officer understands how much less trouble and money retention costs than recruitment. Colleges commonly spend $1,000 or more per student to attract students to the campus in that first semester. Keeping the student there now becomes a significant priority. For the same reason we work to retain effective leaders. There is no foolproof formula for retention, but here are some helpful guidelines.

1. *Begin with a definite term of service.* A college or seminary contract, for example, is dated for one fiscal year. We hire faculty for one year at a time, though we hope the good ones will stay for twenty or thirty. It's exactly the same thing with volunteers in the church. We may ask a youth sponsor to serve from September to August, but hope we have a long-term leader who will serve that ministry for many years.

2. *Use a fair system of promotion.* To be sure, merit should be the issue here. But sometimes people are promoted simply because they have been in an organization for a long time. The Peter Principle warns us that we may be promoted beyond

the level of our competence. Sometimes people gain promotion because they have special connections with the president or senior pastor, and their advancement vaults them ahead of others whose quality of work qualifies them more obviously for the available post. Of all organizations in which employees and volunteers serve, Christian ministries ought to demonstrate the most equitable system of promotion and titling.

    *3. Set specific goals.* I keep coming back to this because it's so important. Already in this chapter we have said that evaluation is based on previously agreed-upon goals. People who understand the objectives of their ministries and agree that they are fair and achievable will be motivated by that achievement and will be much more likely to stay with the organization.

    *4. Provide adequate support.* People leave ministry posts because we ask them to achieve without adequate resources. The support might be human (a part-time secretary) or material (a fax machine). But more important is our own personal support and encouragement affirming the quality of the work so essential to what God has called our ministry to do.

    *5. Build in rewards and recognition.* In a volunteer situation, make sure plaques, notes, verbal gratitude, and public recognition find a place. For employees, make sure the salary and benefits package is commensurate with the demands of the job and the qualifications of the workers. On these points many Christian organizations have compiled a dismal record. It seems to me that we demonstrate distorted priorities when a church that underpays its staff by 30 percent decides to begin plans for a million-dollar sanctuary, or a college with similar salary deficiencies takes a half million dollars out of the general fund for student scholarships. *Christian organizations that do not take care of their people deserve to lose them.*

    *6. Use a separation checklist.* Talking about losing people forces the question of how we go about severing relationships with someone who has served the organization, sometimes for years or even decades. Whether the person is being terminated or has decided to resign, we want to know the answers to several important questions:

1. Had the job been adequately described?
2. Did this employee adequately understand the job?
3. Did we set fair evaluation criteria?
4. Was the employee evaluated regularly and justly?
5. Did the employee understand the evaluation results?
6. Might this ministry post be modified to make it more adaptable to this person?
7. Have we examined whether the person might serve some other place in the organization?
8. Has job location assistance been offered where appropriate?

An effective termination interview deals with all of these things. I once served in a leadership conference with Peter Drucker and heard him describe four questions a leader must ask before he terminates an employee :

- Can this employee do this job?
- Can this employee do this job better than any other job?
- Can this employee do this job better than any other job in this organization?
- Can this employee do this job better than any other job in this organization under my leadership?

GUIDELINES FOR EVALUATION

The evaluative process will always be subjective at best, but after more than thirty-five years at the task I think a few general guidelines might be drawn from experience:

*The evaluator must know what to look for if the evaluation is to culminate in a competent report.* The seasoned leader

388

can analyze most aspects of the organization and feel the temper of its effectiveness. The nonprofessional visitor could look at the same data and not be able to identify the positive and negative factors which make up the dynamics of that ministry situation. Knowing what to look for, however, is not to be construed as an *a priori* conclusion—jumping before fair observation.

*Evaluation is sometimes best done by a person not involved with your organization.* An academic dean is no doubt qualified to analyze programs which he has set up and actually supervises all the time. That personal connection, however, may result in something less than an objective evaluation. The stigma of "a prophet in his own country" might also argue for evaluation from outside.

*Every written evaluation report should contain specific recommendations for improvement.* These are presented in a manner which clearly states that their implementation may require a period of months and probably even years.

*An evaluation report should be presented to all key leaders, not just to a board or committee.* In the final analysis, the trench line soldier and not the chairman of the board must make ministry programs effective. When an evaluation report is presented, each leader should have opportunity to ask for clarification and to become involved in whatever action steps will be necessary as a result of the evaluation.

*Proper evaluation always keeps the mission of the organization in central focus.* Any analysis of a church or ministry which treats the organization as a secular corporation can never provide the necessary spiritual guidance for growth and improvement.

FOR FURTHER READING

Leslie, David W., and E. K. Fretwell, Jr. *Wise Moves in Hard Times.* San Francisco: Jossey-Bass, 1996.

McKillip, Jack. *Need Analysis: Tools for the Human Services and Education.* Newbury Park, Calif.: Sage, 1987.

Pohly, Kenneth. *Transforming the Rough Places: The Ministry of Supervision.* Dayton, Ohio: Whaleprints, 1993.

Rusbuldt, Richard E., Richard K. Gladden, and Norman M. Green, Jr. *Local Church Planning Manual.* Valley Forge, Pa.: Judson, 1977.

Thompson, Robert R., and Gerald R. Thompson. *Organizing for Accountability.* Wheaton, Ill.: Harold Shaw, 1991.

Williams, Dennis E., and Kenneth O. Gangel. *Volunteers for Today's Church.* Grand Rapids: Baker, 1993.

## NOTE

1. Bobb Biehl and Ted Engstrom, *Increasing Your Boardroom Confidence* (Phoenix: Questar, 1988), 162.

# —23—
# DELEGATING
## TASKS AND AUTHORITY

Amazing as it seems, one can peruse the indexes of numerous leadership books (as I have done in preparation for this chapter) and find no entries at all under the term "delegation." Sometimes that occurs because the author has focused on one specific aspect of leadership, such as conflict management for example. More commonly, however, the book deals only theoretically with its topic and therefore pays little more than lip service to the actual functions that make leadership possible.

In my view, one should not suggest that any one aspect of leadership is more important than the rest. For example, can we say that decision making is more important than planning? Might organizing be a more significant ingredient than human relations? Such value judgments seem futile because team leadership is a seamless garment of variable activities, each interwoven with the rest. But on the firing line, delegation comes as close to being indispensable as any characteristic we could name.

Delegation has to do with a leader's assigning of certain tasks, and authority for those tasks, to other persons in the organization. The process is rather simple to define, but exceedingly difficult to carry out. Bower, in his excellent chapter on delegation, speaks to its importance:

> The larger an organization becomes, the more important it is for an administrator to apply the principles of delegation. Those on the staff of a moderately large and growing church will of necessity concern themselves increasingly with more abstract operations, such as policy-making, supervision, counseling, and coordination. These more important activities can be adequately carried out, however, only if lesser important duties are delegated to Sunday-school superintendents, sponsors of youth groups, adult fellowship officers, and other leaders. As a matter of fact, the aim of the administrator ought to be that of utilizing the delegation process as frequently as possible. . . . "The making of decisions," according to Pfiffner, "should ordinarily be delegated to the lowest possible level of the hierarchy." This will then permit him to devote himself to those administrative operations which demand the presence and skill of a full-time, well-trained staff person and will assure a continuing expansion of the church program.[1]

Such delegation fits precisely with the view of team leadership described in this book. It focuses attention on the achievement of group goals rather than the retaining of authority and power by leaders. The autocratic leader will generally be ineffective at delegation. The free-rein leader, on the other hand, may allow too much flexibility to achieve essential results.

In many Christian organizations the delegation process seems complicated by the leader's constant dealing with volunteer workers. She can only *ask* someone else in the organization to take a task and carry it out even though such authority may be consistent with the organizational chart. But difficult though it may be, delegation stands central to leadership roles carried out by pastors, associate staff, and other team leaders.

## THE NECESSITY OF DELEGATION

### Why Should Leaders Delegate?

One basic reason we can so easily support delegation is its *biblical foundation*. Moses found himself strained almost to the breaking point under his responsibilities as the single leader of a wilderness nation. Such unilateral responsibility was unnecessary, however, and at the suggestion of Jethro, Moses divided his leadership among others capable of assuming the assignment of such duties (Ex. 18).

In the New Testament the Lord Himself certainly used delegation. Even while on earth He consigned many tasks of ministry to His disciples. At the time of His ascension, He passed on to them the entire responsibility for the ongoing church. All biblical commissions (such as those found in Matthew 28 and John 20) delegate first to the disciples and then through them, to every Christian.

Another argument for delegation is *sheer necessity* in order to get the job done. The physical and mental weight of team leadership cannot be carried by one or even a few people. Their incapacity to function adequately under the burden should be an obvious argument for delegation.

A third case for delegation reminds us that it serves in the important task of *training future as well as present leadership* for the church's program. Leaders who will someday bear heavy responsibility must first learn to bear lighter responsibility in some followership role. Involving young people in the planning of their own programs exemplifies delegation, which should result in more maturity and leadership responsibility on their part. People who have things done for them all the time never learn to do things for themselves. Consequently, they rarely do things for others.

Professionals place a great deal of trust in this kind of team leadership behavior. Kouzes and Posner write:

393

You demonstrate your trust in others through your actions—how much you check and control their work, how much you delegate and allow people to participate. Individuals who are unable to trust other people often fail to become leaders. They can't bear to be dependent on the words and work of others and consequently end up doing all the work themselves. Conversely, people who trust others too much may also fail, because they can lose touch and a sense of connectedness to their team. Delegation becomes abdication.[2]

## Why Do Some Leaders Fail to Delegate?

Delegation tends to be fraught with fear of the unknown. Without saying so, many leaders hesitate to delegate simply because they *fear giving up authority* which they claim as theirs. One can sense a certain amount of carnality here as selfish pride wins the day. Often, however, leaders just *don't know how.*

Most delegatees will not perform the assigned task to the same level of competence the leader himself would have performed it. However, after exercising the responsibilities for a period of time, the level of competence will rise considerably and even approach that of the mentor. This can be both a blessing and a *threat to the leader* who might already be somewhat skeptical of the delegation process.

Some leaders fail to delegate because *they do not want to commit the necessary time.* In the initial stage, delegation takes more time than doing the task oneself. Making the assignment, issuing reminders, checking and double-checking results, possibly making some corrections, and other aspects of the delegation process tempt us to say, "I'd rather do it myself." But like planning, delegation is not an expense but an investment. Unfortunately, because the returns of the investment do not always appear immediately, discouragement can set in and lead some to forsake the process.

## What Kinds of Tasks Cannot Be Delegated?

At first glance it would appear that good leaders delegate almost without limitation, but some restricting guidelines must be observed.

*Items assigned in a job description.* If, for example, a church has hired a pastor of discipleship to plan and carry out an annual leadership-training retreat, that job should not be passed on to someone else in the congregation.

*Tasks for which the basis and authority of delegation is not clear.* The person asked to accept the assignment should know that the leader asking her has the right to do so. This necessitates an understanding of the entire organizational structure by all concerned.

*Something which belongs to someone else's area of authority.* An academic dean should not delegate responsibilities relative to college finance. A missions field director should not delegate aspects of ministry related to another field.

Generally the literature on delegation suggests that leaders delegate everything they do not absolutely have to do themselves. This may be an overstatement, but it generalizes the great importance placed upon delegation in leadership.

## DEGREES OF DELEGATION

Delegation must carry with it the authority to carry out the task. Certainly the task and its authority constitute a responsibility, and to that extent responsibility is delegated. In another sense, however, the leader can never delegate accountability.

Assume, for example, that a senior pastor asks his assistant to plan the program for the February workers' conference. She, in turn, passes the responsibility on to the chairman of the board of Christian education. If at conference time no program is prepared, the assistant, not the chairman, is ultimately accountable.

In identifying ways to learn leadership, Callahan reminds us that "people learn leadership best in an environment wherein there is a high delegation of authority, not responsibilities." He points out that the scale of competency must be in balance with the range of authority; neither should run ahead or behind the other: "People develop their competencies in direct relation to the authority that has been delegated to them, not the responsibilities they have been asked to take. In any organization, the higher the delegation of authority, the higher the level of competencies and *the more leaders the organization helps to nurture forward*."[3]

It should be immediately obvious that if we overload a developing leader with authority far beyond his competence, he'll end up in frustration. On the other hand, if we withhold authority as competence develops, we get the same result. As in so many aspects of leadership behavior, balance becomes crucial.

The trick in delegation is to realize that leaders can never give away ultimate accountability. We transfer tasks and even responsibility, but ultimately we are accountable for what we delegate to subordinates. That is why some managerial scientists talk about different degrees of delegated authority.

*Executive Authority*

This highest level carries with it full authority to see the task through to its completion. The leader assigns to the delegatee some given responsibility and then no longer concerns himself with it. In the illustration of the conference above, the pastor may have said, "Please plan the February workers' conference," and never thought again about what the program would be.

The pastor's inattention to follow-up may pervert proper delegation process, but it serves also as an example of complete authority. In this illustration it would also include the expenditure of funds for speakers and conference facilities.

## *Reporting Authority*

In a reporting type of delegation, the delegatee undertakes a task but must report to her supervisor at predetermined points in the process. Reports may be single or multiple, but the supervisor asks to be kept informed of decisions made in carrying out the task.

### GUIDELINES FOR EFFECTIVE DELEGATION

Recognizing that delegation is essential; understanding why one fails to delegate; knowing what tasks cannot be delegated; understanding the degrees of delegation; and acknowledging ultimate accountability—all these are guidelines. But in the actual process of delegating itself, we recognize certain rubrics, certain patterns that lead to effectiveness in this key leadership behavior.

### *Make Duties Clear*

Clearly define any delegated task. Generalization is the bugaboo of successful delegation. Delineate specifically what you expect of the delegatee; what time or date you want the task finished; and, if necessary, what form the finished product should take. Provide all necessary information to accomplish the task.

### *Do Not Assign Methods*

Delegate according to results, not methods. The "how" of the task need not be communicated in delegation. Maybe people will do things quite differently than we would. Assuming they achieve the same results, no problem. At times it may be necessary to say that the end does not justify the means, but in the simple mechanics of delegation followers should be free to choose their own approaches.

397

## Set Up Controls

Establish built-in controls to pinpoint difficulties at an early stage. How foolish to go all the way to the date of that February workers' conference only to discover no one has properly planned the program. Periodically from the point of delegation to the point of conclusion, the pastor could have reminded his colleague; and the educator should have followed up with the chairman of the board of Christian education.

We can put such reminders in the form of simple questions, such as, "How are the plans for the workers' conference coming, Susan?" But a more effective system of control is a regular reporting system such as that which should be required from every ministry leader periodically throughout the year.

## Give Praise and Credit

Offer reinforcement when people successfully complete the delegated task. This important step of reinforcement is dealt with by Brethower and Rummler:

> Since behavior is influenced by its consequences, there are several things the manager or management can do to realize the optimum effect of this relationship:
>
> 1. Train only when the behavior trained will be reinforced on the job.
> 2. Design jobs so rewards for the desired behavior exceed punishment for failure.
> 3. Arrange conditions so an employee can see which of his acts are being reinforced.
> 4. Arrange the reinforcement so it is given in time to be linked to the act.
> 5. Select reinforcers that are in fact reinforcing to the employee.[4]

## DELEGATING IN AN ANTI-AUTHORITY CULTURE

By now you know that I believe the New Testament does not support a leadership style based on authoritarian attitude. Authoritarian leadership behavior refers to a relationship between persons, not only to attributes of one individual. It involves exercise of social control which rests on followers' willing compliance with certain directives from their leaders.

Consider, for example, a dean of students in a small Christian college. She wants to maintain a warm climate of rapport so that she can be a friend and confidante to students in counseling situations. But she is hired to enforce rules as well, and her authority rests on the sanctions she can impose on violators. The more she must appeal to this authority, the less attractive she will be in her role of personal counseling.

The question of authority and reaction to authority is crucial to the process of delegation. One cannot delegate without authority, yet abusing authority can cripple the effectiveness of delegation. The gentleness and kindness of the leader filled with God's Spirit stands against the ancient conflict between labor and management and always emphasizes the team concept of the people of God at work together.

The Bible is full of passages on the unity of the body, but few are as poignant as Paul's words to the church at Philippi.

> If you have any encouragement from being united with Christ, if any comfort from his love, if any fellowship with the Spirit, if any tenderness and compassion, then make my joy complete by being like-minded, having the same love, being one in spirit and purpose. Do nothing out of selfish ambition or vain conceit, but in humility consider others better than yourselves. Each of you should look not only to your own interests, but also to the interests of others. Your attitude should be the same as that of Christ Jesus. (Philippians 2:1–5)

We have talked frequently throughout these pages about

empowering other leaders as a central strength of the team leadership concept. Other than the decision-making process, few areas of leadership lend themselves more to empowerment than the process of delegation. Consider the words of Clark and Clark:

> The appropriate distribution of power, authority, and influence is critical to the smooth functioning of an organization. There is a word for it: *Empowerment*. The theme of the empowerment movement is that power to make decisions should be located at the place in the organization where the optimal amount of information exists on which to base the decisions. . . . Every worker in a plant, every member of a community organization, every citizen in every community should be watching for ways to solve problems; there should be willing participants in any campaign for improvement.[5]

Delegation builds the future leadership of ministry. Its elements include responsibility, authority, and accountability, all within proper perspective in the delegation process. Someone has said that with all the evidence to commend it, failure to delegate is an emotional problem, not a rational one. The team leader who can effectively delegate tasks to people and then effectively supervise them in those tasks demonstrates the gift of administration and contributes much to the overall ministry.

## DELEGATION REQUIRES
### PAYING THE PRICE OF LEADERSHIP

James offered wise, experienced counsel when he said, "Not many of you should presume to be teachers" (James 3:1). The price of leadership is not small; it includes faithfulness and self-denial. The time, the privacy, and the personal life of the average person may be sacrificed in the role of leadership. Study and preparation consume hours in a week, weeks in a year, and years in a lifetime. The responsibility never abates.

When we make the investment in other people, we expect a return in the form of appreciation and thanks. Instead, there is often the offense of some who misunderstand and retaliate negatively for all our efforts on their behalf. At moments like this the limelight dims, and the life of leadership can become the life of loneliness.

The leader is often the dreamer, the idealist, the crusader for a cause. He finds himself bucking the tide of popular opinion and standing against the crowd. Probably something of a perfectionist, the leader is her own most severe critic and tends to deal most harshly with herself. That's why developing a leadership team to share the burden becomes so crucial.

This pattern marked the lives of the great leaders of the Old Testament, the disciples and apostles of the New Testament, and our Lord Himself. Yet somehow amid pressing demands of ministry, Jesus took time to carry on the most successful delegation the world has ever seen. He discussed theology with Nicodemus and living water with an adulterous woman. He shared intimate moments with the young apostle John and prayed personally for impetuous Peter. He visited briefly with two disciples after the Resurrection and took time to make a special appearance to the skeptical Thomas.

Jesus' delegative relations with people reflected His relationship with the Father. He did not deal in horizontal communication alone but constantly represented the Father to those with whom He came in contact. In return, their lives were ever brought to the Father in prayer, perhaps never more significantly than in John 17. Such completely spiritual human relations marked the ministry of Jesus Christ. May those same markings be found in the ministry of His team leaders who serve ministry organizations into the twenty-first century.

#### FOR FURTHER READING

Callahan, Kennon L. *Effective Church Leadership*. San Francisco: Harper & Row, 1990.

Clark, Kenneth E., and Miriam B. Clark. *Choosing to Lead*. Charlotte, N.C.: Iron Gate, 1994.

Kouzes, James M., and Barry Z. Posner. *The Leadership Challenge*. Rev. ed. San Francisco: Jossey-Bass, 1995.

Malphurs, Aubrey. *Maximizing Your Effectiveness*. Grand Rapids: Baker, 1995.

Thompson, Robert R., and Gerald R. Thompson. *Organizing for Accountability*. Wheaton, Ill.: Harold Shaw, 1991.

Tillapaugh, Frank R. *Unleashing the Church*. Ventura, Calif.: Regal, 1982.

## NOTES

1. Robert K. Bower, *Administering Christian Education* (Grand Rapids: Eerdmans, 1964), 75–76.

2. James M. Kouzes and Barry Z. Posner, *The Leadership Challenge* (San Francisco: Jossey-Bass, 1987), 146.

3. Kennon L. Callahan, *Effective Church Leadership* (San Francisco: Harper & Row, 1990), 155.

4. Dale M. Brethower and G. A. Rummler, "For Improved Work Performance: Accentuate the Positive," *Personnel Magazine* (September-October 1966): 9.

5. Kenneth E. Clark and Miriam B. Clark, *Choosing to Lead* (Charlotte, N.C.: Iron Gate, 1994), 143.

# —24—

# COMMUNICATING
# IN THE ORGANIZATION

Seconds before the opening of the crucial Green Bay Packer/San Francisco 49er football game on January 6, 1996, one of the cameras focused on defensive end Reggie White, well known for his solid and vocal Christian commitment. He had gathered all the non-starting players, those who normally spend most of the game on the bench, and above the noise of the crowd shouted at them: "Keep focused on the game. Don't you think about nothing else. Be ready to play. Be ready to come in when we need you." As the camera panned the faces of his hearers, one could see how clearly that basic message had penetrated their understanding.

Communication describes the transmission of ideas between (among) persons in a language common to both (all). Such communication forms a basic ingredient of sound team leadership. In recent years Christian leaders have become increasingly aware of the significance of solid communication theory in developing satisfactory witnesses for the gospel (either as individual Christians or the collective assembly). A *Christianity Today* article several years ago expressed the significance the field of communication has for the church:

> These theories and others like them hold new insight for all Christians who will study and apply them. Not only the intended meanings of the words used but also the meanings which the hearer's experience gives to them are essential to communication. Attention to communication theory can be the basis of greater effectiveness in witnessing to the gospel of Christ.[1]

This chapter deals broadly with the principles and problems of communication as they occur in almost all phases of Christian relationships. The communication process is dynamic, always in operation when people confront each other. These principles affect relations between husband and wife and between parents and children. They operate in every classroom situation. The dynamics come into play when a Sunday school superintendent consults a church member about the possibility of teaching a class, or when the mission board meets to discuss plans for opening a new field.

We do these things all the time without thinking about them. That's why the process of communication can fall into error and carelessness. Many of the problems we face today in the evangelical community result from a breakdown in communication between people. If we want to repair this breakdown, leaders must understand the communication process.

## DEVELOPMENT OF THE COMMUNICATION PROCESS

Donald Ely wrote, "There is nothing quite so wonderful as a good idea; there is nothing so tragic as a good idea which cannot be communicated."[2] From his vantage point as director of the audiovisual center at Syracuse University, Ely developed a model for the understanding of communication that I have reproduced here because of its simplicity and effectiveness.

**Fields of Experience**

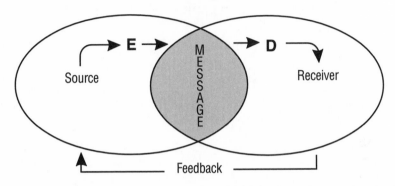

## ELY COMMUNICATION MODEL
*Figure 17*

Notice that at the heart of Ely's diagram is the message we want to communicate. The centrality of the message in communication ought to be of significant interest to evangelicals. Notice also that the message does not travel the entire route from source to receiver unless the process of communication operates properly. This general model can help our understanding and perception of almost any aspect of communication.

*Source*

The source of an idea in person-to-person communication begins in the mind of the communicator. From here the thought or idea is transmitted to the thought patterns of another. In a teaching situation, of course, the source is the mind of the teacher and the message is the content that the teacher wants to communicate to her students during a given class period.

In a very real sense the ultimate source of the Christian's

message is not the mind of the teacher but the mind of God. He has revealed Himself through His Word, the Bible. The teacher studies the Bible, illuminated in her study by the Holy Spirit. Now she must go on to communicate those revealed and illuminated ideas to her students.

It should be obvious even to the casual observer that an idea that exists only in the mind of the source is of no value to anyone else. The Christian who knows the gospel but does not share it cannot fulfill biblical commands to witness and therefore does not assist unsaved friends to know God.

### Encoding

When a message has been decided upon, it must be verbalized or symbolized in some way so it can be communicated to other people. Encoding is not all verbal, as every good leader knows. In most forms of human communication it will consist largely of verbalization, but good communication will also include visualization. People who neither speak nor hear can communicate quite effectively through sign language. Without sound, encoded ideas are transmitted from a source to a receiver.

In communication people do not always say what they mean nor mean what they say. Sometimes we wonder whether our ideas can be encoded verbally. We explain, "I know what I want to say, but I can't explain it to you." As long as we persist in that attitude, we negate the communication process.

No information can be transmitted unless we first encode it. The young man who is "too in love for words" had better find some words fast lest his fair love wander off to another who may not have as much love but knows better how to express it.

### Decoding

Encoding is futile unless it is accompanied by an adequate process of decoding. When decoding works the message is received and comprehended by the receiver. Decoding is insepara-ble from encoding. A word must be heard; a picture must be seen; the succulent aroma of sizzling steaks must be smelled. Note that our sensory experiences play an important role in both encoding and decoding.

Two things are significant here. First, if we want people to understand us, we must take pains to encode our messages clear-ly. Furthermore, we must be somewhat confident that the receiv-er has the wherewithal to decode our meaning.

How foolish, for example, to speak to a young child in Russian if we know in advance that he understands no language other than English. One could encode most distinctly; yet, since decoding would be impossible, no communication could take place. The navy flagman standing on the deck of his ship speaks no words verbally to his colleague on another ship in the convoy. The positions of the flags encode by semaphore. If both have been properly trained, the reception decoding and feedback of the message are handled completely by flag positioning.

Defective decoding can result from problems other than the failure of encoding or the receiver's inability to understand the language of the message. One common flaw is the introduc-tion of a negatively charged emotional element into the commu-nication process. A husband who wishes to speak seriously with his wife about some matter does not begin the conversation by complaining about supper or condemning his mother-in-law. Conceivably, whatever he might say after such a beginning would possibly be heard, but the understanding might be perverted by anger that would distort the decoding.

## Receiver

The receiver is the person for whom the message is intend-ed, perhaps an individual, as in a counseling situation, or a group such as the Sunday morning congregation. Desired results may vary in widely dissimilar situations. Nevertheless, *the principles of communication do not change.* If team leaders want to motivate followers to action and behavioral change, they must go through basically the same process of encoding and decoding that the counselor uses when helping a client understand and solve her own problems.

## Feedback

The major process distinction between preaching and counseling is feedback. Of course every preacher gets feedback. Every time a person smiles, offers a hearty "amen," yawns, looks at his watch, or gets up and walks out, the pastor receives feedback. Nonverbal feedback tells us what is happening in the communication process.

Feedback helps the communicator interpret whether or not the receiver has understood and internalized the message. In short, we need to find out whether we are "getting through." When Mom says, "Johnny, didn't you hear me?" she is asking for feedback. When the classroom teacher asks for questions on the lesson, he solicits feedback. You can see that a teacher who allows students to participate a lot during the class will be in a better position to use effectively the minutes he speaks.

The team leader who suggests an innovative idea and then keeps ears open for the next two weeks to gather comments (negative and positive) is sensitive to feedback and will be rewarded for efforts at improving and refining the idea. Ely reminds his readers that feedback can be both simple and complex:

> The degree of success which a given message has achieved can be determined by *feedback*. Feedback provides a teacher with information concerning his success in accomplishing his objective. The feedback may be covert or overt. A perceptive question stemming from the message is one of the simplest examples of feedback. The learner who asks a pertinent question indicates his degree of understanding. Most feedback is more complex, particularly in the case of value judgments and atti-

tude changes which may not be as easy to process. A teacher should attempt to elicit feedback to determine how well he is achieving his purpose. Feedback assists in determining how future messages will be encoded.[3]

How much feedback you really want directly relates to your philosophy of leadership. The autocrat speaks and expects everyone to listen and do what he asks without question. The team leader, on the other hand, is sensitive to what people think and concerned whether or not her purposes and actions are properly understood by the group. Clark and Clark warn us, "Stereotypes about being in charge interfere with communication between persons of different status. A suggestion from a superior to change behavior produces a sizable emotional response that impedes communication."[4]

## Field of Experience

Communication does not take place in a vacuum. We dare not reduce it to a series of words encoded by a source and decoded by a receiver. The total context or environment in which any message is given and/or received consists of more than words and ideas; it forms a veritable matrix of human relationships.

The field of experience may refer to how much the receiver understands. We would not teach a Sunday school lesson in advanced eschatology to primary-age students because their background and learning level would be insufficient to grasp it. The wife who spends $200 for a new dress may discover after only a few weeks of married life (if indeed she does not already know it by common sense) that her husband's reaction to such news may be more favorable after an evening out together.

We can also speak of the field of experience in terms of the ecological significance of communication. People both act upon and are acted upon by their environment. That environment may refer to a room in which we sit when a certain message is transmitted. It may describe the social and cultural frame of reference in which we have been brought up. Considered broadly, it is the entire global situation at the end of the twentieth century.

The effective team leader takes all these factors into consideration in structuring the communication process. She realizes that the receiver's mind consists not only of internal life (sin, worry, frustration) but also of the mass communications that permeate society today. Whether pastor, parent, president, principal, pedagogue, or simply a person who wants to relate more effectively to others, each of us must recognize that relationship cannot effectively take place without communication. And effective communication does not happen by chance.

## THE MESSAGES OF COMMUNICATION

Someone has pointed out the wide diversity of information that can enter the communication process as the various "messages" in the process progress from element to element. The cyclical pattern repeats itself over and over as it passes various distortion points.

### What the Source Intends to Say

The message originates in the mind of the speaker. Once she has some understanding of what she wants to convey to other people, she then frames a sequence of words or symbols that will serve as the transportation vehicle for her ideas. At this point the message is known only to her and exists only in this form.

### What the Source Actually Says

Unfortunately, what one intends to say and what one actually says may not match completely. Who among us has not had the occasion to say, "I didn't mean to say that," or, "That didn't come out just the way I wanted it to." In only its second stage of communication, the message has been subjected to the possibility of distortion. The mouth is not always an accurate channel for the mind.

### What the Source Thinks He Has Said

When we do not take into proper consideration the hearer's field of experience, the emotional state in which he found himself at the time of the encoding, or deficiencies in the encoding process itself, we create further difficulty. Many arguments in the family begin on just this point. She argues that he said a certain thing, and he argues that he never said any such thing. Who was right? Unfortunately, without some kind of record or third-party witness, the argument must end in capitulation or a "draw."

### What the Receiver Wants to Hear

A counselee listening to the counselor offer some possible alternatives to his problem may very well already have in mind the kind of answers he expects to hear. Indeed, they may be so firmly entrenched in his mind that regardless what the counselor actually says, the counselee goes away thinking that he has heard a certain solution. Two students may sit in a class, later discuss the lecture, and be surprised to find that they each understood the teacher to say a completely different thing or offer seemingly divergent answers to the same question. Every hearer brings to a communication situation some expectation of what she will hear. We frame this expectation by our own personal desires, the prompting of others, or the reputation of the speaker.

### What the Receiver Hears

It is possible and even probable that the original message in the mind of the source, what the speaker says, what the speaker thinks he says, and what the receiver wants to hear may all be different from what the receiver actually hears! We want to believe that what the speaker says and what the hearer hears must be the same since only one set of words or symbols could be involved. But such a conclusion fails to take into consideration the variable factors in the encoding-decoding process.

What the receiver hears is colored by what he wants to hear, what he understands about the subject, and the makeup of his own mind. Sometimes even the basic words themselves fail to get through. How much more problematic the meaning which those words convey. *Words are only vehicles to carry thoughts.* The great prophet of the general semanticists, Alfred Korzybski, once reminded all communicators that "the map is not the territory." Words are to an idea what a road map is to a road—merely a picture or representation of the reality. Hearing the words is relatively unimportant compared to understanding the idea.

### What the Receiver Thinks He Heard

This is similar to the problem of what a leader thinks he has said. A young executive, scolded by her boss for having routed a business order in the wrong direction, responds, "But, sir, I distinctly understood you to say that _____." Remember— the receiver acts not upon what the speaker thought he said, nor upon what the receiver heard, but rather what she thinks she heard.

If all six versions of the message mentioned above can be harmonized, then the communication process is in good shape. Feedback provides the built-in control factor which lets us know whether the messages have gone through on the same wavelength. All team leaders must recognize the points at which misunderstanding may enter the communication process. You will need to keep a constant vigil against distortions of the message if you want interpersonal relationships to be carried on smoothly within your ministry.

As Sam Canine and I put it in a work which vastly expands the material in this chapter:

Our purpose is certainly not to memorize models nor pit the values of one against another. The idea is to understand communication so that we may practice it more effectively. For that to happen, we must understand the various component parts and how they all come together to form a communication system or network. Communication between husband and wife seems very different than communication between boss and employee. However, when analyzed in accordance with accepted models, those differences quickly shrink leaving us with very dependable patterns and principles which relate to virtually every communication situation.[5]

## SUGGESTIONS FOR IMPROVING COMMUNICATION

### In Leadership Situations

*Avoid verbal instructions alone.* Use written memos or e-mail to reinforce and clarify oral communication whenever possible.

*Use informal settings to facilitate dialogue.* Try to break down the barrier that sometimes exists between a leader and the team.

*Use careful planning before any group presentation.* A pastor confronting the board with a building project, for example, should have carefully thought through how he will make the presentation, what possible questions might be raised, and how he will answer them.

*Try to speak to small groups whenever possible.* We can enhance good audience contact by limiting the size of the group.

*Know the audience.* Understand your team and speak directly to them.

*Know your subject matter well.* Do not attempt to bluff your way through a presentation.

*Attempt to establish rapport with your people.* Spend time with them; know and understand their problems and needs; and demonstrate interest and Christian love toward them as persons.

*Be sincere.* Genuine sincerity can cover and atone for a multitude of technical errors. Often this depends upon the love a team leader brings to the group. Koestenbaum attacks this point head-on:

> Do not underestimate the power of love, perhaps the greatest known energy. We all recognize the importance of love in life— how we need it to be happy, to grow, even to be healthy. But, regrettably, many people feel it has no place in business. Love means that you really care about people, whether you are a mother or a general. To love is to communicate intimately in the sense of establishing an intersubjective field, a joint ego or communal self. Love establishes a higher unity, a spiritual connection, an emotional bond.[6]

## In Personal Relationships

*Be friendly, polite, and considerate.* Avoid being cold, overbearing, and offensive.

*Cultivate the practice of listening.* This is important not only for feedback but as a courtesy to the person with whom you are speaking. Like the praying of the Pharisees, the leader is not heard because of his much talking.

*Use positive words in speaking with people.* Avoid offensive terms. Referring to teenagers as "children," for example, is the first sentence of the book on how not to communicate to young people. Be careful with gender exclusive or offensive language.

*Give praise whenever possible.* This should be honest praise, not flowery speech. Cute expressions and showy words may put off some people who would see you as an insecure person—trying to dress up an ineffective presentation.

*Avoid jargon that may confuse.* Do not try to overwhelm others with technical gobbledygook. In speaking to people either individually or in groups, the effective team leader uses simple and sincere words that clearly express the thoughts he wants to communicate.

*Avoid ambiguity.* This problem looks like the one above. The ability to live with ambiguity in thought process may mark a philosopher, but speaking in ethereal and cloudy language does not create good communication.

*Demonstrate clearly your dependence on and expectation of results.* When a Sunday school superintendent encourages a teacher to visit, he ought to visit not for the sake of the superintendent, but for the sake of Christ and the students. In communication the receiver should never go away wondering what you really asked.

*Listen carefully to feedback.* See if anything the receiver says or does will help understand him better and therefore enable you to communicate with him more effectively.

The issue of human relationships in communication plagues secular business and industry as well as Christian organizations. Warren Bennis wastes no words in attacking the problem in our nation's business community:

> If these arrogant American chieftains do not begin to see the world as it is, do not finally acknowledge that their employees are their primary asset, not their primary liability, then all their jealously held power, prerogatives, and perks will sooner or later count for nothing, because their companies will be acquired, merged, or sunk.[7]

## HUMAN NEEDS:
### BASIS FOR EFFECTIVE COMMUNICATION

Because of the leader's position in the organization, she has the greater responsibility to develop positive human relations through proper use of interpersonal communication. One outstanding psychologist has indicated that a person's usefulness is enhanced proportionally as his linkages with life multiply. The multiple relationships which a leader maintains depend upon her ability to keep tabs on all the variable factors which sustain those relationships. This is largely accomplished by means of face-to-face interaction during working hours.

In the realm of Christian ministry, a proper vertical relationship with Christ as the head of the church and the director of all its leaders is essential before we can develop and maintain satisfying and profitable horizontal relationships.

## Understanding People's Needs

Part of the problem many leaders face in effective human relations is the very driving nature of their own personalities. Effective leaders often demonstrate a high level of personal accomplishment. They have learned how to get things done, to achieve goals, to obtain results, and to maintain a tight rein on their own time. Consequently, they frequently appear to subordinates and colleagues as cold, calculating, and unapproachable. Such an image immediately puts them at a disadvantage in developing satisfying relationships through interpersonal communications.

I have dealt elsewhere with the basic needs of people in groups. When we apply them to organizational relationships, we come up with a crucial list:

- Sense of belonging
- Share in planning
- Clear understanding of what is expected
- Genuine responsibility and challenge
- Feeling of progress toward organizational goals
- Intense desire to be kept informed
- Desire for recognition when it is due
- Reasonable degree of security for the future

Although research supports all these items and more, most team leaders could become aware of human need without the research. The problem with some of us is that we become so entangled with our own problems and personal overload that we fail to recognize and deal with the things we really know are important.

## Interpersonal and Intrapersonal Relations

Dynamic forces operate within human personality that produce profound effects upon our interactions with other people on the team. *Intrapersonal relations* describes the phenomena existing within us as feeling, thinking, and expressing persons. *Interpersonal relations* focuses on our visible encounters with each other and interaction within the organization.

In one sense, we could say that there is no communication without the interpersonal dimension, since mutuality forms a basic ingredient of communication. But the inner factors of personal equilibrium influence the communication process. We place meanings upon words as we listen to another's communication through his grid of emotional, social, religious, and political prejudices.

If a leader genuinely wants to understand and relate to one of her colleagues, she recognizes that *interpersonal communications are being greatly affected by two sets of intrapersonal factors, her own and those of the other person.*

## Structuring for Communication

The desirability of breaking up leadership responsibility into smaller units relates to the basic theory of communication and decision making. Such decentralization enables us to "touch all the bases" in a more comprehensive, yet intensive, fashion in our relationships with other people in the organization. Good leadership is multidimensional, so there are always a number of diverse factors that elude the autocratic leader who fancies himself *the* leader.

A para-church ministry director, for example, might decide to create a climate of openness and mutually happy interpersonal relations among his staff. One of his objectives for the year might be regular staff meetings which follow a carefully prepared agenda to explore mutual concerns. Another objective might be to spend time individually with each member of the leadership team as an attempt to build through a spirit of rapport and mutual exchange of ideas. As we become more specific in delineating goals for such meetings, we will consider our role as listener, our response to questions, and our openness in providing thorough information at staff meetings and in one-on-one situations.

Some experts argue that communication is relative to the centrality of a person in a group. People on the periphery, they suggest, tend to be negative and contribute less to the solution of group problems. Obviously, in a highly centralized bureaucracy there are many more people on the periphery. Decentralization secures an increasing involvement of personnel.

## Avoiding Communication Breakdown

If communication breakdown also means a breakdown in human relations in the organization (and it can), then we must pay careful attention to the problems we might encounter here. Experts tell us that the loss of communication can be traced primarily to factors such as foggy detail, distortion of words, retention of emotional concepts, and an attachment to the facts of innate prejudice. In the process, certain central ideas seem to hang on, whereas obscure or misunderstood concepts fade into even greater ambiguity.

We must emphasize the centrality of important ideas, and look for comprehension, not memorization, during feedback. Any good college teacher has come to grips with the relationship between *knowing* and *understanding*. Parents should not be as concerned that little Johnny can memorize huge portions of Scripture as that he understands what God is saying in the Bible.

Living within a society without becoming part of it has been a difficult task for Christians since earliest days. Somehow we must recognize that biblical separation represents neither isolation nor insulation from the culture.

Christian leaders' openness to the ideas and innovative suggestions of their teams ought to characterize the flow of communication in any Christian organization. In an excellent article that appeared in *Personnel Administration* back in 1968, John Anderson spoke about the blockades to upward communication. It might be helpful at least to identify the factors delineated in Anderson's analysis of the problem. In the following list B represents the subordinate and A the leader:

1. It must occur to B that it matters whether he says anything.
2. Once aware that he has significant information, B must choose to pass it on.
3. B must have an opportunity to make his information available to A.
4. If B does speak, A must be able to receive his message.
5. Having listened to and understood B's message, A needs to act on it.[8]

If at any one of these points the communication process goes awry, it can destroy the attempts of a staff member to communicate with his leader about matters that might be of extreme importance to both.

In *Interpersonal Communication and the Modern Organization,* the authors delineate, from the many case studies with which they worked, a profile of the communicating leader. In the profile, they isolated six characteristics which supposedly mark the person who recognizes that communication with others in the organization is especially crucial to the survival of his leadership and the ongoing productivity of the organization.

1. *Do not play the role of manipulator.* When a person in

an organization constantly uses others to serve his own ends, or even the ends of the organization, he will soon find himself without a leadership role.

2. *Be willing to pay the price.* In their research, Bormann and his coauthors discovered that almost every person of the work group wanted to be a leader because of the obvious rewards of leadership, but few wanted to be leaders badly enough to assume the enormous responsibility and work load.

3. *Talk up.* The quiet, reticent member of the group is rarely chosen as leader because it does not appear that she has sufficient interest in the group. On the other hand, it is not the quantity of words which makes the difference, but the clarity of the group's objectives and the leader's seeming ability to help the group achieve those objectives.

4. *Do your homework.* Members who emerge as leaders have sensible, practical ideas and state them clearly.

5. *Give credit to others.* Most people are not interested in working toward the glory of their leader, but they seem quite willing to work for their own glory and perhaps even for the glory of the group, assuming they are in complete harmony with its objectives and directions. Obviously, in a Christian organization, we emphasize working for the Lord's glory (Col. 3:22–4:1).

6. *Raise the status of other members.* "People who emerge as leaders compliment others when the latter do something for the good of all. . . . In short, they are honestly disinterested in whether they emerge at the top of the pecking order or not—so long as the team does well."[9]

Perhaps one warning can be offered in closing. Effective communication patterns cannot be achieved overnight. We must discipline ourselves to perform satisfactorily in all the various aspects and elements of the process. We must learn to listen rather than talk. We must learn to speak clearly rather than mumble. We must learn to convey our ideas accurately rather than depending upon other people's efforts to make sense out of what we say.

Effective communication, however, is not necessary only for leaders. All Christians must learn how to speak to other people. Ely says, "Where does one start? Start where you are, with what you have. You can do no more, but as a Christian communicator, you can do no less."[10]

## FOR FURTHER READING

Bennis, Warren. *Why Leaders Can't Lead*. San Francisco: Jossey-Bass, 1991.

Clark, Kenneth E., and Miriam B. Clark. *Choosing to Lead*. Charlotte, N.C.: Iron Gate, 1994.

Gangel, Kenneth O., and Samuel L. Canine. *Communication and Conflict Management*. Nashville: Broadman, 1992.

Koestenbaum, Peter. *Leadership—The Inner Side of Greatness*. San Francisco: Jossey-Bass, 1991.

Schmuck, Richard A., and Philip J. Runkel. *The Handbook of Organization Development in Schools and Colleges*. Prospect Heights, Ill.: Waveland, 1994.

## NOTES

1. George L. Bird and Lillina H. Dean, "Christians Can Learn from Communications Theorists," *Christianity Today* (January 20, 1967): 10.

2. Donald P. Ely, "Are We Getting Through to Each Other?" *International Journal of Religious Education* (May 1962): 4.

3. Ibid., 5.

4. Kenneth E. Clark and Miriam B. Clark, *Choosing to Lead* (Charlotte, N.C.: Iron Gate, 1994), 171.

5. Kenneth O. Gangel and Samuel L. Canine, *Communication and Conflict Management* (Nashville: Broadman, 1992), 31–32.

6. Peter Koestenbaum, *Leadership—The Inner Side of Greatness* (San Francisco: Jossey-Bass, 1991), 167.

7. Warren Bennis, *Why Leaders Can't Lead* (San Francisco: Jossey-Bass, 1990), 89.

8. John Anderson, "What's Blocking Upward Communication?" *Personnel Administration* (January-February 1968).

9. Ernest Bormann et al., *Interpersonal Communication and the Modern Organization* (Englewood Cliffs, N.J.: Prentice-Hall, 1969), 75–77.

10. Ely, "Are We Getting Through?" 5.

# –25–
# RELATING TO
# OTHER LEADERS

I n the late twentieth century, churches rarely split or even fight over substantive issues. Seventy-five years ago entire denominations splintered as they hotly debated such matters as the deity of Christ, the bodily resurrection, the promise of the Second Coming, and other such foundational biblical truths. Many evangelical congregations and denominations existing today came out of those conflicts.

But today we fight over interpersonal issues. More accurately, the petty matters that cause our problems draw us into emotional struggles with other Christians. Then the relationship between and among people becomes the focal issue, and we forget that the reason we no longer speak to certain people is that they vigorously campaigned for contemporary worship styles—a decision which, in our opinion, ruined our church forever.

Leaders face a different level of this problem. For us, relationships always stand at the foreground of what we try to do. Efficiency and competence may operate on a very high level, but if our people skills break down (or never develop) we will very quickly face major problems in carrying out the leadership task.

One business magazine carried an interesting article entitled "Ten Fatal Flaws of Business Executives" and listed them as follows:

1. Insensitivity to others
2. Coldness, aloofness, arrogance
3. Betrayal of trust
4. Overt ambition
5. Performance problems (incompetence)
6. Over-managing
7. Inability to staff effectively
8. Inability to think strategically
9. Inflexibility–especially in adapting to superiors
10. Weak or insufficient communication[1]

With a possible exception of numbers 5, 6, and 8, every item on the list has to do with interpersonal relations.

## STAGES OF CHURCH MINISTRY DEVELOPMENT

Mark Senter contributed an excellent article to *Leadership* journal some years ago.[2] He claims there are five stages of church ministry development and they look something like the chart on the following page.

The flow of Senter's article is well captured in the model. But let's analyze the implications in each of the five main boxes.

### Getting Acquainted

During this stage the team leader talks to as many people as he can and asks the key questions about the church, its philosophy of ministry, and its vision; through all of that he tries to get a handle on his unique fit in this particular group of people.

# FIVE STAGES IN CHURCH MINISTRY DEVELOPMENT

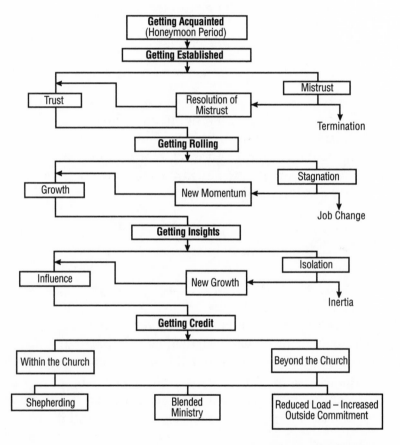

Mark H. Senter III, "Five Stages in Your Ministry Development", Leadership Journal, Spring 1989. Used by permission.

*Figure 18*

Senter also suggests arranging public visibility during this time, some evidence of effectiveness such as planning a retreat, developing a training program, rewriting job descriptions—some indication that there is a new kid on the block with something to contribute.

Obviously, throughout all this the leader works on the job control we discussed in an earlier chapter.

### Getting Established

During this time leaders build people's trust. Goal achievement continues to be important, but relationship building rises to the fore. The leader begins to establish solid, ongoing programs, which build trust over the long haul. If that trust does not develop, as Senter notes, termination of employment or leadership position may very well result.

### Getting Rolling

How does one measure growth in leadership? The leader receives wider responsibilities both within the congregation and outside it; she can now anticipate some support in failure as well as in success, no small step in the credibility process. By now she should have job control, well aware of what happens and why.

But what if stagnation sets in? How can we recognize it? One of the first signs of this is sheer physical exhaustion. When things do not go well, we often work harder trying to turn them around, and our bodies remind us that not all is well in this particular role. But the absence of some of the items mentioned just above can also serve as red flags—no opportunities for ministry beyond the congregation; no support in failure; no confidence in job control. Often a leader struggling with stagnation resorts to hiding mechanisms to excuse the real problem and perhaps will begin to find interest and satisfaction in something beyond the primary leadership role.

## *Getting Insights*

At this stage the leader enrolls in a D.Min. or a D.Miss. program. Or on a less formal basis, he may sign up for continuing education seminars or make some observation visits to effective ministries around the country. She enjoys the acceptance of her peers. He begins to see recognition of his role as a professional. In short, there is "new growth" which serves as a buffer against inertia.

## *Getting Credit*

According to Senter, this probably won't develop until about five years in the leadership role. It comes because of efficiency in ministry, shepherding relationships, and the development of new programs or approaches to ministry. Team leaders are now involved in professional organizations, perhaps holding office or preparing papers for national meetings. They recognize a shepherding rather than a hireling role within the church and a blended ministry of wider responsibility and lesser specialization (speaking, writing, consulting).

This all happens because of firm relationships with people who accept us and make it possible for us to move all the way to stage five. Senter wryly observes that we cannot get stuck in stages one and two because termination will probably shake us loose. But three and four represent great danger, and many who might otherwise be leaders of significant influence have found themselves instead in the ruts of stagnation or inertia.

## DEVELOPING INTERPERSONAL RELATIONSHIPS

Many readers of this book will be long-established team leaders in their congregations and ministry organizations. Others will have made a recent move (or are contemplating one) and, despite their veteran status, may face the same interpersonal issues all over again. Still other readers will be neophytes, ready to establish positive relationships and therefore effective ministries where God has led them to serve. To these latter two groups, but especially to the rookies, I address these next few paragraphs. They attempt to answer the question, "How can you behave like an experienced leader even if you are not?"

## Know and Be Known by the Key Players

At first glance this sounds like raw politics, but that is hardly my intent. The fact is, most leaders cannot escape visibility. Chief executive officers or senior pastors stand up front at meetings, chair important gatherings, and meet with boards and executive committees on a regular basis. But middle management associate staff, for example, tend to be much less visible. In a large church or Christian organization, an associate could be on board for almost a year before many folks know he has arrived. So without being pushy or appearing self-serving, the new leader stays in contact with the senior pastor, the rest of the staff, key elders or deacons, and key leaders in all phases of the church's ministry.

## Never Consider Yourself Indispensable

One of the great sins of Christian leadership is to think one is irreplaceable in an organization. Leaders who delegate reluctantly, who always seem to have much more work than any of their staff members, who never take a vacation of any length, and who constantly complain about stress and overwork may very well fall into this category. But you can measure an attitude of indispensability by staff behavior as well as by your own.

1. Have your subordinates' skills been static over the past year?
2. Do people tend to come and go in your organization without any significant longevity or tenure?

428

3. Do staff members rarely come to you with ideas?
4. Is it impossible to keep the organization functioning when you are out of the office for a time?

Such people fail miserably as team leaders and cannot work at producing new leadership for their organizations. This attitude runs counter to the biblical text. The parable of the servant in Luke 17 helps us grasp our proper role.

> Suppose one of you had a servant plowing or looking after the sheep. Would he say to the servant when he comes in from the field, "Come along now and sit down to eat"? Would he not rather say, "Prepare my supper, get yourself ready and wait on me while I eat and drink; after that you may eat and drink"? Would he thank the servant because he did what he was told to do? So you also, when you have done everything you were told to do, should say, "We are unworthy servants; we have only done our duty." (Luke 17:7–10)

What does Jesus mean? What exactly is an "unworthy" servant? The King James text renders this word "unprofitable." Apart from the humility that Christ's servants must always show (we have only done our duty), there is a hidden idea here worth exploring. The word translated "unworthy" in the NIV is a form of the word *achreios,* which literally means "without need." Establishing that, one could conclude that it is the servant who has no need, but that does not seem to be the point of the parable. Rather, we might substitute the word "dispensable" and capture the spirit of the text.

The Master has no indispensable servants. We do our duty, follow our orders, and a sovereign God determines when our time in a given leadership position is complete. That's one reason why it seems so foolish to argue vociferously to maintain a leadership position in a Christian organization when others (particularly those in authority) seem intent on dismissing us.

## Leadership That Affirms Relationships

Wherever I lecture or consult with churches, people ask about training programs. What should we be teaching? When can training programs take place? How can we motivate people to come? The answer lies in the interpersonal atmosphere your church or organization currently maintains.

To put it in another way, the issue of recruitment and training ultimately comes down to the kind of ministry team you ask others to join. Do they want to be a part of your organization? Can you develop people with the intent of their taking over leadership positions?

### Team Leadership

Central to creating a positive climate for Christian leadership is the team approach we have been talking about throughout this book. Current research in leadership theory and practice emphasizes the significance of the breadth and reliability of leadership development. Ulrich puts it this way:

> In an increasingly interdependent world, leadership must be created through relationships more than through individual results. Leaders of the future will have to master the art of forming teams and learning to work with boundaryless teams. Instead of coming from individual heroes, future successes will come from teams that share resources and that learn to overlook personal ambition for the sake of the team. Leaders who learn to collaborate through teams rather than directing through edicts see the value of team success. In almost every team sport, good teams will beat good talent.[3]

### Participatory Leadership

Once again, we come back to something which has occupied our attention throughout the book. Genuine participation pushes decision-making authority to the trenches. It invites leaders at all levels to make decisions in areas which pertain to their direct work responsibilities. It avoids the upward surge of power in a bureaucratic organization. When a board of deacons or elders gives off an aura of cultic authority, rather like hooded Klansmen gathered deep in the woods for a secret meeting, they place the entire congregation in danger. Such procedure destroys the universal priesthood so central to a properly functioning church.

## Biblical Leadership

As we seek other leaders, it becomes absolutely essential to know and follow biblical requirements. In one pastors' conference after another, in one D.Min. class after another, I have heard congregational leaders discuss deacons and elders (and sometimes even pastors) who do not meet biblical qualities and yet hold office. Like cities, states, and entire countries, people often deserve the leadership they get. God has clearly identified biblical qualities of leadership, and if we ignore them or deny them, we should expect to pay the consequence.

## Tolerant Leadership

In his book *Effective Church Leadership* Ken Callahan talks about "excellent mistakes." He points out that the level of creativity in developing leaders is directly commensurate with the positive recognition for excellent mistakes. To state it more directly, the more positive the recognition for excellent mistakes, the higher the level of creativity.[4]

Greg was a beginning youth pastor in a suburban Midwestern church. He knew all about hayrides and lock-ins, but he wanted to try something different. With full authority of the pastor and elders, he designed a "Teen Ministry Sunday" in which every Sunday school class and every other ministry carried on in that church would be done by a teenager. Sound creative? You bet it was. Sound productive? Not in this case. Maybe with a few more months of preparation it would have worked, but hitting it cold as they did, the kids "blew the assignment."

Now what? The board turns down all future ideas from Greg? The teenagers get no more cracks at public ministry in the congregation and are confined to summer trips in Mexico? Not if we follow the principle of flexible leadership. It may have been a mistake to let the teens take over the church that Sunday, but it was an excellent mistake. Greg gets high points for creativity, and his supervisors help him work out the kinks so that three or four months from now he can try the idea again, probably with outstanding results.

## Relationships and the Workaholic Syndrome

One of the reasons we train other leaders is to share the burden. Autocratic leaders take the yoke, but they don't share the burden. As people develop under our guidance they, like John Mark, become "profitable for the ministry" and help us avoid stress and overwork, problems common to ministry leadership.

### What Are the Marks of the Workaholic?

People who specialize in this area suggest several behavior patterns that mark someone obsessed with his or her work to the point of what is called "performance dependency."

1. Inability to accept failure
2. Incessant work patterns
3. Guilt over low productivity
4. Anxiety and depression
5. Subjective standards of success
6. Leisure time guilt
7. Time consciousness
8. Self-denial

9. Future orientation
10. Impatience

These are not character flaws. Nor are they all negative behavior patterns. Self-denial is a strong New Testament characteristic. Future orientation is essential for long-range planning. But taken as a package, or even a cluster of six or seven, we begin to see a syndrome. Without delving into the oft-described Type A personality, we can certainly see that the person described in this list—driven, task-oriented, goal-focused—moves through life leaving others in her wake. Without time to develop other leaders, the syndrome only worsens and ultimately medical help of some kind may become necessary.

## Suggestions for Defeating Workaholism

Yes, psychologists, counselors, and therapists can "treat" this syndrome over a period of months or even years if necessary. But as Christian leaders we can go a long way toward alleviating these problems in our own lives once we recognize them. Though the following list is not as long as the first, it offers practical suggestions to shed the workaholic patterns that mark too many of us:

1. See people and respond to them as people.
2. Give of yourself instead of things.
3. Enhance your sensory awareness.
4. Develop a capacity for spontaneity.
5. Make yourself slow down.
6. Find a pleasant avocation or hobby.

All of these are valuable for leaders immediately coping with the problem, of course, but they are essential as well in relationships. We not only develop leaders, we have a tendency to develop leaders who are like us. God help the congregation in which a driven senior pastor cultivates driven associates until the whole staff looks like a herd of stampeding buffalo.

So watch out for those nervous habits, missed dates and appointments, slipping work quality, and other symptoms of workaholic stress. And above all other solutions, remember that in such times "Jesus often withdrew to lonely places and prayed" (Luke 5:16).

## RELATING TO NEW LEADERS

Developing new leaders implies that somewhere along the line we have made choices regarding those with whom we will work, into whose lives we will pour our own. The following principles relate to a pastor hiring his first assistant, a Sunday school superintendent looking for teachers, a para-church ministry director combing college campuses for staff, and a dozen or even a score of other leadership development situations. There are pitfalls in the road.

### Pitfalls in Leadership Selection

1. *Availability bias.* Sadly, many Christian organizations ask three basic questions when a leadership position becomes available: Who's handy? Who's visible? Who's cheap? Certainly a handy, visible, and inexpensive leader may also be competent and long-term, but that is not likely. Availability bias betrays laziness in our processes of leadership recruitment and development.

2. *Association bias.* This refers to some connection with existing leadership. It might just be a long-term relationship, such as a pastor recommending to the official board that a youth pastor who has served the church for five years now be appointed associate pastor.

In its ugliest form, association bias deteriorates into nepotism. We have all seen it—Christian organizations passed on from father to son or husband to wife as though they were family businesses. Certainly strong relational leaders draw followers. And people closely associated to the present leader may be the logical selections for leadership needs. But it can be a pitfall, a danger zone. Keeping "power" within the family may be typical of Old Testament monarchical times, but we find no evidence whatsoever of such behavior in the New Testament.

3. *Agreement bias.* Here the present leader asks, "Who's like me? Who thinks like I do? Who won't rock the boat? Who won't change what we've developed here in our organization?"

Like availability and association, agreement hardly represents a mortal sin. In some situations, agreement may be essential (for example, in doctrinal matters). But if we follow the leadership principle "lead to your strength and staff to your weakness," it may very well be wise for leaders to find those who have some differences and disagreements in order to help the organization toward its future.

## Process of Leadership Selection

If leaders are to develop other leaders effectively, at least four steps must be in place—and in order. The basic idea comes from Gilmore's fascinating book, but the embellishment, I must confess, is my own.[5]

1. *Choose the right follower.* No amount of mentoring, training, patience, or long-suffering can undo a bad choice. By "bad choice" I do not mean an unworthy person or one who could not be of great use and success in another leadership role. When Elijah chose Elisha, he selected someone very unlike himself. To be sure, the former was given to theatrics and public performances to attract attention to the Lord's message. But Elijah's high/low temperament and mood swings were no match for the bizarre behavior of his follower. Nevertheless, in this situation it was the right follower, God's choice for Israel at a crucial time in its history.

Numerous tests and measurements can help us narrow

this decision. Myers/Briggs personality profiles, production capability prediction analyses—all are helpful and probably should be used for major leadership posts. But ultimately God's Holy Spirit can give us assurance of the person or persons in whom we should invest our leadership lives.

2. *Create an acceptable climate.* Here I offer the example of Jesus' disciples. And we swing back to an emphasis earlier in the chapter. Our Lord developed His own life to a point of maturity (defined in human framework) before He attracted to Himself those who would be His followers. Upon joining Him, they embraced a climate unlike any they had seen before. Selfish aggressiveness now turned to meekness and gentleness, an attitude they were very slow to grasp. Right up to the time of the Crucifixion, they still debated with one another regarding their relative greatness and authority in the group. Nevertheless, for three and a half years the Lord directed them through experience after experience, which formed a climate of growth which had been pre-designed to achieve the goals He had for them.

3. *Control the pre-arrival factors.* Since forty years would seem to be enough time to design and control pre-arrival factors for a new leader, we look with confidence to Moses and Joshua on this point. Moses could hardly be accused of association bias since God Himself made the choice of his successor. But for forty years Joshua had been waiting in the wings. I have never met an assistant pastor who waited forty years to become a senior pastor, but such was Joshua's experience. And when he "took over," both God and Moses had so designed the patterns of leadership responsibility that Joshua could step right in and lead the nation forward.

4. *Cope with post-arrival factors.* Whatever one plans before the new leader's arrival, something will change after he or she gets on the job. According to Peters, "Leaders, especially early in their tenure, do not get fully developed options from which they select a path. Rather, a direction begins to emerge from a sequence of choices—about people, issues, resources—and from serendipity."[6]

These traps (patterns of misunderstanding) arise from the inability to discuss the situation freely before arrival and after one is on the job.

What do we look for should we wish to avoid these arrival traps?[7]

- *Patterns of delegation.* Insofar as it is possible, we should know about the leadership style of the new leader before he or she arrives. That style will to a significant extent determine how work is apportioned to others and whether centralization or decentralization will be the order of the day. Obviously, when a participatory leader develops another participatory leader, team leadership style should emerge.
- *Internal/external priorities.* Consider Saul and David. Saul's internal priorities were to hold on to the kingdom he saw slipping from his grasp almost from the first. His external priorities focused on keeping the Philistines away from the door at any cost. One could argue that David was Saul's protégé in a way, having watched Israel's first king "up close and personal" for many years. But when David became king, the priorities of the kingdom changed dramatically, and the people needed to learn those differences.
- *Resistance to change.* Again, Saul serves us as a negative model. At times, when his senses were collected, he realized how foolishly he had behaved in his relationship to the one who would be the next leader of the kingdom. But in jealousy for himself, for Jonathan, and for his entire tribe, he resisted change literally to the death.

  In appointing new leaders, resistance to change may appear on the part of the outgoing leader or the group being led. In any case, it is a part of the overall process of development. We cannot pretend these traps do not exist, nor can we dispense with them. We can only know they offer ongoing difficulties which must be watched.

I conclude this chapter by offering a passage that reflects the leadership transition from Moses to Joshua. In reality, it is a passionate prayer for a successor, a total commitment to the new leader's success. Let us not limit our understanding of this passage to a leadership change, that is, the team leader departs and a new leader takes charge. This should be true of leaders who continue to work together after the trainee's appointment.

> Then the Lord said to Moses, "Go up this mountain in the Abarim range and see the land I have given the Israelites. After you have seen it, you too will be gathered to your people, as your brother Aaron was, for when the community rebelled at the waters in the Desert of Zin, both of you disobeyed my command to honor me as holy before their eyes." (These were the waters of Meribah Kadesh, in the Desert of Zin.)
> Moses said to the Lord, "May the Lord, the God of the spirits of all mankind, appoint a man over this community to go out and come in before them, one who will lead them out and bring them in, so the Lord's people will not be like sheep without a shepherd."
> So the Lord said to Moses, "Take Joshua son of Nun, a man in whom is the spirit, and lay your hand on him. Have him stand before Eleazar the priest and the entire assembly and commission him in their presence. Give him some of your authority so the whole Israelite community will obey him." (Numbers 27:12–20)

Multitudinous lessons present themselves from this passage; I offer only seven.

1. Christian leaders should pray about their colleagues and successors (16a).
2. Christian leaders are divinely appointed (16b).
3. Christian leaders serve in offices of authority (16c).

4. Christian leaders bridge the gap between God and His people (17a).
5. Christian leaders serve the people they lead (17b).
6. Christian leaders exercise a shepherding role (17c).
7. Christian leaders should reproduce themselves (18–20).

## FOR FURTHER READING

Callahan, Kennon L. *Effective Church Leadership.* San Francisco: Harper & Row, 1990.

Dyer, William. *Team Building: Issues and Alternatives.* Reading, Mass.: Addison-Wesley, 1977.

Gangel, Kenneth O. *Feeding and Leading.* Wheaton, Ill.: Victor, 1989.

Gilmore, Thomas N. *Making a Leadership Change.* San Francisco: Jossey-Bass, 1988.

Peters, T. J., and N. Austin. *A Passion for Excellence.* New York: Random House, 1985.

## NOTES

1. John Ramos, "Ten Fatal Flaws of Business Executives" *Across the Board,* vol. 31, no. 10, Nov./Dec. 1994, 22.

2. Mark H. Senter III, "Five Stages in Your Ministry Development," *Leadership* (Spring 1989): 88–95.

3. Dave Ulrich, "Credibility X Capability," in *The Leader of the Future,* ed. Francis Hesselbein, Marshall Goldsmith, and Richard Beckhard (San Francisco: Jossey-Bass, 1996), 213.

4. Kennon L. Callahan, *Effective Church Leadership* (San Francisco: Harper & Row, 1990), 221.

5. Thomas N. Gilmore, *Making a Leadership Change* (San Francisco: Jossey-Bass, 1988).

6. Quoted in ibid., 136.

7. Ibid., 136–40.

# CONCLUSION

Ending the final chapter with a "prayer for a successor" certainly indicates that I don't believe most of us will spend our entire adult lives in one ministry leadership role. My career has spanned four different institutions in nearly forty years, and that average tenure per post is dramatically greater than most leaders.

A special report released by *Your Church* indicates that "since the mid-1970s pastoral tenure has declined from an average of seven years per church to about five years (4 years, 11 months). This means the typical pastor has changed churches three times and is nearing the mid-term of his fourth pastorate."[1] I should observe here that the pastors surveyed averaged forty-six years of age and eighteen years in ministry. At an average tenure of five years and a ministry life of forty (serving from age twenty-five through sixty-five), the average pastor in this survey would serve eight different churches during his career.

When asked their reasons for moving, the pastors indicated numerous possibilities but focused on the following four as the main motivation:

1. A new vision or sense of call to a new place.
2. A sense of resolution that ministry was complete or could go no further.
3. Opportunity to do something more elsewhere.
4. Unresolved or ongoing tension or trouble in the present ministry.

Most of the pastors indicated a strong call from God to make the move, and we must honor that, though the tenure figures don't look like much of a divine plan.

Perhaps the biggest question Christian leaders face has to do with whether to stay or leave a present situation. Might the factors involved in analyzing that choice depend upon something other than a "gut level" or divine appointment recognition? Obviously, whether one is still getting along with one's coworkers is a significant factor in deciding to stay or leave a ministry post. Change of leadership above us is a major factor. Sometimes we can feel very comfortable with the present boss but uncomfortable under the leadership style of a new one. Often a church will grow beyond the ability of a pastor to lead it, or the Christian leader won't keep up professionally with the changing demands of the ministry. This could happen to any of us—pastors, presidents, mission executives.

Credibility is crucial. It should build through the years rather than diminish. An ongoing or perhaps a fresh vision for the ministry is surely essential as well.

But perhaps the most important question we must ask before leaving any leadership post is, "Is God finished with me here?" If we cannot get a clear-cut affirmation to that question, then the second one is irrelevant: "Where does God want me to go next?"

This book argues that a properly developed team leadership style will increase tenure and make ministry more effective. I am genuinely committed to the idea that practicing these principles will enable Christian leaders to work with other leaders, boards, volunteers, and to do so within virtually any polity or framework. Servant leadership is an attitude with which we approach the leadership task; it is not bound by the situations in which we find ourselves, though certainly it is exercised more or less easily depending on the context.

The biblical emphasis allows us few options—the early Christians carried out their ministry in teams because that's what Jesus taught them to do. To quote Van Auken, "Teams engaged in Christian ministry are supernaturally empowered, generating a rare kind of fruitfulness nurtured by team member unity, vision and sacrifice. God lovingly shepherds His teams, helping them succeed despite human fallibility and frailty."[2]

NOTES

1. John C. LaRue, Jr., "Profile of Today's Pastor: Transitions," *Your Church* (May/June 1995): 56.

2. Philip Van Auken, *The Well-Managed Ministry* (Wheaton, Ill.: Victor, 1989), 238.

# APPENDIX A

## GLOSSARY OF LEADERSHIP TERMS

ADMINISTRATION—The management of resources in an organization necessary to achieve goals.

ANTHROPOLOGY—The scientific study of the nature of man.

AUTOCRATIC LEADERSHIP—Leadership that focuses on the importance and authority of the "top man."

AXIOLOGY—The scientific study of values.

BUDGET—Funds allocated to an organizational unit for any given fiscal year identified in a written and quantified statement of management's goals and plans for both sources and uses of money.

BUREAUCRACY—A term describing the size and administrative detail characteristic of large organizations, usually reflecting extensive control and detail specialization.

CENTRALIZATION—A philosophy of organization that vests authority or programming in a few persons, places, or ideas.

CENTRICITY—Attitudes and activities of group members that cause them to reflect inwardly on themselves rather than the group.

COMMUNICATION—The transmission of ideas from one person to another in a language that is common to both.

COMPENSATION—A mechanism that enhances self-esteem by overcoming a failure or deficiency in one area through achieving recognition in another area.

CONFLICT—Dispute between individuals or groups which will either facilitate or hinder the attainment of organizational goals.

CONTROL—The extent of regulation upon group members by the leader or the group itself.

COUNSELING—The process of helping other people to understand, face, and solve their own problems.

CYBERNETICS—An attempt to bring together and reexamine lines of research; study of behavior on the basis of a theory of machines, particularly computers.

DECENTRALIZATION—A philosophy of organization that vests authority or programming in as many persons, places, or ideas as possible.

DELEGATION—The consigning of certain tasks and authority to other persons in the organization.

DELPHI TECHNIQUE—Coordinating the communication of ideas and decision making through questions and summarized responses.

DEMOCRATIC LEADERSHIP—Leadership that focuses on the group and its goals, ideas, and decisions.

DIFFERENTIATION—The process of correctly discerning or identifying the perspective between two items that appear to be similar.

## GLOSSARY OF LEADERSHIP TERMS

EMERGENT LEADERSHIP—Leadership that is neither elected nor appointed but develops from among the group itself, probably as a result of the situation.

EMPATHY—Identifying oneself with the members of the group.

ENVIRONMENT—Elements outside the organization that affect its operations and its future.

EPISTEMOLOGY—The scientific study of the nature and limits of knowledge.

EQUALITARIANISM—The leader treating group members as equals.

FRUSTRATION—A state of being unable to discharge a painful or uncomfortable excitation.

GROUP—A collection of individuals united by perceived unity, common goals, and face-to-face interaction.

GROUP ATTRACTIVENESS—The degree to which a group promises rewards to its members.

GROUP EFFECTIVENESS—The degree to which a group rewards its members and achieves the goals it sets out to perform.

HABITUATION—The process of forming patterns of behavior which become almost automatic through repetition.

HAWTHORNE EFFECT—The behavior that occurs in individuals as a result of noncontrolled variables in an experimental situation.

HEDONIC TONE—Satisfactory group relationships. The atmosphere that makes a member "like" his group.

HETEROGENEITY—The degree to which outsiders are able to get into a group. Also, the diverse makeup of the group itself.

HOMOGENEITY—The degree to which members of the group are similar with respect to socially relevant characteristics.

HOSTILITY—A feeling of enmity or antagonism between people or perhaps on the part of one person toward others.

IDEATION—The process of thinking which produces ideas.

IDIOGRAPHIC ORGANIZATION—Organization that places heavy emphasis on the needs and personal goals of individuals, possibly to the point of insufficient concern for the achievement of the institution.

INITIATIVE—The leader or a member of the group originating ideas, developing new procedures, and starting the group out on progress.

INSIGHT—One's ability to perceive the underlying or genuine nature of things.

INTERACTION—Confrontation between group members (usually verbal).

INTIMACY—The degree to which members of the group are mutually acquainted with one another and familiar with personal details of one another's lives.

JOB DESCRIPTION—A specification of the duties and responsibilities that accompany a given task. Sometimes called "role definition" or "job analysis."

LAISSEZ-FAIRE RELATIONSHIPS—Leadership that withdraws authority and control in favor of extreme permissiveness.

LINE-STAFF RELATIONSHIPS—Line relationships refer to vertical positions of authority or subordination as shown on the organizational chart. Staff relationship is shown horizontally and generally depicts equal authority. Any leader is in line and/or staff relationship to someone else in the organization.

MEDIA—Plural of medium: the channel used to communicate the message, such as a recorder, film, etc.

MENTORING—Using one's experience and wisdom to assist less mature leaders in improving their skills.

GLOSSARY OF LEADERSHIP TERMS

METAPHYSICS—The scientific study of the nature of reality.

MISSION—The purpose of an organization, its reason for being in existence, and its distinction from other similar organizations.

MOTIVE—A conscious or subconscious factor that serves as an impetus in determining behavior.

NOMOTHETIC ORGANIZATION—Organization that places heavy emphasis on the goals and achievements of the institution without proper consideration to the individuals who work in it.

ORGANISM—A living being or body; the church of Jesus Christ.

ORGANIZATION—The structure of a company or institution which reflects lines of authority, span of control, and flow of information.

ORGANIZATION CHART—An explicit diagram of formal roles and relationships in an organization.

PERCEPTION—Any differentiations the individual is capable of making in his perceptual field, whether an objectively observable stimulus is present or not.

POLARIZATION—The centering of interest, discussion, or thought on one person or idea.

PROJECTION—The process of shifting the responsibility for an act or thought from oneself to an outside agency or to another person; taking an attitude of oneself and attributing it to someone else.

RADICITY—Attitudes and activities of group members that cause them to reflect on the group and its projects rather than themselves.

RAPPORT—The relationship between people marked by attitudes of friendliness, harmony, and cooperation.

RATIONALIZATION—A device whereby the individual provides plausible reasons for his behavior rather than the actual reasons which are too painful to acknowledge; the substitution of a socially approved motive for a socially disapproved one.

REGRESSION—The process of relieving anxiety or threat by falling back upon the thoughts, feelings, or behavior which worked successfully during an earlier period of life.

REINFORCEMENT—Rewards and recognition that will serve as an impetus for group members to continue to perform in a constructive capacity.

REPRESSION—An unconscious process wherein shameful thoughts, guilt-producing memories, painful experiences, or distasteful tasks are removed from awareness or forced below the level of consciousness.

ROLE—A description of how a person is supposed or expected to behave in a given situation.

ROLE SET—A structure of defined relationships involving two or more people in given positions.

SELF-ACTUALIZATION (Self-realization)—The process of "becoming" a complete person, realizing one's own abilities and goals and accepting one's self realistically.

SELF-CONCEPT—One's image or evaluation of himself. It has been determined by his environment in the past as well as internal spiritual factors. Now it governs the way he behaves in various situations.

SPAN OF CONTROL—The number of officers in an organization over which a given leader has authority and for whose work he bears responsibility.

STABILITY—The extent to which a group persists over a period of time with essentially the same characteristics.

STRATIFICATION—Process of a group's placing its members in status hierarchies.

SUBSTITUTION—A device that makes it possible to discharge tensions by diverting one's energies from a desired goal to an alternative goal.

SUPERVISION—The directing of the activities of other people toward the accomplishing of organizational goals.

SURGENCY—Generally defined in terms of personality, talkativeness, outreach, and gregariousness.

SYNTALITY—The prediction of group performance or effectiveness.

TRANSACTIONALISM—An attempt to reconcile structurally and otherwise the goals and needs of the organization with those of the individuals who work in the organization.

TRANSFERENCE—Reaction toward people in present situations motivated and controlled by one's attitudes toward important people earlier in life.

VALUE SYSTEMS—The importance and truth that a person places upon concepts or people, which in turn determine the way he treats them.

VISCIDITY—The group's acting as a unit, working together toward group goals.

VISION—The way an organization intends to implement its mission in the future.

# Appendix B

## Sample Form for Leadership Recruitment

P & R Sheet
(Privilege and Responsibility)
for Christian Service

*P* The privilege of being a Christian is difficult to describe, for mere words are insufficient vehicles to express the wonders of salvation, redemption, peace, and spiritual joy. This privilege is best experienced by an active faith, constantly nourished by daily communion with the Lord through His Word and prayer, and best expressed by sacrificial service through the agency of the local church.

Therefore, as you read the list below, do so with a sense of gratitude to God and a willingness to demonstrate your faith by service in the areas indicated.

*R* Check your desired area of service:

Sunday School

    1. Teacher _____

    2. Helper _____

3. Secretarial work _____

4. Transportation _____

Please note age group preferred and approximate years of experience _____

_____

## Other Agencies of Youth or Children's Work

1. Youth sponsor _____
2. Home open for youth parties _____
3. Transportation to youth events _____
4. Vacation Bible school teaching _____
5. Helping in VBS _____
6. AWANA leader _____
7. Mothers' day out _____
8. Children's church _____
9. Graded prayer groups _____

## Music

1. Pianist _____
2. Choir _____ (part you sing) _____
3. Vocal soloist _____
4. Instrumental soloist_____ (type of instrument) _____
5. Song leading _____

## Committee Work

1. AWANA _____
2. Camp _____
3. Christian education _____
4. Building _____
5. Hospitality _____

## SAMPLE FORM FOR LEADERSHIP RECRUITMENT

6. Missions _____

7. VBS _____

Miscellaneous

1. Ushering _____

2. Nursery worker _____

3. Manual service _____ (list what type) _____

Name _____ Address _____

Telephone _____

 

This sheet is your invitation to Christian service through your local church. We are interested in helping you train for and then faithfully and joyfully serve the Lord in a position. This P & R sheet will greatly facilitate the total service program of our church. Thank you.

Christian Education Committee

# Appendix C

## Planning Team Evaluation

### Will You Need Assistance in this Planning Process?[1]

Complete each of the following statements so it best fits your preference or probable action. Don't think long about your choice since your first and immediate reaction is probably more accurate.

Place the letter corresponding to your choice in the "My Choice" blank at the end of each statement. You will be shown how to score your choices when you have finished. Statements marked with an asterisk (*) are for clergy only.

There are no "right" or "wrong" choices. The purpose is to discover the degree of help needed in your use of this planning process. Honesty in completing these statements is essential.

1. Richard E. Rusbuldt, Richard K. Gladden, and Norman M. Green, Jr., *Local Church Planning Manual* (Valley Forge, Pa.: Judson Press, 1977), 101–5. Reprinted with permission of the publisher, Judson Press, 1-800-458-3766.

|  | My Choice | Score |
|---|---|---|

1. All other circumstances being equal, I would rather:
   (a) grow as much of our family's food as possible
   (b) purchase as much as possible from the store

2. If I were able, I would prefer to be:
   (a) a TV emcee
   (b) a TV producer-director

3. If skills, time, and money made no difference, I would prefer to:
   (a) build my own house
   (b) buy a house already built

4. If I were a teacher, I would prefer to teach:
   (a) physical education
   (b) geometry

5. I am the kind of person who prefers to:
   (a) do a job myself
   (b) teach someone else how to do it
   (c) ask for volunteers and let them do the job on their own

6. When I wake up, I need:
   (a) no extra help or encouragement
   (b) some assistance
   (c) lots of help, encouragement, etc., to get me out of bed

*7. If I were not a pastor, I would most likely have a job where:
   (a) I could set my own schedule and assignments
   (b) I could work on an hourly basis and be told what to do

## PLANNING TEAM EVALUATION

|  | My Choice | Score |
|---|---|---|

(c) I could be paid a salary and work as a supervisor
or department head          ＿＿＿  ＿＿＿

*8.  I am strongest in:
(a) preaching          ＿＿＿  ＿＿＿
(b) visitation          ＿＿＿  ＿＿＿
(c) administration          ＿＿＿  ＿＿＿

*9.  In relationship to our Sunday church school I feel:
(a) I know the people, leaders, materials, and what is
happening          ＿＿＿  ＿＿＿
(b) I am removed and not familiar with what is
happening          ＿＿＿  ＿＿＿
(c) I am involved in planning, training, or teaching          ＿＿＿  ＿＿＿

10.  If time and money were not important and I had and
used a fireplace, I would rather:
(a) cut and haul my own wood          ＿＿＿  ＿＿＿
(b) purchase the wood and have it delivered to
my home          ＿＿＿  ＿＿＿

11.  My leisure reading is usually:
(a) books under 200 pages in length          ＿＿＿  ＿＿＿
(b) books over 200 pages in length          ＿＿＿  ＿＿＿
(c) newspapers and magazines          ＿＿＿  ＿＿＿

12.  If I purchase a bicycle, I would prefer that:
(a) it come already assembled          ＿＿＿  ＿＿＿
(b) it come disassembled so I could put it together          ＿＿＿  ＿＿＿

13.  When sitting in meetings where I am not in charge or
have little or no responsibility, my tolerance level is
usually reached after:
(a) 1 hour          ＿＿＿  ＿＿＿

|  | My Choice | Score |
|---|---|---|

(b) 2 hours ⎯⎯ ⎯⎯

(c) 3 hours or more ⎯⎯ ⎯⎯

*14. I usually plan my sermon topics:
    (a) week by week ⎯⎯ ⎯⎯
    (b) one or two months at a time ⎯⎯ ⎯⎯
    (c) three months or more at a time ⎯⎯ ⎯⎯

15. The person who manages my finances is:
    (a) myself ⎯⎯ ⎯⎯
    (b) another ⎯⎯ ⎯⎯

16. If I were asked what my personal and/or professional goals are for the next 1–5 years:
    (a) I could say definitely ⎯⎯ ⎯⎯
    (b) I could not say ⎯⎯ ⎯⎯
    (c) I would have a general idea ⎯⎯ ⎯⎯

17. When operating a new machine or appliance for the first time, I usually:
    (a) read, reread, and carefully follow the operator's manual ⎯⎯ ⎯⎯
    (b) figure I know how to operate it and proceed to do so, reading the manual only if I have problems ⎯⎯ ⎯⎯

18. Given a fairly normal week, those closest to me:
    (a) know at all times where I can be reached in case of an emergency ⎯⎯ ⎯⎯
    (b) do not know where to reach me ⎯⎯ ⎯⎯

*19. In planning a worship service, I would prefer:
    (a) to choose a theme and then fit hymns, sermon, Scripture, etc., around it ⎯⎯ ⎯⎯

## PLANNING TEAM EVALUATION

|  | My Choice | Score |
|---|---|---|
| (b) to write the sermon and then fit the rest of the service around it | —— | —— |
| (c) to use a published guide for worship services | —— | —— |

20. I would rather be:
    (a) a newspaper sports reporter    ——    ——
    (b) a newspaper photographer    ——    ——
    (c) a newspaper editor    ——    ——
    (d) a newspaper publisher-manager    ——    ——

21. If age, talent, and money were no problem, I would rather be:
    (a) a professional baseball player    ——    ——
    (b) a professional baseball manager    ——    ——
    (c) a professional baseball club owner–general manager    ——    ——

22. In games, what counts most to me is:
    (a) playing to win    ——    ——
    (b) being with people    ——    ——
    (c) having fun    ——    ——

23. If I were given $50,000, I would most likely:
    (a) spend most on some things I've wanted for a long time    ——    ——
    (b) spend some but deposit most in a bank    ——    ——
    (c) invest all of it    ——    ——

*24. I use the following amount of time most weeks in preparing for the Sunday morning sermon:
    (a) under 2 hours    ——    ——
    (b) 2–3 hours    ——    ——
    (c) 3–4 hours    ——    ——
    (d) 4 or more hours    ——    ——

|  | My Choice | Score |
|---|---|---|

25. I:
    (a) enjoy putting together difficult picture puzzles      ____    ____
    (b) do not enjoy this activity      ____    ____

*26. I prefer:
    (a) to keep my work schedule flexible and not be tied
        to a pattern      ____    ____
    (b) to set a definite schedule and stick to it except for
        emergencies      ____    ____

27. If able, I would rather be:
    (a) a physical education teacher      ____    ____
    (b) a librarian      ____    ____
    (c) a high school principal      ____    ____
    (d) a superintendent of school

28. I believe a car owner should:
    (a) try to do most of his or her own service and repairs    ____    ____
    (b) have someone else work on the car      ____    ____

29. In solving a problem, I prefer to:
    (a) work with the smallest group possible      ____    ____
    (b) work on the problem alone      ____    ____
    (c) involve the maximum number of persons      ____    ____

30. What I know about systematic planning:
    (a) turns me on      ____    ____
    (b) turns me off      ____    ____
    (c) gives me mixed feelings      ____    ____

## PLANNING TEAM EVALUATION

| | My Choice | Score |
|---|---|---|
| 31. When people ask questions in meetings: | | |
| (a) I am annoyed | —— | —— |
| (b) I feel good | —— | —— |
| (c) I am not affected | —— | —— |
| 32. I would prefer to: | | |
| (a) put together a TV kit | —— | —— |
| (b) buy a TV from a store | —— | —— |
| 33. My vacations are usually planned by: | | |
| (a) myself | —— | —— |
| (b) another | —— | —— |
| (c) myself and others | —— | —— |
| 34. If given a choice, I would rather: | | |
| (a) watch TV | —— | —— |
| (b) read a good book | —— | —— |
| (c) do something with another person | —— | —— |
| 35. If the washing machine breaks down, I would: | | |
| (a) attempt to fix it myself | —— | —— |
| (b) call a technician without trying to fix it myself | —— | —— |
| (c) tell someone else to fix it or to call a technician | —— | —— |
| (d) forget about it for a while and suggest the laundry be done at the Laundromat | —— | —— |
| 36. Regarding this questionnaire: | | |
| (a) I think I know what it is trying to determine | —— | —— |
| (b) I'm not really sure | —— | —— |
| (c) I really don't know and don't particularly care | —— | —— |

## SCORING

Note: Listed below is the number of each statement and the possible choices. Each choice has a point value. Using this list as a guide, put the point value of your choice for each statement in the blank provided. Then add the total points and place that figure in the blank opposite the words "Total Score."

You will then be informed about what your total score means.

| Statement Choice | Point Value | Statement Choice | Point Value | Statement Choice | Point Value |
|---|---|---|---|---|---|
| 1 a | 2 | 10 a | 2 | b | 3 |
| b | 1 | b | 1 | c | 2 |
| 2 a | 1 | 11 a | 2 | 20 a | 1 |
| b | 2 | b | 3 | b | 2 |
| 3 a | 2 | c | 1 | c | 3 |
| b | 1 | 12 a | 1 | d | 4 |
| 4 a | 1 | b | 2 | 21 a | 1 |
| b | 2 | 13 a | 1 | b | 2 |
| 5 a | 1 | b | 2 | c | 3 |
| b | 3 | c | 3 | 22 a | 2 |
| c | 2 | *14 a | 1 | b | 3 |
| 6 a | 3 | b | 2 | c | 1 |
| b | 2 | c | 3 | 23 a | 1 |
| c | 1 | 15 a | 2 | b | 2 |
| *7 a | 1 | b | 1 | c | 3 |
| b | 2 | 16 a | 3 | *24 a | 1 |
| c | 3 | b | 1 | b | 2 |
| *8 a | 2 | c | 2 | c | 3 |
| b | 1 | 17 a | 2 | d | 4 |
| c | 3 | b | 2 | 25 a | 2 |
| *9 a | 2 | 18 a | 1 | b | 1 |
| b | 1 | b | 2 | *26 a | 1 |
| c | 3 | *19 a | 1 | b | 2 |

## PLANNING TEAM EVALUATION

| Statement Choice | Point Value | Statement Choice | Point Value | Statement Choice | Point Value |
|---|---|---|---|---|---|
| 27 a | 2 | b | 1 | 34 a | 1 |
| b | 1 | c | 2 | b | 2 |
| c | 3 | 31 a | 1 | c | 3 |
| d | 4 | b | 3 | 35 a | 4 |
| 28 a | 2 | c | 2 | b | 3 |
| b | 1 | 32 a | 2 | c | 2 |
| 29 a | 2 | b | 1 | d | 1 |
| b | 1 | 33 a | 2 | 36 a | 3 |
| c | 3 | b | 1 | b | 2 |
| 30 a | 3 | c | 3 | c | 1 |

* If you are not clergy, disregard scoring those numbers with an *

TOTAL SCORE _____

Interpreting your score:

If you answered all questions (the "clergy" form) your score should fall between 36 (minimum) and 99 (maximum). If you omitted the asterisked questions (the "layman" form) the possible range is 29–88.

If your score is between . . .          your planning skills rate as . . .

    75–99 (clergy) or                    very good: should have little difficulty
    65–88 (layman)                       directing the planning process.

    60–74 (clergy) or                    adequate: should seek consulting
    50–64 (layman)                       help at critical points.

    36–59 (clergy) or                    a poor risk: seek help through the
    29–49 (layman)                       planning process.

# BIBLIOGRAPHY

Anderson, Carl R. *Management*. Dubuque, Iowa: Wm. C. Brown, 1984.

Anderson, Leith, et al. *Mastering Church Management*. Portland, Oreg.: Multnomah, 1990.

Anthony, Michael J. *The Effective Church Board*. Grand Rapids: Baker, 1993.

Apps, Jerold W. *Ideas for Better Church Meetings*. Minneapolis: Augsburg, 1975.

Armerding, Hudson T. *The Heart of Godly Leadership*. Wheaton, Ill.: Crossway, 1992.

Arnold, John, and Bert Tompkins. *How to Make the Right Decisions*. Milford, Mich.: Mott Media, 1982.

Bennett, Thomas R. *The Leader and the Process of Change*. New York: Association, 1962.

Bennis, Warren. *Why Leaders Can't Lead.* San Francisco: Jossey-Bass, 1990.

Bennis, Warren, et al. *The Planning of Change.* New York: Holt, Rinehart & Winston, 1961.

Blumenthal, L. H. *How to Work with Your Board and Committees.* New York: Association, 1954.

Brammer, Lawrence M. *The Helping Relationship.* Englewood Cliffs, N.J.: Prentice-Hall, 1973.

Bratcher, Edward B. *The Walk-on-Water Syndrome.* Waco, Tex.: Word, 1984.

Buchanan, Paul C. *The Leader and Individual Motivation.* New York: Association, 1964.

Callahan, Kennon L. *Effective Church Leadership.* San Francisco: Harper & Row, 1990.

Cedar, Paul A. *Strength in Servant Leadership.* Waco, Tex.: Word, 1987.

Cedar, Paul A., Kent Hughes, and Ben Patterson. *Mastering the Pastoral Role.* Portland, Ore.: Multnomah, 1991.

Clark, Kenneth E., and Miriam B. Clark. *Choosing to Lead.* Charlotte, N.C.: Iron Gate, 1994.

Collins, Gary R. *How to Be a People Helper.* Santa Ana, Calif.: Vision House, 1976.

Colson, Charles. *Kingdoms in Conflict.* Grand Rapids: William Morrow/Zondervan, 1987.

Coppedge, Allan. *The Biblical Principles of Discipleship.* Grand Rapids: Francis Asbury, 1989.

Cormack, David. *Team Spirit.* Grand Rapids: Zondervan, 1989.

Deboy, James J., Jr. *Getting Started in Adult Religious Education.* New York: Paulist, 1979.

Drucker, Peter F. *The Effective Executive*. New York: Harper & Row, 1967.

_____. *The New Realities*. New York: Harper & Row, 1989.

Dyer, William. *Team Building: Issues and Alternatives*. Reading, Mass.: Addison-Wesley, 1977.

Edwards, Mary A. *Leadership Development and the Worker's Conference*. Nashville: Abingdon, 1967.

Engstrom, Ted W. *The Making of a Christian Leader*. Grand Rapids: Zondervan, 1976.

Engstrom, Ted W., and Edward R. Dayton. *The Art of Management for Christian Leaders*. Waco, Tex.: Word, 1976.

_____. *The Christian Executive*. Waco, Tex.: Word, 1979.

Finzel, Hans. *The Top Ten Mistakes Leaders Make*. Wheaton, Ill.: Victor, 1994.

Ford, Leighton. *Transforming Leadership*. Downers Grove, Ill.: InterVarsity, 1991.

Gangel, Kenneth O. *Feeding and Leading*. Wheaton, Ill.: Victor, 1989.

_____. *Lessons in Leadership from the Bible*. Winona Lake, Ind.: BMH, 1980.

_____ *So You Want to Be a Leader!* Harrisburg, Pa.: Christian Publications, 1973.

Gangel, Kenneth O., and James C. Wilhoit. *The Christian Educator's Handbook on Adult Education*. Wheaton, Ill.: Victor, 1993.

_____. *The Christian Educator's Handbook on Spiritual Formation*. Wheaton, Ill.: Victor, 1994.

Gangel, Kenneth O., and Samuel L. Canine. *Communication and Conflict Management.* Nashville: Broadman, 1992.

George, Karl, and Warren Bird. *The Coming Church Revolution.* Grand Rapids: Revell, 1994.

Getz, Gene. *Loving One Another.* Wheaton, Ill.: Victor, 1979.

Gilmore, Thomas N. *Making a Leadership Change.* San Francisco: Jossey-Bass, 1988.

Grenz, Arlo. *The Confident Leader.* Nashville: Broadman & Holman, 1994.

Habecker, Eugene B. *The Other Side of Leadership.* Wheaton, Ill.: Victor, 1987.

Harris, Ben M. *Supervisory Behavior in Education.* New York: Prentice-Hall, 1963.

Henricksen, Walter A. *Disciples Are Made Not Born.* Wheaton, Ill.: Victor, 1988.

Hesselbein, Francis, Marshall Goldsmith, and Richard Beckhard, eds. *The Leader of the Future.* San Francisco: Jossey-Bass, 1996.

Howard, J. Grant. *The Trauma of Transparency.* Portland, Oreg.: Multnomah, 1979.

Hull, Bill. *The Disciple-Making Pastor.* Old Tappan, N.J.: Revell, 1988.

Johnson, Douglas W. *The Care and Feeding of Volunteers.* Creative Leadership Series, ed. Lyle E. Schaller. Nashville: Abingdon, 1978.

_____. *Empowering Lay Volunteers.* Creative Leadership Series, ed. Lyle Schaller. Nashville: Abingdon, 1991.

Johnson, James L. *The Nine-to-Five Complex, or the Christian Organization Man.* Grand Rapids: Zondervan, 1972.

Kilinski, Kenneth K., and Jerry C. Wofford. *Organization and Leadership in the Local Church.* Grand Rapids: Zondervan, 1973.

Koestenbaum, Peter. *Leadership—The Inner Side of Greatness.* San Francisco: Jossey-Bass, 1991.

Koivsto, Rex A. *One Lord, One Faith.* Wheaton, Ill.: Victor, 1993.

Kouzes, James M., and Barry Z. Posner. *Credibility.* San Francisco: Jossey-Bass, 1993.

_____. *The Leadership Challenge.* Rev. ed. San Francisco: Jossey-Bass, 1995.

Leas, Speed. *Leadership and Conflict.* Nashville: Abingdon, 1982.

Lewis, Phillip V. *Transformational Leadership.* Nashville: Broadman & Holman, 1996.

Longenecker, Harold L. *Growing Leaders by Design.* Grand Rapids: Kregel Resources, 1995.

Luft, Joseph. *Group Processes: An Introduction to Group Dynamics.* Palo Alto, Calif.: Mayfield, 1970.

MacArthur, John, Jr. *The Church, the Body of Christ.* Grand Rapids: Zondervan, 1973.

Madsen, Paul O. *The Person Who Chairs the Meeting.* Valley Forge, Pa.: Judson, 1973.

_____. *The Small Church—Valid, Vital, Victorious.* Valley Forge, Pa.: Judson, 1975.

Malphurs, Aubrey. *Maximizing Your Effectiveness.* Grand Rapids: Baker, 1995.

_____. *Pouring New Wine into Old Wineskins.* Grand Rapids: Baker, 1993.

471

_____. *Values-Driven Leadership*. Grand Rapids: Baker, 1996.

Maslow, A. H. *Motivation and Personality*. New York: Harper, 1954.

Mason, David E. *Voluntary Non-Profit Enterprise Management*. New York: Plenum, 1984.

McKillip, Jack. *Need Analysis: Tools for the Human Services and Education*. Newbury Park, Calif.: Sage, 1987.

Means, James E. *Leadership in Christian Ministry*. Grand Rapids: Baker, 1989.

Miller, Calvin. *The Empowered Leader*. Nashville: Broadman & Holman, 1995.

Nanus, Burt. *Visionary Leadership*. San Francisco: Jossey-Bass, 1992.

Peters, T. J., and N. Austin. *A Passion for Excellence*. New York: Random House, 1985.

Pohly, Kenneth. *Transforming the Rough Places: The Ministry of Supervision*. Dayton, Ohio: Whaleprints, 1993.

Ratcliffe, Donald, and Blake J. Neff. *The Complete Guide to Religious Education Volunteers*. Birmingham, Ala.: Religious Education, 1992.

Richards, Lawrence O., and Clyde Hoeldtke. *A Theology of Church Leadership*. Grand Rapids: Zondervan, 1980.

Robinson, Haddon. *Decision-Making by the Book*. Wheaton, Ill.: Victor, 1991.

Rogers, Carl A. *A Therapist's View of Personal Goals*. Wallingford, Pa.: Pendle Hill, 1966.

Rosenbach, Wm. E., and Robert L. Taylor, eds. *Contemporary Issues in Leadership*. Boulder, Colo.: Westview, 1984.

Rusbuldt, Richard E., Richard K. Gladden, and Norman M. Green, Jr. *Local Church Planning Manual*. Valley Forge, Pa.: Judson, 1977.

Sanders, J. Oswald. *Spiritual Leadership*. Rev. ed. Chicago: Moody, 1980.

Saucy, Robert L. *The Church in God's Program*. Chicago: Moody, 1972.

Schaller, Lyle E. *The Decision Makers*. Nashville: Abingdon, 1974.

_____. *Effective Church Planning*. Nashville: Abingdon, 1979.

_____. *Getting Things Done*. Nashville: Abingdon, 1986.

Schaller, Lyle E., and Charles A. Tidwell. *Creative Church Administration*. Nashville: Abingdon, 1975.

Schmuck, Richard A., and Philip J. Runkel. *The Handbook of Organization Development*. 4th ed. Prospect Heights, Ill.: Waveland, 1994.

Senter, Mark. *Recruiting Volunteers in the Church: Resolve Your Recruiting Hassles*. Wheaton, Ill.: Victor, 1990.

Smith, Dennis R., and L. Keith Williamson. *Interpersonal Communication*. Dubuque, Iowa: Wm. C. Brown, 1977.

Snyder, Howard A. *The Community of the King*. Downers Grove, Ill.: InterVarsity, 1977.

Stabbert, Bruce. *The Team Concept*. Tacoma, Wash.: Hegg Bros., 1982.

Stedman, Ray C. *Body Life*. Revised and expanded. Glendale, Calif.: Regal, 1977.

Stevens, R. Paul. *Liberating the Laity: Equipping All the Saints for Ministry*. Downers Grove, Ill.: InterVarsity, 1985.

Sutherland, Sidney S. *When You Preside.* Rev. ed. Danville, Ill.: Interstate, 1969.

Thompson, Robert R., and Gerald R. Thompson. *Organizing for Accountability.* Wheaton, Ill.: Harold Shaw, 1991.

Tillapaugh, Frank R. *Unleashing the Church.* Ventura, Calif.: Regal, 1982.

Tournier, Paul. *The Meaning of Persons.* New York: Harper & Row, 1957.

_____. *To Understand Each Other.* Richmond, Va.: John Knox, 1966.

Van Auken, Philip M. *The Well-Managed Ministry.* Wheaton, Ill.: Victor, 1989.

Ver Straten, Charles A. *How to Start Lay-Shepherding Ministries.* Grand Rapids: Baker, 1983.

Walton, Mary. *The Deming Management Method.* New York: Putnam, 1986.

Westing, Harold J. *Make Your Sunday School Grow Through Evaluation.* Wheaton, Ill.: Victor, 1976.

_____. *Multiple Church Staff Handbook.* Grand Rapids: Kregel, 1985.

Williams, Dennis E., and Kenneth O. Gangel. *Volunteers for Today's Church.* Grand Rapids: Baker, 1993.

Wilson, Gerald L., et al. *Interpersonal Growth for Communication.* Dubuque, Iowa: Wm. C. Brown, 1985.

Wortley, Judy. *The Recruiting Remedy: Taking the Headache Out of Finding Volunteers.* Elgin, Ill.: David C. Cook, 1990.

# INDEX

self-control, 260–61
Senter, Mark, 424–27
separation, 387–88
servanthood, 58–59
servant leadership, 313, 362
service, 321
shared power, 59–60
simultaneity, 40
society, 90–91
spiritual gifts, 34, 357–58
staff, 123
staff relationships, 38
stewardship, 59
strengths, emphasis on, 363–64
success, 47–48
supervision
  defined, 96, 365–66
  principles of, 368–71
  process of, 366–68

Taylor, James, 83–84
teachableness, 86
teaching, 258, 259, 268–69
Tead, Ordway, 95, 97, 100
team leadership
  defined, 12, 64
  examples of, 315–17
team spirit, 243
tensions, 383–84
testing, 374
theological perspective, 53
Theory X and Theory Y, 236–37

time management, 114–16, 162, 290, 322
Timothy, 62
tolerance, 431–32
total perspective, 264
total quality management (TQM), 109
training, 238
*Training of the Twelve*, 72
transactionalism, 214, 217–18, 248, 249
transformational leadership, 249
trend analysis, 280

unity, 29–30, 134–35, 312–13
unity in love, 39
universal church, 19, 21, 29

values, 224
Van Auken, Philip, 307–8
vision, 251–52, 277, 327–28, 378
volunteers, 346–47
vulnerability, 200

willingness and competence, 323–24
women's leadership, 248–50
workaholism, 432–34
worship, 25

Zaleznik, Abraham, 207, 237–38, 358–59

Moody Press, a ministry of Moody Bible Institute,
is designed for education, evangelization, and edification.
If we may assist you in knowing more about Christ
and the Christian life, please write us without obligation:
Moody Press, c/o MLM, Chicago, Illinois 60610.